BOLLINGEN SERIES LX

SAMOTHRACE

EXCAVATIONS

CONDUCTED BY THE INSTITUTE OF FINE ARTS

OF NEW YORK UNIVERSITY

KARL LEHMANN

Editor

Volume 2, PART I

SAMOTHRACE

THE INSCRIPTIONS

ON STONE

BY

P. M. FRASER

BOLLINGEN SERIES LX·2·1

PANTHEON BOOKS

THIS IS PART ONE OF THE SECOND VOLUME
IN A SERIES OF WORKS ON SAMOTHRACE
CONSTITUTING NUMBER LX IN BOLLINGEN SERIES,
SPONSORED BY AND PUBLISHED FOR
BOLLINGEN FOUNDATION

Library of Congress Catalogue Card No. 58–8985

Manufactured in the U.S.A. by Kingsport Press, Inc.,
Kingsport, Tenn.
Designed by Andor Braun

FOREWORD TO VOLUME TWO

THE TWO PARTS of this volume complete the publication of the written documents relating to ancient Samothrace hitherto known. They contain all the Greek and Latin inscriptions discovered between 1938 and 1957 in the course of the excavations carried out by the Archaeological Research Fund Expedition of the Institute of Fine Arts of New York University.

During these twenty years, the number of known inscriptions on stone has been substantially increased by stones found in the excavations and, to an even greater extent, by inscriptions rescued by us from the territory of the ancient city, the main village of Chora, and other scattered sites on the island. The ancient city—that is, what is today called Palaeopolis proper—remained inhabited, if sparsely so, throughout the Middle Ages. At the end of that period, in the fifteenth century, a large number of ancient inscribed blocks were re-used by the Genoese in the construction of a fortress in its territory. Since the Middle Ages, the inhabitants of Chora and to a lesser extent of other villages, as well as the builders of churches in other parts of the island, have also used such blocks, as elsewhere in Greece. From 1938 on, we have tried to rescue them, often by extracting the stones from extant buildings or ruins. We are indebted, in many instances, to inhabitants of the island who allowed us to do so. These documents are now sheltered in the Museum of Samothrace, for the most part in the peristyle courtyard that we constructed for this purpose. This collection includes all that remains of an assemblage of inscriptions providentially made around the turn of the century by the late Dr. N. Phardys and deposited in the main church of Chora, where, alas, after his death it was badly neglected. Hence some items seen there and published by C. Fredrich in *Inscriptiones Graecae* (XII, 8) along with the other then known inscriptions of Samothrace have since disappeared. The collection also includes a few items found and deposited in a local house in the hamlet of Palaeopolis by Professors F. Chapouthier and A. Salač in the early twenties of this century. On the other hand, we have left some of the major dedicatory inscriptions and inscribed building blocks found in the excavations of the Sanctuary on or near the buildings to which they belong. We had to refrain from extracting inscribed blocks from the standing Genoese towers and from such medieval ruins as the Monastery of Christos, where they are integral parts of post-antique monuments in themselves worthy of preservation.

The reader will thus appreciate the extent as well as the limits of the new stone inscriptions presented in this volume by Mr. P. M. Fraser, of All Souls College, Oxford. The task of preparing this edition has been particularly difficult because of the fragmentary state of many documents and the friable character of the Thasian marble material. While I felt it desirable in my preliminary reports in the *American Journal of Archaeology* and in *Hesperia* to make known immediately any important newly discovered inscription, in the nature of things these preliminary notices contained many gaps and errors that have been filled and corrected by Mr. Fraser in the present volume. If, in some instances, he and I have not been able to agree fully about the reading, restoration, or evaluation of an individual document, as he points out in his own preface, such disagreement does not diminish my deep appreciation of his invaluable readiness to edit this material. In future volumes dealing with the various areas of the Sanctuary of the Great Gods and with the character of their rites, whatever remains controversial will be re-examined.

The inscriptions on ceramics and other minor objects which I edit in the second part of this volume are also to be found in the Samothrace Museum in so far as they are now preserved. Owing to circumstances of the second World War that have been described in *Archaeology*, 1 (1948), 44 ff., uncertainties have arisen in regard to some of the inscriptions both on stone and on ceramics and minor objects. Bulgarian soldiers invading our storage places disturbed accession labels, emptied containers of stratified material, and, in one case, broke an inscribed marble stele. Provenances have been obscured in many instances. Wherever the catalogued items in both Parts I and II of this volume are marked "provenance unknown," the uncertainty is the result of these acts of vandalism.

In 1948 and 1949, with the zealous assistance of Phyllis Pray Bober and Elsbeth Dusenbery, we were able to rescue and identify a great deal of the disturbed material by means of our inventories (which had been taken to America), our sketches of all the inscribed items, and such photographs as existed. In spite of these endeavors, the provenance of a number of items could not be re-established, and some of the objects themselves published in Part II have been irretrievably lost. In these instances, the drawings made at the time and published in this volume are the only records available. In general, these drawings were made by various members of our staff.

The majority of the photographs reproduced on the plates of both parts of this volume we owe to a well-known professional photographer, Anna Wachsmann, who volunteered in 1954 to come with us to Samothrace without remuneration and who worked there during a whole campaign under primitive conditions in order to provide us with the basic photographs needed for this publication. Other photographs included in this volume we owe to the skill of another outstanding photographer, Alison Frantz, who has repeatedly visited us in Samothrace and unselfishly given us her help and advice. Less expert photographs, some of good quality, were made as the work progressed, by various members of our staff; and, for the developing of campaign photographs, we often availed ourselves, again, of the expert assistance of Miss Frantz's laboratory at the quarters of the American excavations in the Agora at Athens.

To our colleagues at the Agora excavations we are indebted for assistance always generously given. Professor B. D. Meritt has provided me over the years with the necessary stock of squeeze paper. I need not repeat the acknowledgment due throughout this publication to our sponsors and helpers of all kinds. As this second volume goes to press, I am, as always, keenly aware of their part in it. But special acknowledgment is here due the editorial staff of Bollingen Series. This volume has presented many intricate problems with which they have dealt in a spirit of co-operation that has proven a delight.

KARL LEHMANN

Athens
May 1957

PREFACE

THE INSCRIPTIONS here published have been found mainly by the members of the New York University Archaeological Research Fund Expedition to Samothrace, either in the excavations of the Sanctuary, or in the village of Chora, or elsewhere on the island. Only internal evidence can determine the original provenance of those from Chora and outlying parts of the island, since they can have been taken from either the city or the Sanctuary.

The texts as here presented are, with the exception of **88**, based on readings of the stones by myself in 1954 and again in 1956 and 1957, and on study of the squeezes. All the stones—except the major fragments **9–11**, and **45**, which have remained on the site of the excavations, and **88**, now in Paris—are in the Museum of Samothrace.

In the commentaries to the individual inscriptions I have, when possible, tried to restrict my remarks to points of epigraphy and factual interpretation, reserving for the Introduction the wider questions which some of them raise.

I must express here my debt to Professor Lehmann, the leader of the expedition, at whose request I undertook the publication of the inscriptions. His practical assistance, both in Samothrace and by correspondence, has facilitated my task in every way, and I have also benefited from his study of my manuscript. It will be evident to the reader that there are a good many matters, of varying degrees of importance, on which we have not been able to reconcile our opinions, but I hope that in all such instances I have made Professor Lehmann's own views available.

I owe a particular debt to two friends. Professor G. E. Bean spent long hours revising some of these very illegible texts with me, and his skill in deciphering solved some problems that had baffled me, while common study solved other difficult problems. Professor Ronald Syme discussed the Latin inscriptions with me, and these texts have profited considerably from his expert suggestions. In addition Mr. W. G. Forrest and Professor I. A. Richmond both made suggestions while the work was in proof. To all I express my warmest thanks.

I am also indebted to Monsieur J. Charbonneaux, Conservateur-en-Chef of the Musée du Louvre, for providing photographs of the inscriptions from Samothrace now in the Louvre, and to Miss Lucy Talcott for enabling me to purchase squeeze paper from the supplies of the American excavations of the Athenian Agora.

The spelling of the English manuscript has been altered to current American usage, and the apparatus has been somewhat modified from my usual practice to conform to the style of the series.

P. M. F.

All Souls College, Oxford
October 1958

ACKNOWLEDGMENTS FOR PHOTOGRAPHS

By Anna Wachsmann:

PL. I: 1, 2, 5; PL. II: 7, 8; PL. III; PL. IV; PL. V: 10a, c; PL. VI; PL. VII: 12; PL. VIII: 17a, b; PL. IX: 19; PL. X: 21, 22a, b; PL. XII: 26, 27, 35, 37; PL. XV; PL. XVI; PL. XVII; PL. XVIII: 44, 47; PL. XIX: 48, 49, 50, 51; PL. XX: 53 *right;* PL. XXI: 55, 56, 59; PL. XXII: 57, 60, 61; PL. XXIV; PL. XXV; PL. XXVI: 70, 74; PL. XXVII: 71, 73, 75, 77, 79; PL. XXVIII; PL. XXIX: 83a, b, 84, 85a, b.

By Alison Frantz:

PL. XI: 23; PL. XII.

By Phyllis W. Lehmann:

PL. VII: 1, 2, 5; PL. VIII: 13, 14; PL. XIX: 45; PL. XXII: 61; PL. XXVI: 68, 69; PL. XXVII: 72; PL. XXIX: 91.

The photographs for PL. XX, 53 *left* and 53 *bis,* we owe to the courtesy of the Kunsthistorisches Museum, Vienna.

CONTENTS

CONTENTS

ABBREVIATIONS

AEMÖ	*Archäologisch-epigraphische Mitteilungen aus Österreich (-Ungarn).*
AEp	*L'Année épigraphique.*
AJA	*American Journal of Archaeology.*
AJP	*American Journal of Philology.*
AM	*Mitteilungen des deutschen archäologischen Instituts, Athenische Abteilung.*
AnzWien	*Anzeiger der Akademie der Wissenschaften,* Vienna: philosophisch-historische Klasse.
ATL	B. D. Meritt, H. T. Wade-Gery, and M. F. McGregor. *The Athenian Tribute Lists.* American School of Classical Studies, Princeton, 1939–53. 4 vols.
AZ	*Archäologische Zeitung.*
BCH	*Bulletin de correspondance hellénique.*
Beloch, *GG*	Karl J. Beloch. *Griechische Geschichte.* 1st edn., Strassburg, 1893–1904, 3 vols.; 2d edn., Berlin and Leipzig, 1912–27, 4 vols.
Berl. Abh.	Deutsche Akademie der Wissenschaften, Berlin: philosophisch-historische Klasse, *Abhandlungen.*
Berl. Ber.	——, *Monatsberichte.*
BMI	*Collection of Ancient Greek Inscriptions in the British Museum.* London, 1874–1916. 4 pts.
BS[R]AA	*Bulletin de la Société [royale] d'archéologie d'Alexandrie.*
CAH	*Cambridge Ancient History.* Cambridge, 1927–39.
Chapouthier	F. Chapouthier. *Les Dioscures au service d'une déesse.* Paris, 1935.
Choix	F. Durrbach. *Choix d'inscriptions de Délos.* Vol. 1 (all published), Paris, 1922.
CIG	*Corpus Inscriptionum Graecarum.*
CIL	*Corpus Inscriptionum Latinarum.*
CRAI	*Comptes rendus de l'Académie des inscriptions et belles lettres.*
Degrassi, *Fasti Consolari*	A. Degrassi. *I Fasti Consolari dell' Impero Romano.* Rome, 1952.
DenkschrWien	Akademie der Wissenschaften, Vienna: *Denkschriften.*
EphDac	*Ephemeris Dacoromana.*
FdDelphes	*Fouilles de Delphes.* Paris, 1909– . Vol. 3, *Epigraphie,* in 6 pts.
FGrHist	F. Jacoby. *Die Fragmente der griechischen Historiker.* Berlin and Leiden, 1923– .
GGM	C. Müller. *Geographi Graeci Minores.* Paris, 1855–61. 2 vols. and *Tabulae.*
GöttNachr	*Nachrichten von der Gesellschaft der Wissenschaften zu Göttingen.*

Guide	Karl Lehmann. *Samothrace. A Guide to the Excavations and the Museum.* New York, 1955.
Guide[2]	Ibid. 2d revised edn., Locust Valley, New York, 1960.
Hemberg	B. Hemberg. *Die Kabiren.* Uppsala, 1950.
HN[2]	B. V. Head, G. F. Hill, G. MacDonald, and W. Wroth. *Historia Numorum.* 2d edn., Oxford, 1911.
HTR	*Harvard Theological Review.*
IG	*Inscriptiones Graecae.*
IGLS	L. Jalabert and R. Mouterde. *Inscriptions grecques et latines de la Syrie.* Paris, 1929– . 4 vols. to date.
IGRR	R. Cagnat, J. Toutain, P. Jouguet, and G. Lafaye. *Inscriptiones Graecae ad Res Romanas Pertinentes.* Paris, 1906–27. 3 vols. (1, 3, 4).
ILS	H. Dessau. *Inscriptiones Latinae Selectae.* Berlin, 1892–1916. 3 vols. in 5 pts.
Inscr. Délos	*Inscriptions de Délos.* Paris, 1926– .
Inscr. Lindos	C. Blinkenberg. *Lindos, Fouilles de l'Acropole, 1902–14.* Vol. II, *Inscriptions.* Berlin and Copenhagen, 1941. 2 vols.
JDAI	*Jahrbuch des [kaiserlichen] deutschen archäologischen Instituts.*
JEA	*Journal of Egyptian Archaeology.*
JHS	*Journal of Hellenic Studies.*
JOAI	*Jahreshefte des österreichischen archäologischen Instituts in Wien.*
JRS	*Journal of Roman Studies.*
Kock	T. Kock. *Comicorum Atticorum Fragmenta.* Leipzig, 1880–88. 3 vols.
LS[9]	H. G. Liddell and R. Scott. *A Greek-English Lexicon.* 9th edn., revised by H. Stuart Jones. Oxford, 1940. 2 vols.
Michel	C. Michel. *Recueil d'inscriptions grecques.* Vol. 1, Brussels, 1900; Suppl. 1, Paris, 1912; Suppl. 2, Brussels, 1927.
Muratori, *Thesaurus*	L. A. Muratori. *Novus Thesaurus Veterum Inscriptionum.* Milan, 1739–64. 4 vols. and Suppl.
OGIS	Wilhelm Dittenberger. *Orientis Graeci Inscriptiones Selectae.* Leipzig, 1903–1905. 2 vols.
Pape-Benseler	W. Pape. *Wörterbuch der griechischen Eigennamen.* 3d edn., G. E. Benseler. Brunswick, 1875.
PCZ	C. C. Edgar. *Zenon Papyri.* Cairo, 1925–40. 5 vols. Vol. 5, ed. O. Guéraud and P. Jouguet.
PIR	*Prosopographia Imperii Romani.*
PPetr	J. P. Mahaffy and J. G. Smyly. *The Flinders Petrie Papyri.* Dublin, 1891–1905. 3 vols.
PRyl	A. S. Hunt, J. de M. Johnson, V. Martin, C. H. Roberts, and E. G. Turner. *Catalogue of the Greek Papyri in the John Rylands Library of Manchester.* Manchester, 1911–52. 4 vols.

PTeb	B. P. Grenfell, A. S. Hunt, J. G. Smyly, and C. C. Edgar. *The Tebtunis Papyri.* London, 1902–38. 3 vols. in 4 (Vol. 3 in 2 pts.).
RE	G. Wissowa et al. *Paulys Real-Encyclopädie der classischen Altertumswissenschaft.* Stuttgart, 1894– .
REG	*Revue des études grecques.*
RevPhil	*Revue de philologie.*
RFIC	*Rivista di Filologia e d'Istruzione Classica.*
RhM	*Rheinisches Museum für Philologie.*
RM	*Mitteilungen des deutschen archäologischen Instituts, Römische Abteilung.*
Rostovtzeff, *SEHHW*	M. I. Rostovtzeff. *The Social and Economic History of the Hellenistic World.* Oxford, 1941. (Corrected reprint by P. M. Fraser, 1953.) 3 vols.
Rubensohn	O. Rubensohn. *Die Mysterienheiligtümer in Eleusis und Samothrake.* Berlin, 1892.
S,I	A. Conze, A. Hauser, and G. Niemann. *Archäologische Untersuchungen auf Samothrake.* Vienna, 1875.
S,II	A. Conze, A. Hauser, and O. Benndorf. *Neue Archäologische Untersuchungen auf Samothrake.* Vienna, 1880.
SB	F. Preisigke, F. Bilabel, and E. Kiessling. *Sammelbuch griechischer Urkunden aus Ägypten.* Strassburg, Berlin, Leipzig, Heidelberg, and Wiesbaden, 1915– . Vols. 1–6 (1) to date.
SEG	*Supplementum Epigraphicum Graecum.*
Syll [3]	Wilhelm Dittenberger. *Sylloge Inscriptionum Graecarum.* 3d edn., Leipzig, 1915–24. 4 vols.
TAM	*Tituli Asiae Minoris.* Vienna, 1901– .
Tod, *GHI*	M. N. Tod. *A Selection of Greek Historical Inscriptions.* Vol. 2, Oxford, 1948.
Trans. Int. Num. Congr.	*Transactions of the International Numismatic Congress, 1936.* London, 1938.
ZNum	*Zeitschrift für Numismatik.*

SAMOTHRACE:

THE INSCRIPTIONS ON STONE

Introduction

THE INSCRIPTIONS published in this volume, though on the whole disappointing in both substance and preservation, add a good deal to our knowledge of the Sanctuary but very little to that of the political history of the city. Nevertheless, to be able fully to estimate the significance of the new material relating to the Sanctuary, we must first discuss briefly the fortunes of the city, particularly during the Hellenistic period, from which almost all of our evidence dates.

I

The first inscription (1) is of prime importance in connection with the history of the city, not only because it is probably half a century or more older than any other surviving decree but also because the Aeolic words in it indicate a corresponding Aeolic element, hitherto unattested, in the colonizers of the island. At the same time the appearance, in 5, of the Ionic month *Maimakterion* should mean that there was also an Ionic element in the city. The Aeolic strain was evidently predominating, and it is significant that archaeological evidence also points to early connections with the opposing mainland of Asia Minor.[1] Evidence is lacking whether the Aeolic and Ionic colonists were contemporary or whether, as often, they came in successive groups.

The Archaic and Classic periods of the city receive no enlightenment from the new evidence, though in this connection the identification, within recent years, of the archaic coinage of the city should not be forgotten.[2] Samothrace is thereby known to have issued its own coinage some two centuries earlier than had previously been supposed.[3] Other evidence for the history of the city, already familiar, is listed elsewhere [4] and need not detain us.

1. Lehmann, *Guide,* p. 13.
2. See W. Schwabacher, *Trans. Int. Num. Congr., 1936* (1938), pp. 109 ff.; cf. id., American Numismatic Society, *Museum Notes,* 5 (1952), 49–51. The hoard appears to have been buried ca. 470 B.C. (see pp. 119–20).
3. B. V. Head, *HN* [2], p. 263, says, "The coins of this island seem to be all subsequent to the death of Lysimachus."
4. See Vol. 1, *The Ancient Literary Sources.*

The history of the city in the Hellenistic period has been interpreted in the past largely in terms of the suzerainty exercised over it by this or that royal house.[5] To this end, evidence from the Sanctuary and from the city has been indifferently evoked. It is perhaps time for a general reassessment in this respect. Questions of principle face us at the outset. Can royal dedications in the Sanctuary be used as evidence of fluctuations of political suzerainty over the city? Can the Sanctuary itself be regarded as having been subject to this power or that, in the same way as the city may have been? Is there any reason to suppose that the Sanctuary enjoyed the restrictive protection of one power, which surrendered that protection only when forced to do so, and that it was not accessible to all powers, and all heads of states, to make dedications? It is unfortunate, in a matter where so much might be answered by the force of analogy, that the status of Delos is uncertain in this respect. It remains a matter of controversy whether the dedications of vase-festivals and other acts of patronage there—by Ptolemies, Seleucids, and others—represent acts of sovereignty or testify to a peaceful coexistence in respect of a religious center.[6] So also at Samothrace, the question must to some extent be answered in principle. So far as the present writer is aware, there is no good reason for suggesting that the Sanctuary was restricted. Samothrace possessed no strategic importance and was not the center of a lively commercial, or even political, activity, as was Delos in the third century, when, notwithstanding, it may have been accessible to all. Samothrace in the third century should perhaps rather be compared with Delos in the second century, when the suzerainty of the Aegean had passed to Rhodes and the island had lost much of its importance. In the same sense we may compare a letter of Philip V to the Athenian cleruchs on Lemnos, in which he accepts an invitation to patronize τὰ παρ' ὑμῖν ἱερά.[7] Here there is no question of Philip's having exercised political control over Lemnos. In the absence, therefore, of evidence to the contrary, it does not seem necessary to accept the proposition that a dedication made by a sovereign in the Sanctuary of the Great Gods presupposes that the island—city and Sanctuary—was subject to him.

The conspectus of the history of the city and Sanctuary drawn up by Fredrich,[8] the main attempt up to the present to give a continuous history of Samothrace, needs considerable revision in the light both of the argument elaborated in the preceding paragraph and of a more careful interpretation of the scanty evidence. For the early Hellenistic period

5. Cf. H. Braunert, *JDAI*, 65–66 (1950–51), 259, who says that the history of the island "so recht ein Spiegelbild bietet für die Kämpfe der Diadochenreiche." Cf. Fredrich, *RE*, s.v. *Samothrake*, col. 2226, who says, "Seit dem Tode Alexanders spielte sich die grosse Geschichte der Zeit auch in der der Insel ab."
6. For a bibliography see P. M. Fraser and G. E. Bean, *The Rhodian Peraea and Islands* (London, 1954), p. 164, n. 6.

7. See the republication of the letter by Fraser and McDonald, *JRS*, 42 (1952), 81 ff. (*SEG*, XII, 399). The general interpretation remains true, even if the supplement proposed, ibid., for line 12 is not certain.
8. *IG*, XII (8), 37 ff. The same author's article in *RE*, s.v. *Samothrake*, is extremely jejune. As we shall see, Fredrich's Samothracian annals are marred by considerable carelessness.

we have no information of significance, and no new information. The political status of the island has first to be considered in connection with the decree of thanks passed by the city in honor of Lysimachus, presumably when he was king of Macedon (287–281 B.C.), for having rescued the Sanctuary from some ἀσεβεῖς who attacked it at night and attempted to set fire to it.[9] This decree describes the relationship of Lysimachus to the city in language which shows that it regarded him as its benefactor. It orders the erection of an altar to Lysimachus Euergetes, part of the dedicatory inscription of which may survive (12), and the performance of regular ceremonies in his honor.[10] There is, however, nothing in the language which inevitably implies that the city was dependent on him at the time. Such ceremonious honors, including worship with a cult-title, are attested beyond doubt in cities that were wholly autonomous, and nothing can be argued from them.[11] The description of the operation by which Lysimachus saved the Sanctuary makes no reference to a garrison, and the king's presence may have been casual,[12] and connected with his own participation in religious ceremonies. There is no evidence, therefore, in the inscription itself that Samothrace was not independent at the time. Nevertheless, the alternative possibility remains, and perhaps is probable on general grounds.

The period from 281 to 197 B.C. is divided by Fredrich as follows: 281 to 265, "Insula Aegyptiorum est"; 265 [as a result of the battle of Kos] to 245, "In Seleucidarum potestate est"; 246 / 245 [conquest of Thrace by Euergetes I] to 228–225, "Aegyptiorum rursus est"; 228 [lost to Antigonos Doson] to 197 / 196, "Macedonum est."[13]

The selection of the year 281 for the first acquisition of the island by Egypt derives from the fact that Arsinoe after her marriage to Ptolemy Keraunos fled to Samothrace.[14] Subsequently, the argument runs, Ptolemy Philadelphus dedicated the Propylaea ("Ptolemaieion") of the Sanctuary (11). The assumption, therefore, is that Arsinoe retained possession of the island, as she did of Samos, and that it became Egyptian on her marriage to Philadelphus.[15]

9. *IG,* XII (8), 150 = *Syll*[3] 372.

10. Lines 23 ff.: ἱδρύσασθαι βωμὸν | [β]ασιλέως Λυσιμάχου εὐεργέτου | [ὡ]ς κάλλιστον καὶ θύειν κατ' ἐνιαυτὸν | [κ]αὶ πομπεύειν τοὺς ἐννέα ἄρχοντας | [κ]αὶ στεφανηφορεῖν τοὺς πολίτας | [πά]ντας τῆι ἡμέραι ταύ-τηι, ποεῖν δὲ ———— |.

11. See my note on the cult of the Ptolemies in Byzantium and Rhodes in *Opuscula Atheniensia,* 4°, III (1960), p. 30, n. 1, p. 38, n. 1. The document is normally regarded as proof that Lysimachus was master of Samothrace: see W. W. Tarn, *Antigonos Gonatas* (Oxford, 1913), pp. 117–18; 135, n. 48; id., *CAH,* VII (1928), 92–93; Fredrich, above, n. 8.

12. Lines 12 ff.: παραγενόμενος ὁ βασιλεὺ[ς | εἰ]ς τοὺς τόπους δέδωκεν ἐγδότους | [τ]ῆι πόλει καὶ ἀφέσταλκε πρὸς τὸν [δῆμ]ον, κ.τ.λ. C. Habicht, *Gottmenschentum und griechische Städte* (Zetemata, 14, 1956), pp. 39–40,

argues from Lysimachus' presence on the island that it belonged to him. I do not think this a necessary conclusion, in view of the general considerations already noted.

13. *IG,* XII (8), 38; cf. *RE,* s.v. *Samothrake,* where the same divisions are given without the supporting evidence.

14. Justin 24.3 (see Vol. 1, 102): "ex urbe protracta Samothraciam in exilium abiit, eo miserior quod mori ei cum filiis non licuit."

15. See Beloch, *GG,* 1st edn., III, pt. II, 280 = 2d edn., IV, pt. II, 347: "Von den Inseln an der thrakischen Küste ist Samothrake dem Ptolemäerreiche durch Arsinoe zugebracht worden"; M. Fritze, *Die ersten Ptolemäer und Griechenland* (Halle, 1917), pp. 61–62: "Arsinoe hatte die Insel mit dem Ptolemäerreich vereinigt."

This argument, however, does not stand examination. If the island had previously belonged to Lysimachus, it presumably belonged to Keraunos at the time Arsinoe went there,[16] and her presence there would not necessarily give her control over it, either then or after Keraunos' death, when she moved to Egypt. Alternatively, if the island were independent and she fled there because it was outside Macedonian territory and because the Sanctuary had previously been patronized by her (10) and by Lysimachus (see above) when they ruled Thrace, it would be as a refugee that she arrived there—perhaps to take advantage of the recognized asylum of the Sanctuary [17]—and she would not be in a position to transfer the island to Egypt. Consequently, though Ptolemy may have favored the Sanctuary because of the reception it had granted Arsinoe, this does not constitute a reason for supposing that the city passed at that time into Ptolemaic control.[18] In any case, there are in fact good grounds for believing that Philadelphus' dedication of the Propylaea occurred not after his marriage to Arsinoe, but while Arsinoe was still queen of Macedon.[19] If this is correct, the last trace of evidence for Philadelphus' control of the island is gone. It is quite likely that the city retained

16. Thus B. Niese, *Geschichte der griechischen und makedonischen Staaten* (3 vols., Gotha, 1893–1903), II, 10–11, says, "Arsinoe wurde verstossen, aus Makedonien vertrieben und nach Samothrake verbannt"; and Tarn, *CAH*, VII, 99, writes, "[Keraunos] allowed her to take sanctuary in Samothrake." The first at least of these statements clearly implies that Keraunos was master of Samothrace, and the latter may do so. Haussoullier thought it was already Seleucid at this time: see below, n. 21. J. Pouilloux, *Recherches sur l'histoire et les cultes de Thasos* (Paris, 1954), I, 384, speaking of Egyptian influence in the Thracian area, says, "L'influence d'Arsinoé à Samothrace fut considérable," but this is misleading, since the evidence for her influence belongs to the period before she was queen of Egypt.

17. Thus Fritze, *Die ersten Ptolemäer*, p. 62, in continuation of the sentence quoted above, n. 15, writes, "nach der Ermordung ihrer Söhne durch ihren zweiten Gatten Ptolemäos Keraunos war sie als Schutzflehende an den Altar der μεγάλοι θεοί geflüchtet." I am inclined to share this point of view, but I do not see how Fritze can combine this with her view that Arsinoe united the island to Egypt.

18. This is already the conclusion of Haussoullier, *Études sur l'histoire de Milet et du Didymeion* (Paris, 1902), p. 83. Speaking of the dedication of the Propylaea (which he unfortunately confuses with the "Arsinoeion"), he says, "Nous n'avons pas le droit de conclure de cette royale offrande que l'île appartenait à Philadelphe; Ptolémée III seulement en deviendra le maître" (Fredrich, *IG*, XII [8], 38, refers to Haussoullier, but does not indicate that the latter's

view is directly opposed to his own); so also Dittenberger, *OGIS* 225, n. 23, and, more recently, G. Corradi, *Studi ellenistici* (Turin, 1929), p. 82, n. 2, and pp. 195–97, who gives the best statement on this.

19. Corradi, p. 196, pointed out, on general grounds, that Philadelphus may have dedicated the Propylaea during Lysimachus' lifetime, in the years of their friendship based on their matrimonial connection. This conjecture can be supported by a precise argument. In the dedicatory inscription of the Propylaea (11) the parents of Philadelphus are described simply as Σωτῆρες, not θεοὶ Σωτῆρες. I have shown in detail in *BS[R]AA*, 41 (1956), 50, n. 2—with particular reference to Egyptian documents—that this formula is characteristic only of the earliest dedications of the reign of Philadelphus, before 280 / 279 B.C., and in a formal dedication such as that of the Samothracian Propylaea strict court protocol would probably be followed. This seems a strong argument in favor of the view that the dedication should be dated 285–281. A comparison of the hands of the two dedications also suggests that the dedication by Philadelphus would not be later than that of the "Arsinoeion." Beloch, *GG*, 1st edn., III, pt. II, 280, and 2d edn., IV, pt. II, 347, maintains that Philadelphus could not have made his dedication if another king had controlled the island. If the relations between Lysimachus and Philadelphus, his brother-in-law, were good, and if Lysimachus was indeed master of the island, as he may have been, there seems, on the contrary, every reason why Lysimachus should have permitted, even welcomed, such a dedication by a friendly sovereign: cf. above, p. 4.

its independence in these years, when the main exertions of the warring kings were being made farther south, and there is no need to replace Philadelphus by another suzerain.

The next stage in the history of the island, as envisaged by Fredrich, occurs when city and Sanctuary became Seleucid sometime before 253, and therefore either during the second Syrian War or earlier.[20] Once more, on examination the argument appears insufficient. It is based on the fact that in 254 / 253 Antiochus II ordered the text of his sale of land to Laodike to be set up in the Sanctuary.[21] However, since Delos is mentioned in an earlier Seleucid document as one of the places for its exposition at a time when Delos, if protected by any power, was protected by Egypt, no political significance can safely be attached to the mention of Samothrace here.[22] The Sanctuary was the most natural place for the publication of a text in the north Aegean, as Delos was for the central and southern areas. To maintain on this ground—and there is no other—that the island was under Seleucid control would obviously be unwise.[23]

Thus, though the proximity of Samothrace to the Thracian mainland means that the island very easily might have become subject to the power of Macedon, and may have been so at least before 281, it is likely enough that in the troubles which followed the death of Seleucus it was left in peace and enjoyed independence, even if it had not done so earlier. The view that it was subsequently a Ptolemaic, and then a Seleucid, possession depends on a seeming misunderstanding of the status of the Sanctuary, and the significance of the dedications made there. These dedications should be taken as a sign of the growing fame of the Sanctuary.

With the Ptolemaic conquest of Thrace and the Hellespontine region, the position changes. The well-known Samothracian decree in honor of Hippomedon, the Ptolemaic

20. See Niese, *Geschichte*, III, 380 (addend. to p. 28); Beloch, *GG* (above, n. 19), maintains that Egypt lost the island as a result of the battle of Kos, and he is followed by Fredrich, *IG* and *RE*. Tarn, *Antigonos Gonatas*, pp. 324–25, *CAH*, VII, 712, places it in a different context, ca. 256 B.C., in the second Syrian War. In each case the reason is expressly stated to be the inscription quoted in n. 21, below.

21. *OGIS* 225 = C. B. Welles, *Royal Correspondence in the Hellenistic Period* (New Haven, 1934), 18, lines 27 ff.: καὶ τὴν ὠνὴν ἀναγράψαι εἰς τὰς βασιλικὰς γραφὰς| τὰς ἐν Σάρδεσιν καὶ εἰς στήλας λιθίνας πέντε· τού|των τὴμ μὲν μίαν θεῖναι ἐν Ἰλίωι ἐν τῶι ἱερῶι τῆς Ἀθηνᾶς|, τὴν δὲ ἑτέραν ἐν τῶι ἱερῶι τῶι ἐν Σαμοθράικηι, τὴν δὲ ἑτέ|ραν ἐν Ἐφέσωι ἐν τῶι ἱερῶι τῆς Ἀρτέμιδος, τὴν δὲ τε|τάρτην ἐν Διδύμοις ἐν τῶι ἱερῶι τοῦ Ἀπόλλωνος, τὴν | δὲ πέμπτην ἐν Σάρδεσιν ἐν τῶι ἱερῶι τῆς Ἀρτέμιδος. The commentators on this (except Welles, see n. 22, below) have also accepted this as evidence for Seleucid control of the island: see Haussoullier, *Études*, p. 83

(followed by Dittenberger, *OGIS* 225, n. 23), who believed that the island became Seleucid after Curupedion, and remained so until the reign of Ptolemy Euergetes I. Haussoullier also believed that τὸ ἱερὸν τὸ ἐν Σαμοθράικηι refers not to the Sanctuary of the Great Gods but to the temple of Athena in the city where Samothracian decrees were erected (see below, p. 37), a view seemingly accepted by Dittenberger, *OGIS*, loc. cit.; cf. Hemberg, p. 63, n. 2. I do not think this at all likely. The parallel text—quoted below, n. 49—expressly mentions the Sanctuary of the Great Gods.

22. This is pointed out by Welles, *Royal Correspondence*, p. 99, n. 30. The document in question is *OGIS* 335, the Pergamene text concerning the boundary dispute between Mytilene and Pitane, which includes (lines 132 ff.) a description of the sale of land to Pitane by Antiochus I, record of which was inscribed on stelai erected at Ilium, Delos, and Ephesos.

23. Cf. Welles, loc. cit.

στρατηγὸς τοῦ Ἑλλησπόντου καὶ τῶν ἐπὶ Θράικης τόπων, clearly shows that at this time the city was subject to Egypt,[24] as is evident from the fact that Hippomedon had taken military measures to secure the safety of the Samothracian continental possessions; [25] that the city had to ask his permission to import grain free of tax [26]—probably one of the taxes which were still imposed by Egypt on her foreign dependencies at the end of the century; [27] and that it requested him to undertake the resettlement of the Peraea with citizen-cleruchs.[28] Hippomedon, it may be noted, had been himself initiated in the mysteries after taking up his appointment [29]—thus creating a precedent for the Roman officials of Macedonia—and had embellished the Sanctuary with offerings. Another more recently discovered Samothracian decree [30] in honor of the Ptolemaic governor of Maroneia, Epinikos, records in very similar language the assistance given by him in the defense of the Peraea when invaded by barbarians. Both these decrees show very clearly that Samothrace was an Egyptian dependency. The natural occasion for the acquisition is the conquest of Thrace, ca. 245 B.C.[31] Fredrich accepted the view that the decree in honor of Hippomedon should be dated 228–225, on the ground that the dispatch of troops mentioned in the decree represents measures taken in a campaign against Antigonos Doson at this time. The conjecture, as expressed by Fredrich, seems to rest in part on a misunderstanding,[32] but in any case it seems quite clear

24. The text of this inscription—*IG*, XII (8), 156 = *Syll*³ 502—is given below, pp. 39–40. The best commentary on it is that of H. Bengtson, *Die Strategie in der hellenistischen Zeit* (3 vols., Munich, 1937–52), III, 178 ff.; cf. Rostovtzeff, *SEHHW*, I, 335; further references are given by P. Treves, *Euforione e la storia ellenistica* (Milan, 1955), p. 53, n. 8; cf. Fraser, *Gnomon*, 29 (1956), 581.

25. See below, p. 39, A, lines 8 ff.; P. Roussel, *BCH*, 63 (1939), 137 ff.

26. Below, p. 40, B, lines 15–16: σίτου ἐξαγωγὴν καὶ ἀτέλειαν δοῦν[αι | τ]ῆι πόλει Χερρονήσου καὶ ἄλλοθεν ὅθεν αὐτῶι εὔκαιρον φα[ί]|νηται εἶναι, κ.τ.λ.

27. For the general significance of the measure see the passages quoted by Bengtson, p. 180, n. 2; Rostovtzeff, loc. cit. For the Thracian φόρος, still paid at the end of the third century, see *PTeb* 8, and cf. Fraser, *JEA*, 39 (1953), 91, n. 5.

28. Below, p. 40, B, lines 18 ff.: καὶ παρακαλεῖν αὐτὸν συμπρᾶξαι τῆι π[ό|λ]ει εἰς τὸ συντελεσθέντος αὐτο[ῦ] κατασταθῆναι τῶμ πολ[ι|τῶ]ν τοὺς κληρουχήσοντας καὶ γεωργήσοντας τὴν χώραν, κ.τ.λ.

29. Ibid., A, lines 6 ff.: ἔσπευσεν παρα[γενό]μενος εἰς τὴν νῆσον μετασχεῖν τῶν μυστηρίων, κ.τ.λ.

30. This inscription was originally published by G. Bakalakis and R. L. Scranton, *AJP*, 60 (1939), 452 ff., based on independent copies made by them in 1935. Subsequently the stone was badly damaged, and affected by weathering (see the detailed history of the stone after its discovery, given by Scranton, p. 452).

Subsequent publications and corrections (see the bibliography in Bengtson, *Strategie*, III, 183, n. 1) are based on the published text. Since 1938 the stone has been in the Epigraphical Museum in Athens (EM 13042), where I collated it in 1954. The whole of the left part is badly shattered for lines 1–20 (this part has been stuck together, but pieces are missing), while from line 20 onward the whole of the left part is lost. The whole surviving stone is worn beyond the limits of legibility, and nothing is served by republishing it.

31. The earliest dated document is the decree of Ainos, *Asylieurkunden aus Kos, Berl. Abh.*, 1952 (1), no. 8, dated to 242 B.C.; cf. Fraser, *JEA*, 39 (1953), 91, n. 5; id., *Opuscula Atheniensia*, 4°, III (1960), p. 37, n. 3. It is natural, however, to connect the conquest with the operations of the third Syrian War, since Thrace is not listed in the Adulis inscription (*OGIS* 54) among the territories inherited by Euergetes (cf. Bengtson, *Strategie*, III, 178, n. 1), though it must be admitted that the modality of the acquisition is quite unknown. Treves, *Euforione*, pp. 77 ff., tries to establish the background of the conquest, but I cannot accept his hypotheses: see *Gnomon*, 29 (1956), 581.

32. He says, "Hippomedon insulam ab Antigono Dosone defendere iussus erat, sed paulo post Antigonus S. cepit (de bello cf. Niese, *Geschichte*, II, 169)." But Niese in the passage in question (p. 169, n. 3) refers the inscription to the reign of Demetrius II, i.e., 239–229. However, numerous scholars before and since have adopted the fictitious connection with

that even if the lines in question refer to an actual defensive operation in the Peraea, there is no suggestion that Macedon was involved. There is no reference to Macedon or to royal troops, and it is natural to suppose that the enemy, if any, were Thracian tribesmen, as they were on the occasion of the services rendered by Epinikos.[33] The inscription can, on paleographical grounds, be placed considerably earlier in the reign of Euergetes, and since we know that Hippomedon was governor by ca. 240–230, there is no objection to the earlier date.[34] We must therefore be content with the knowledge that it refers to the reign of Euergetes.

The question now arises, how long did Ptolemaic rule in Samothrace persist? According to Fredrich, the island was Macedonian from 228–225 to 197/196. This appears to rest on two alleged pieces of evidence: first, that already shown to be unfounded, that the island became Macedonian in the reign of Doson; and secondly, that a single Samothracian occurs in the list of new citizens of Larisa in the letter of Philip V of 214 B.C.[35] To this may be added the fact that in the treaty concluded between Philip and Lysimachia the Lysimachian oath of observance is made on the Samothracian deities.[36] However, if the foundation of this argument is removed—the capture of the island by Macedon in 228–225—these two other points lose substance. The fact that a single unknown Samothracian occurs among the new citizens of Larisa clearly can prove nothing as to the status of his native city,[37] and the oath of the Lysimachian treaty only attests yet again the growing prestige of the Sanctuary.[38] Substantial evidence for a Macedonian occupation at this time has thus still to be

Antigonos Doson: see A. Bouché-Leclercq, *Histoire des Lagides* (4 vols., Paris, 1903–1907), I, 281, n. 1; W. Otto, *RE*, s.v. *Hippomedon* (14), cols. 1885 f.; F. Hiller von Gaertringen, *Syll³* 502, n. 2. Roussel, *BCH*, 63 (1939), 139, has already rejected the view that the island was ever Seleucid at this time (see esp. p. 139, n. 4, where he lists further adherents of the view that Doson acquired the island).

33. Cf. Roussel, pp. 135–36.

34. Hippomedon must have left Sparta soon after the collapse of the reforms of his cousin Agis IV in 241 (see Otto, col. 1884), and Teles' speech (p. 23, Hense), in which Hippomedon is called ὁ Λακεδαιμόνιος ὁ νῦν ἐπὶ Θράκης καθεστάμενος ὑπὸ Πτολεμαίου, was delivered in Megara sometime after this; but, as Wilamowitz saw when he originally dated it (Wilamowitz-Moellendorff, *Antigonos von Karystos*, Berlin, 1881, pp. 302 ff.), the lower limit is uncertain: cf. Roussel, *BCH*, 63 (1939), 139, n. 1. Otto (op. cit., n. 32, above) makes a point independent of his adherence to the theory that Hippomedon was concerned in a war with Antigonos Doson, namely, that though he may have been governor of Thrace by ca. 240 or earlier, some time must have elapsed during which he manifested that good will for which honors were bestowed on him, and he therefore prefers a date in the twenties for the inscription. If, however, he had been governor since the

conquest, ca. 245, the argument against a date ca. 240 would disappear.

35. *IG*, IX (2), 517 (= *Syll³* 543 = F. Schroeter, *De regum . . . stilisticae* [Leipzig, 1932], 30/1—both without the list of names), line 48, the first name: Σαμόθρακες· ῎Αρχιππος Καλλιφούντειος. Objections to the force of this argument have already been raised by Otto, op. cit., col. 1886, and Roussel, p. 139, n. 4.

36. G. Oikonomos, Ἐπιγραφαὶ τῆς Μακεδονίας (Athens, 1915), no. 1, B, lines 5 ff.: ὅρκος Λυσιμαχέων· ὀμνύω Δί[α——|——] καὶ τοὺς θεοὺς τοὺς ἐν Σαμοθράι[κηι ——]. This passage is adduced in its present context in Hiller's note 40 on *Syll³* 543. On Philip's occupation of Lysimachia see also L. Robert, *Hellenica*, 10 (1955), 266 ff., esp. 269–70.

37. The impossibility of determining the status or allegiance of a city from the presence of a single member of it in a particular context should be clear. In this case, as Otto (op. cit., col. 1886) has pointed out, it is clear from lines 4 and 5 of the inscription that those on whom citizenship is bestowed are residents in Larisa.

38. It may also mean that Lysimachia, like Sestos— *OGIS* 88, attribution uncertain: see M. Holleaux, *Études d'épigraphie et d'histoire grecques* (5 vols., Paris, 1938—, ed. L. Robert), IV, 317, n. 3; Hemberg, p. 237—and many cities of the Pontic region, had its own temple of the Samothracian gods; cf. below, p. 36.

found. On the other hand, the Samothracians sent a theoros or ambassador to Alexandria in 220 / 219, and this seems an indication in favor of the view that the city was still Ptolemaic at this time.[39] It therefore probably suffered the same fate as the other Ptolemaic possessions in Thrace, remaining Egyptian at least until the second Macedonian War. It should be noted in passing, both as indicating the early interest of Rome in the shrine, and as providing an example of patronage of the shrine by a distinguished representative of one foreign power during the suzerainty of another, that it was in this period of probable Ptolemaic control, in 212 B.C., that Marcellus, the conqueror of Syracuse, dedicated ἀνδριάντες and πίνακες in Samothrace.[40]

At this point the fate of the island has to be considered in a wider context, and unfortunately there is no reference to Samothrace either in the accounts of Polybius and Livy or elsewhere, during these years. Philip conquered the Ptolemaic possessions in 200 / 199 B.C.,[41] and he may have conquered Samothrace at the same time. Even if he did not, this date probably represents the termination of Ptolemaic power in the area; Egypt would not have left an isolated holding there. In the terms of the senatorial decree recorded by Polybius,[42] containing the conditions to be imposed on Philip in 196, Samothrace, like Ainos and Maroneia, is not mentioned explicitly (as, for example, are Myrina, Lemnos, and Thasos) as to be liberated, and Holleaux has convincingly argued that this is because Polybius has omitted, as being without general interest, reference to those places which Philip was required to restore to Egypt.[43] If Holleaux is correct, it is likely that the Ptolemaic possessions in Thrace, and also Samothrace (if it had been taken by Philip), were restored, in theory if not subsequently in fact, to Egypt at this time.[44]

On this unsatisfactory note of uncertainty our examination of the third century must

---

39. A. C. Merriam, *AJA*, 1 (1885), 21, no. 2 = E. Breccia, *Iscrizioni greche e latine* (Cairo, 1911), p. XVI, no. 2 = H. Braunert, *JDAI*, 65–66 (1950–51), 236, no. 21: L γʹ Δίου ιγ̄ʹ | διὰ Θεοδότου | ἀγοραστοῦ, | Θεώνδου | Σαμόθραικος. For a photograph of this vase I am indebted to the authorities of the Metropolitan Museum: the reading is absolutely clear (Breccia's Θευδότου is wrong). The hand resembles closely that of the main Hadra series, and thus belongs to the reign of Philopator: see my detailed discussion, *JEA*, 39 (1953), 88 ff. (on p. 89, top, for "a year δ̄ (4)" read "a year β̄ (2)"; cf. further *Berytus* 13, p. 160, n. 157). Though Theondas has neither the title πρεσβευτής nor θεωρός, both the fact that the vase came from the same group of burials, and that the deposition of the ashes was due to the same Theodotos, ἀγοραστής, who was responsible for the deposition of the ashes of some of the other πρεσβευταί and θεωροί, indicate that he was an important foreigner and therefore no doubt a representative of his state, like the others. For the various problems connected with the role of the ἀγοραστής see *JEA* (above), p. 87, n. 7. It does not seem probable that in the normal course of things an envoy or theoros would present himself in Alexandria if his city were under Macedonian rule, though exceptional circumstances no doubt could be envisaged in which the situation might arise. I would therefore stop short of regarding this as complete proof of the thesis that the city was still Ptolemaic.

40. Plutarch *Marcellus* 30 = Posidonius, *FGrHist*, 87 F 44 (see Vol. 1, **197**): ἦν δὲ ἀνάθημα Μαρκέλλου δίχα τῶν ἐν Ῥώμῃ γυμνάσιον μὲν ἐν Κατάνῃ τῆς Σικελίας, ἀνδριάντες δὲ καὶ πίνακες τῶν ἐκ Συρακουσῶν ἔν τε Σαμοθρᾴκῃ παρὰ τοῖς θεοῖς, οὓς Καβείρους ὠνόμαζον, καὶ περὶ Λίνδον ἐν τῷ ἱερῷ τῆς Ἀθηνᾶς.

41. On this campaign see F. W. Walbank, *Philip V of Macedon* (Cambridge, 1940), pp. 132 ff.

42. Polybius 18.44.2; cf. Walbank, pp. 178 ff.

43. *CAH*, VIII, 181, n. 1 (*Études*, V, 367).

44. See below, p. 11.

end. In retrospect we see that the history of the city during this long period was probably more uneventful than has been supposed, and it is possible to present a simpler picture in place of the frequent changes of suzerainty envisaged by Beloch, Fredrich, Tarn, and others. In the second half of the third century the main change in the fortunes of the island occurs when it becomes subject to Egypt, but there are no grounds for supposing that Ptolemaic suzerainty ended before 200 B.C., and what if anything happened then is, as we have seen, exceedingly uncertain.

Before examining the evidence for the second century, one aspect of the city under Ptolemaic rule may be briefly noticed. Both the decree for Hippomedon and that for Epinikos refer to the grain situation. In the former the city sought permission to import wheat from the Chersonese and elsewhere if it wished, instead of being restricted to the import of Egyptian wheat. Evidently the pressure of Ptolemaic imperial economy was making itself felt. The second decree, the date of which is also uncertain, sheds light on the gravity of the situation: among Epinikos' benefactions to the city is the gift—whether personal or official we cannot tell—of money free of interest for the purchase of wheat.[45] This provision of money for such a purchase, presumably on the open market, probably implies that the Ptolemaic authorities had relaxed the austerities of the previous system. However, *ad hoc* measures could not solve a chronic problem. It is therefore of great interest to see that at a later date the city introduced legislation of its own (5) to provide a permanent grain fund, and it is much to be regretted that the full sense of the law cannot be recovered.

We may now turn to the history of the second century. Here once more, until toward the end of the reign of Perseus, lack of evidence renders any certainty impossible. It has been pointed out that if Philip V occupied the island during his drive against Ptolemaic possessions in Thrace in 200 / 199, he was probably required to restore them in 197. There is, however, no sign whatever of Ptolemaic authority in the Thracian and northern Aegean area after the war, and it seems clear that Egypt never did reoccupy these regions and that Rome took them under her protection. It is recorded that in 196, after the peace, L. Stertinius liberated the Thracian cities [46]—and Hephaisteia on Lemnos and Thasos are mentioned in this connection, but Samothrace is not. Thus what happened to Samothrace must be left an open question. Fredrich—who, it will be recalled, maintained that the island became Macedonian in 228–225—held that Antiochus III subsequently occupied the island in 196, and that he maintained his hold on it until 190.[47] However, there is no evidence that such was the case, and we can only say that if he did, he probably had to evacuate the island in 190.[48] It

45. Lines 31 ff.: π[ρεσβ]είας τε ἀπο|σταλείσης πρὸς αὐτὸν ἐδά|νεισεν χρήματα ἄτοκα εἰς σι|[τηρ]έσ̣ι̣[ον] ἐν καιροῖς ἀναγκαίοις————(the rest of the inscription is missing); cf. above, p. 8, n. 30.

46. Polybius 18.48.2: Λεύκιος δὲ Στερτίνιος εἰς Ἡφαι-

στίαν καὶ Θάσον ἀφικόμενος καὶ τὰς ἐπὶ Θράκης πόλεις ἐποίησε τὸ παραπλήσιον [i.e., liberated them]; cf. Holleaux, *CAH*, VIII, 186, n. 1 (*Études*, V, 372, n. 1).

47. See *IG*, XII (8), p. 38.

48. See Walbank, *Philip V*, pp. 211–12, 332.

should be noted that in a document of the period in which Antiochus III occupied Lysimachia, it is stated that a copy of the text should be erected in the shrine of the Great Gods in Samothrace.[49] As before, in the absence of other evidence it is wiser to refrain from drawing inferences regarding the status of the city from this reference to the Sanctuary.

The obscurity of the years 200–196 affects our interpretation of the period down to the battle of Pydna. It is commonly assumed that the island, having fallen into the hands of Philip, was retained by him at the end of his life and was inherited by Perseus.[50] This is probably what in general terms did happen, but how or when Philip acquired the island—whether it was for the first or second time—is not clear. Contrary to the wishes of Rome, he reacquired, ca. 187, Maroneia and Ainos, both previously Ptolemaic possessions, and he could have taken the opportunity to occupy Samothrace, the failure of Livy to mention the fact notwithstanding. But, in any case, Ainos and Maroneia were both evacuated by Philip in 183.[51] Perseus made use of Samothrace as early as 172 as a meeting place for himself and some Asian envoys,[52] and Polybius expressly states with reference to the events of 169 that Perseus was master of the island.[53] The probability is that Philip acquired it and Perseus inherited it, rather than that the latter acquired it for himself. The main difficulty is, then, the obscurity round the period from Philip's campaign of 200/199 until his death in 178, and we must be content to say that he probably acquired the island definitively sometime within these limits.

After the battle of Pydna, Perseus took refuge on Samothrace, where he was apprehended by Roman officials.[54] From this point on, the island enjoyed independence under Roman protection, although it continued to suffer piratical raids.[55] As we shall see, the proximity to the Roman province of Macedonia made the shrine a resort of Roman provincial officials from an early date.[56]

49. A. Brückner in W. Dörpfeld, *Troja und Ilion* (2 vols., Athens, 1902), II, 448, no. III:[————τὴν μὲν ἐ]ν | Λυσιμαχείαι παρὰ τὸν βωμὸν τοῦ | Διὸς τοῦ Σωτῆρος, τὴν δὲ ἐν Σαμο|θράικηι ἐν τῶι ἱερῶι τῶν θεῶν [τῶν | μ]εγάλων, noted by Fredrich (above, n. 47).
50. So Fredrich, ibid.: "190–166. Macedonum rursus est."
51. Livy 39.27.10, and Walbank, *Philip V*, pp. 224 ff., for the tortuous negotiations between Rome, Philip, and Eumenes regarding Ainos and Maroneia in these years.
52. Livy 42.25.6, the report of the Roman envoys (see Vol. 1, 108).
53. Polybius 29.8.7: Perseus promised Eumenes that he would send Polemokrates with 1500 talents to Samothrace to act as intermediary there: τῆς δὲ Σαμοθράκης αὐτὸς ἦν κύριος (Vol. 1, 106). It does not follow from Livy 42.50.8 (see Vol. 1, 109: "dum integrae res sint, statuere apud animum Persea debere, utrum singula concedendo nudatus ad extremum opibus extorrisque

regno Samothraciam aliamve insulam petere ab Romanis, ubi privatus superstes regno suo in contemptu atque inopia consenescat, malit. . . .") that because permission would have to be obtained from Rome for him to live there, Samothrace was not part of Perseus' dominions. The speaker envisages Perseus as an exile seeking for permission to reside in a corner of his former kingdom. Fredrich (above, n. 47) unaccountably says of this passage, "Romani deliberant num regem ibi contineant." I do not know what Niese (above, n. 16), III, 28, n. 2, had in mind, when he wrote, "es ist aber möglich, dass die Insel nicht eigentlich zu Makedonien gehört hat; denn die Römer behandeln sie als neutral."
54. See Livy 44.45.15, 45.5–6 (Vol. 1, 111–27).
55. Pliny *Nat. hist.* 4.12.73 (see Vol. 1, 7): "Insula Samothrace libera ante Hebrum." For the piratical raids see above, Vol. 1, 50, 128, 129.
56. See below, pp. 15 ff.

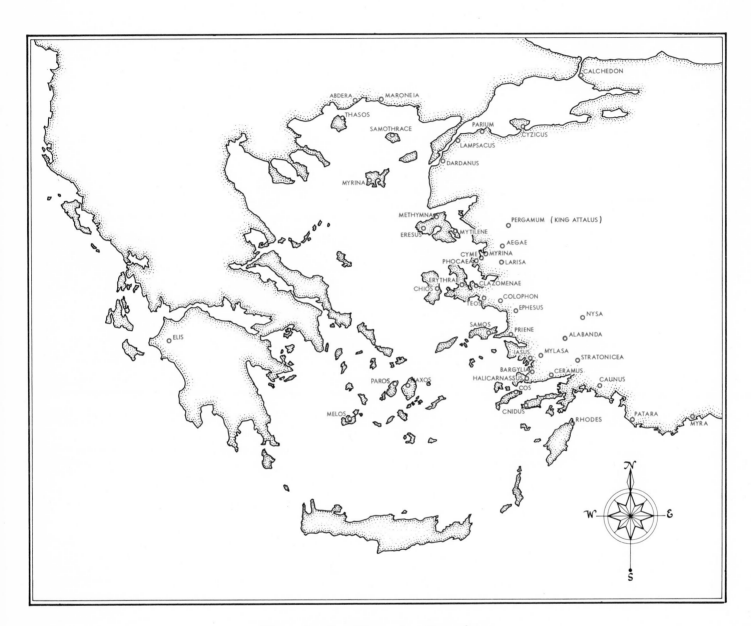

Places Sending Theoroi to Samothrace

II

While the new inscriptions do not add much to our knowledge of the political history of the island, the same cannot be said of our knowledge of the Sanctuary, which is enlarged and enriched by the new material.

The most striking single new item is, in spite of the impossibility of identifying the dedicant beyond dispute, the late fourth-century dedication, **9**. Whoever the dedicant was, the dedication is on a lavish scale, wholly comparable in this respect to those, already familiar, of the "Arsinoeion" (**10**) and of the Propylaea of Philadelphus (**11**). This is material evidence for wealthy patronage, possibly patronage by one of the leading figures of the day, not much less than two decades, and probably more, before the next important dedications, already referred to, and it thus involves a considerable modification of the view that the Sanctuary achieved its popularity, and became a fashionable object of patronage, as a result of the Ptolemaic connection [57]—a view which we have already seen is untenable in its political implications. Evidently a shrine which was presented with such a building as the "Altar Court" had already achieved a considerable measure of fame and popularity. This is important in two ways. First, it serves to lessen the significance of early Ptolemaic influence; secondly, it suggests that the decisive element in the development of the shrine may have been patronage from Macedon. This can be supported by other evidence. It is recorded by Plutarch that Philip II was initiated in the Sanctuary in his youth,[58] and a phrase in the decree in honor of Lysimachus merits particular attention in this respect. The sacrilegious attackers of the Sanctuary are said to have "attempted to steal the dedications erected by the kings." [59] Admittedly, the words ὑπὸ τῶν βασιλέων are not very explicit, but at this comparatively early date, 287–281, it seems natural to refer this to Lysimachus' predecessors as kings of Macedon. Thus the new dedication, evidently made by a Macedonian of wealth, if not of rank, emphasizes the Macedonian environment of the Sanctuary in the early Hellenistic period. This is an environment it never greatly loses.

The new material also adds very considerably to our knowledge of another field, the range of cities which sent theoroi to the Sanctuary (cf. map). The two main considerations, geographical and chronological, established by the Austrian excavators and confirmed by Fredrich, were (1) that the lists of theoroi begin in the later third century B.C. and continue into the first century A.D., and (2) that the theoroi are for the most part from the coasts of Asia Minor and the islands, Greece proper being barely represented, Thrace and Macedonia

57. Cf. Hemberg, pp. 69–70.
58. Plutarch *Alexander* 2 (see Vol. 1, **193**, **194**): λέγεται δὲ Φίλιππος ἐν Σαμοθράκῃ τῇ Ὀλυμπιάδι συμμυηθεὶς αὐτός τε μειράκιον ὢν ἔτι κἀκείνης παιδὸς ὀρφανῆς γονέων ἐρασθῆναι.
59. *IG*, XII (8), 150 = *Syll*³ 372, lines 5–6: [ἐ]γχειρήσαντας συλῆσαι τὰ ἀναθήματα [τ]ὰ ἀνατεθέντα [ὑ]πὸ τῶμ βασιλέωγ καὶ τῶν ἄλλων Ἑλλήνων.

apart.[60] These two considerations are not seriously disturbed by the new material. A few points deserve attention.

(1) The previously known lists of theoroi were almost without exception of theoroi who were made proxenoi of the city. We have now a list of simple theoroi (22) who are not stated to have been made proxenoi, and this list appears to be earlier than the others. The grant of proxeny to theoroi may therefore be a later development. This would not be incompatible with the political evolution suggested above. During the Ptolemaic and Macedonian occupations the constitutional links between the city and the Sanctuary may have been less close than in the subsequent period of independence under Roman rule: none of the lists of theoroi-proxenoi need be earlier on paleographical grounds than the early second century B.C.

(2) None of the lists, including 22, appears to be earlier than the mid-third century B.C. This, however, may be due to chance survival and destruction of records, or to the fact that these particular lists were not inscribed on stone before that date (though if the non-Greek stele, 64, be a list of theoroi, this would not be true). It would be dangerous to argue from their absence that the shrine had not achieved much popularity, since the earliest lists show as wide a geographical range as the later ones, and represent a clientele which cannot have been built up in a short time.

(3) The new cities represented in the lists of theoroi do not change the impression gained from the previously known lists, regarding the areas in which the cities that sent theoroi were situated.[61] Of half a dozen new cities, four—Methymna (22), Larisa-on-Hermos (23), Erythrai (Appendix III A), and Knidos (22)—take their place beside the other cities from the same areas, and fill in some gaps. Thus on Lesbos, Mytilene and Eresos were previously recorded, and Methymna rounds off the Lesbian representation. Erythrai fills a major gap on the northern Ionian coast—otherwise represented by Teos, Klazomenai, and Phokaia—and Larisa-on-Hermos joins the other Aeolic cities of the coastal region, particularly Myrina. Farther south, Knidos may now be added to the Dorian cities of the southern Aegean and Caria, thickly represented already by Rhodes, Kos, Halikarnassos, Bargylia, Iasos, and others. The islands of the central and western Aegean, on the other hand, are less well attested, largely no doubt because they naturally turned to Delos as their center. Naxos, however, is now joined by Melos (22) and Paros (13).

The new lists of mystae, collective and individual, are of particular importance in that they emphasize the early appearance of Romans in this role. Apart from this (discussed below), there are no striking new features, though there are some well-preserved collective lists of late Republican and early Imperial date: see, particularly, 28, 32, and 36. Apart, how-

60. See below, p. 62, and Fredrich, *IG,* XII (8), 47, lemma to 160 ff.

61. See, in general, Fredrich, loc. cit.; Hemberg, p. 127.

ever, from the Roman officials who visit the Sanctuary, there are evidently few persons of distinction, Roman or Greek, and this bears out the impression derived from the dedications, and from the lists of theoroi, that the Sanctuary, although it continued to enjoy a measure of popularity in the Imperial period, never attained again the fame it had enjoyed in the earlier Hellenistic period.

There is one feature of the evidence, old and new, concerning the lists of theoroi, and to a lesser extent those of mystae, which deserves notice. It is very striking that almost no new foundations of the Hellenistic world seem to have sent them (exceptions are Stratonikeia in **24** and in *IG*, XII [8], 170 and "King Attalus" [II or III] also in no. 170). The cities are not restricted only geographically; they are, in a sense, restricted culturally as well. The Great Gods and their mysteries were cultivated largely by the old Greek cities and were of little interest to the new Hellenistic capitals. This is a striking paradox: although the period in which the Sanctuary enjoyed greatest prosperity was undoubtedly the third and second centuries B.C., it was the old cities which contributed to that prosperity and not the new. This corresponds in general to the picture of the dispersion of the cult of the Samothracian gods outside the island. The θεοὶ Σαμοθρᾳκες were in the main worshiped in the Greek cities of the Black Sea and the northern Aegean and appear rarely in the new cities.[62] It is particularly striking that in all the wealth of cults in Ptolemaic Alexandria there is no trace of the Samothracian gods.[63] To a less extent the same is true of the individual mystae, mostly of Imperial date. The Roman element apart, the majority of them come from the same cities and regions which had sent theoroi at an earlier period: particularly from Thrace and Macedonia, although, as might be expected, individuals from farther afield also occur—for instance in one list we find two ᾿Αντιοχεῖς and an ᾿Αρσινοεύς.

The most striking feature of the evidence, old and new, undoubtedly lies in the prominence of the Roman element among the mystae. This has often been stressed before,[64] and the new evidence makes it even more pronounced. As we have already seen, as early as 212 B.C. Marcellus dedicated some of the booty of Syracuse in the Sanctuary, but, although the truth of this statement need not be doubted, the event which it records may well have been isolated, and no great significance should be attached to it. Some of the Latin lists of mystae belong to the second or early first century B.C., and it is suggested that one (**25**) may possibly date to the time of the third Macedonian War. This possibility is based on a combination of paleographical and prosopographical arguments, and although it is by no means certain we know that political events led to the presence of a group of Romans on the island at the time,[65]

---

62. Hemberg, pp. 212 ff., and his map III, which marks the cult-centers.
63. The evidence from Egypt for the Samothracian gods is very slight: *PCZ* 59.296 (restored), from Philadelphia—cf. E. Visser, *Götter und Kulte im ptolemä-* *ischen Alexandrien* (Amsterdam, 1938), p. 19; Hemberg, pp. 231 ff.—and the dedication from Upper Egypt, *OGIS* 69, and Visser, p. 97.
64. E.g., Hemberg, p. 72; *Guide*, p. 16.
65. See above, p. 12.

and it is quite possible that either then or shortly afterward a Roman official may have been initiated. When, subsequently, Rome established the province of Macedonia (145 B.C.), Samothrace was left independent, but, as at an earlier epoch, proximity to the Macedonian coast brought the new rulers to the Sanctuary. To judge by the surviving lists of mystae, it seems to have become customary, from the first century B.C. onward, for the Roman governor, or members of his staff, to be initiated (**28, 31, 50, 53,** *IG,* XII [8], 232). These initiations and the benefactions bestowed on the Sanctuary and city by individual Romans (cf. **18**) may be in part due to the exercise of political tact by Roman officials anxious not to offend an important sanctuary, but from an early date other Romans—soldiers and officials in transit,[66] merchants, and freedmen—appear in such quantity as to suggest that the island made a particular appeal to Romans.

An explanation of this is probably to be found in those versions of the legend of Aeneas which associate the hero and Rome with Samothrace. This is not the place to investigate fully these stories, but a few words must be said. A version of the wanderings of Aeneas originating, so far as Latin literature is concerned, with the annalist L. Cassius Hemina, who was writing in the middle of the second century B.C., records that it was from Samothrace and not from Troy that Aeneas brought the Penates to Rome,[67] and this story seems to have held its ground in Rome at least until the time of Varro, who modified it.[68] Whatever may be its ultimate source,[69] it seems clear that it originated in Rome with Hemina,[70] and it is probably not a coincidence that just at the time of Roman activity on Samothrace in connection with Perseus a close sentimental link was established between the island and the new power which had replaced Macedon.[71] Such a link, over and above the reasons already

66. Cf. esp. *CIL,* III, 714 = *IG,* XII (8), p. 38, *sub anno* 92 B.C.; Plutarch *Lucullus* 13 (see Vol. 1, **198**): ἐν Σαμοθρᾴκῃ μυούμενος καὶ πανηγυρίζων καθυστέρησε.

67. See, in general, R. H. Klausen, *Aeneas und die Penates* (2 vols., Hamburg and Gotha, 1839–40), I, 326 ff.; G. Wissowa, *Gesammelte Abhandlungen zur römischen Religions- und Stadtgeschichte* (Munich, 1904), pp. 94 ff.; id., *Religion und Kultus der Römer* (2d edn., Munich, 1912), pp. 165–66; and C. Robert, *Die griechische Heldensage* (Vol. 2 of L. Preller, *Griechische Mythologie,* Berlin, 1920–23), pp. 1516 ff., esp. p. 1523, n. 3; cf. also A. Degrassi, *Inscriptiones Latinae Liberae Rei Publicae* (*Biblioteca di studi superiori,* XXIII, Florence, 1957), I, 135–36.

68. See Wissowa, *Abhandlungen,* pp. 107 ff., who shows that Varro introduced the element in the story according to which Dardanos took the Penates from Samothrace to Troy. See also Vol. 1, **182–84**.

69. The story of Aeneas' wanderings in the Thracian region are, of course, considerably earlier, and probably date back to the time of Hellanikos: see E. Wörner, *Die Sagen von den Wanderungen des Aeneas*

bei Dionys und Vergil (Leipzig, 1882), pp. 5 ff.; but the view of Wörner that the connection of Aeneas with Samothrace is of equal antiquity was based on the fact that Parrhasius is said (Pliny *Nat. hist.* 35.10.71) to have painted a group of Aeneas with the Dioscuri, which Wörner maintained referred to Samothrace, where the Cabiri and the Dioscuri were early identified. This view cannot stand today, and there is no direct evidence for Aeneas on Samothrace earlier than Cassius Hemina.

70. On L. Cassius Hemina see H. W. G. Peter, *Historicorum Romanorum Reliquiae* (2d edn., 2 vols., Leipzig, 1906–14), I, CLXIV–CLXXIII, and C. Cichorius, *RE,* s.v. *Cassius* (47). For the relevant fragments see Peter, pp. 98 ff., frgs. 5–7, and Wissowa, *Abhandlungen,* pp. 100 ff. Frg. 6: "alii autem, ut Cassius Hemina, dicunt deos penates ex Samothraca appellatos, θεοὺς μεγάλους, θεοὺς χρηστούς, θεοὺς δυνατούς"; cf. Macrobius *Saturnalia* 3.4.9, quoted ibid. (Vol. 1, **182**), and Servius *in Aeneidem* 3.12 (see Vol. 1, **179**).

71. Wissowa, *Abhandlungen,* p. 105, thought Hemina might either have learned the story from a Greek of the

advanced, satisfactorily accounts for the diligence of Romans of all classes, particularly in the Republican period, in visiting the Sanctuary and being initiated. The persistence of the popularity is clearly attested by the remarkable, bilingual Greek-Latin *lex sacra* (**63**), of the first or second century A.D. There seems to be no parallel to this, and its uniqueness is not surprising, since it implies an unusual state of affairs, that Romans visiting the Sanctuary were not assumed to understand Greek. This is an interesting sidelight on the difference, as a cult-center, between Samothrace and, say, Delos. The Roman merchants and members of corporations who visited Delos were no doubt mostly, or all, Greek-speaking.[72] It is a very different class of person to whom the Latin part of the Samothracian prohibition is addressed: the proconsular Roman and his staff, who might be ignorant of Greek. This is a further aspect of the phenomenon previously stressed, namely that Samothrace was unaffected by those political and social trends of the Hellenistic and Roman periods which led to the growth of syncretism, and that just on this account it forms a significant element in the total picture of Hellenistic religion, in which the survival of the traditional in religious practice is of no less importance than the development and Hellenization of exotic cults.

Scipionic circle, or have invented it himself. However, as he goes on to say, Rome was already aware of Samothrace as a cult-center if we are to believe the story that M. Claudius Marcellus, the conqueror of Syracuse, sent a portion of the booty to the Sanctuary in 212 B.C.: cf. n. 40, above.

72. Of course, documents from the Roman communities in Delos, the dedicatory inscriptions of their own meeting places, etc., were bilingual or Latin. The significant point of the Samothracian law is that it emanates from the administration of the Sanctuary.

CATALOGUE

I. Decrees

1. 53.1. (Pl. I.)

Fragment of block of brownish-gray limestone, broken on all sides except right where edge is preserved at ends of lines 4–5. Preserved height 0.117, preserved width 0.235, preserved thickness 0.17, space between lines ca. 0.003; height of letters ca. 0.015, omicron 0.008. Stoichedon, without guide lines, horizontal checker unit 0.0155, vertical 0.0158.

Found 20 June 1953, in the region of the Genoese Towers, at Palaeopolis.

Mentioned *BCH*, 78 (1954), 145; *JHS*, 74 (1954), 161; *Guide*, p. 13.

```
— — — — — — — — — — — — —
—————————————————ε . . ⁵ . . ιδ̣ . .
——————————————ε Σωκλῆς εὐερ-
[————————————τᾶ]ς πόλιος τᾶς Σα-
[μοθράικων————————τού]ς Ἐπικλέους παῖ-
5  [δας————————ʻΗφα]ιστίωνα καὶ Ἐπι-
————————————————ξόντεσσι προξ[ε]-
————————————————αὐτοὺς π————
— — — — — — — — — — — — — —
```

The inscription probably belongs to the middle, or third quarter, of the fourth century.[1] The stone is a Samothracian limestone, which, as Fredrich noted, was not generally superseded by Thasian marble for documentary use until the mid-third century.[2] It does not necessarily follow from this that the document is a Samothracian decree. If there were no other factors to consider, it could equally well be a copy of a decree for a Samothracian citizen, passed by some other city and erected in Samothrace. This interpretation is at first sight attractive: the dialect is Aeolic, and we hear of no early Aeolic element in the popula-

---

1. There is no other Samothracian inscription of about this date with which to compare it, *IG*, XII (8), 155, being of ca. 300: photo in L. Robert, *Hellenica*, 2 (1946), pl. 1 (cf. ibid., 1 [1940], p. 90).

2. See *IG*, XII (8), 151, note: "N.151–155 decretorum fragmenta sunt scripta saeculo III ineunte in lapide calcario, qui in insula nascitur, cum marmor postea, saepius ex Thaso insula, importatum sit."

tion of Samothrace. However, if the city of origin were not Samothrace, it would have to be a city the name of which begins with Σα- (line 3) — since evidently this could not then refer to Samothrace — and there is no known Aeolic city with these initial letters. For this reason I agree with Lehmann that the inscription is Samothracian.[3] This has obvious consequences for the history of the early settlement of the island.[4]

There is no indication as to how much of the decree is lost at the top, and the restoration [ἐπὶ βασιλέως τοῦ δεῖνος· ἔ]δ[οξε τῶ]ι δ[άμ|ωι—] in line 1 would be rash. The length of line cannot be determined, since there is no certain link between two consecutive lines followed by a complete line. Evidently we have here only a fraction of the whole, considered horizontally, and allowance must be made for a line of very considerable length, while vertically we can have no idea how much is missing. The role of Sokles is not clear. Since he stands in the nominative he is evidently not among those honored, and he is not likely to be a Samothracian since he is apparently a εὐεργέτης of the city, and this title is rarely bestowed on fellow-citizens.[5] In line 2 the epsilon is certain. In lines 4 ff. it looks as if some honors are being bestowed on the sons of Epikles. For example: τοὺ]ς ᾿Επικλέους παῖ[δας τὸν δεῖνα καὶ ῾Ηφα]ιστίωνα καὶ ᾿Επι[κράτη (e.g.) *ethnikon?*—]. After this, for example: [δεδόσθαι δὲ αὐτοῖσι φίλοισιν] ἐόντεσσι προξ[ε|νίαν, κ.τ.λ. —]. αὐτούς (*sic*), with change of case, probably indicates a fresh clause, for example, ἀναγράψαι δὲ] αὐτοὺς π[ροξένους καὶ εὐεργέτας—].[6]

The dialect is not wholly Aeolic, since there are intrusions from the κοινή. Thus we have Aeolic forms in line 3, πόλιος τᾶς, and line 6, ἐόντεσσι, while in line 2, εὐερ- and line 7, αὐτούς, we have common forms. It is to be noted that the decrees of the third century show no dialect forms. This, together with the presence of κοινή forms in this fourth-century text, shows that the latter entered the dialect and dominated it at a relatively early date.

3. *Guide*, p. 13 (cf. *JHS*, 74 [1954], 161).
4. See p. 3.
5. See Oehler, *RE*, s.v. *Euergetai*, col. 981; Busolt-Swoboda, *Staatskunde*, pp. 1246–47; for some exceptions see Rehm, *Didyma*, II (1958), 184, n. 2. For

εὐεργέται and πρόξενοι in general see Wilhelm, *Att. Urk. V* (*SBWien*, 220 [5], 1942), pp. 17 ff., 35 ff.
6. A verbally correct restoration is certainly impossible, in view of the mixture of Aeolic and κοινή forms.

2–4 (**22**, q.v. below).

These stelai of Thasian marble all come from the Roman aqueduct lying on the west slope of the main hill of the city. They were used as roofing for this structure, and **4** and **22** were in position when the aqueduct was uncovered; **2** and **3** had been removed before. They are mostly largely illegible through the action of the water, only **2** and **22** being at all legible. All were found in July 1938.

2. *38.354. (Pl. I.)*

Stele with molding. Complete except at bottom. Preserved height 1.01, width 0.34–38, thickness 0.090–011; height of letters 0.015–018, omicron 0.008. Very worn, especially in lines 15 ff.

"Casual find near E" (i.e., aqueduct) — Expedition diary.

K. Lehmann-Hartleben, *AJA*, 43 (1939), 144; corrections by P. Roussel, *BCH*, 63 (1939), 103; J. and L. Robert, *REG*, 52 (1939), 492, no. 296.

ἔδοξεν τῆι βουλῆι *vv·*
ὁ πρόεδρος Σωσιφά-
νης Σωφάνου εἶπεν·
ἐπειδὴ Ἐπικράτης Μα-
5 ρωνίτης φίλος ὢν καὶ
εὔνους διατελεῖ τῆι
πόλει καὶ χρείας πα-
ρεχόμενος καὶ κοινῆι
καὶ ἰδίαι τοῖς ἐντυγχά-
10 νουσι τῶν πολιτῶν, ἐ-
ψηφίσθαι τῶι δήμωι, ἐ-
παινέσαι ['Επ]ικράτην
Ἀρκεσ[τράτου] Μαρωνίτην
καὶ εἶναι αὐτὸν καὶ [ἐ]γ[γ]ό-
15 νους πρ[οξ]ένους τῆς π⟨ό⟩-
λεω[ς, μετέχ]οντ[ας] πάν-
των [ὧν καὶ οἱ ἄλλ]οι πρό-
18 [ξ]ενοι, [ἀναγράψαι δὲ τόδε]
[τὸ ψήφισμα εἰς στήλην]
[λιθίνην.]

The stone has deteriorated since its discovery, and at some points the original photograph (Pl. I) yields more than does direct study of the stone or of the squeeze. The correct readings were established in the main by Roussel (above), though I have been able to determine those of lines 14–18.

The lettering suggests a date in the middle Hellenistic period, 250–150 B.C.

Line 13. The patronymic, read by Roussel as Ἁλιάρχου (the patronymic of Epikrates of Maroneia, theoros at Samothrace[1]), appears to be Ἀρκεσ[τράτου]: the first four letters are clear, the fifth less so.[2]

Lines 14–15. Roussel read ε[ἶ]ν[αι δὲ α]ὐτὸν [πρόξε]|ν[ον———] for Lehmann-Hartleben's

1. *IG*, XII (8), 161 (for which see below, p. 72).
2. For the mutations χι|χε, κι|κε, common in proper

names in the third century B.C., see E. Mayser, *Grammatik der griechischen Papyri aus der Ptolemäerzeit*

[κ]|αὶ πά[ντας τοὺς Μα]——. The reading is, however, fairly clear, and the supplement natural. At the end of line 15 there is no room for omicron after the pi.

Line 17. The οι read by Roussel from the photograph is no longer visible.

Lines 16–18. For the formula see, e.g., *IG,* XII (8), 151–53, and the newly published Samothracian decree from Thasos.[3]

The πρόεδρος Σωσιφάνης Σωφάνου was identified by Roussel with the βασιλεύς of that name who introduced the Samothracian decree found at Iasos,[4] which, like the present decree and certain others, is a decree of the βουλή.[5] Evidently decrees of the βουλή could be proposed either by the βασιλεύς or a πρόεδρος, though the privilege may not have been restricted to these officials.

The πρόεδροι, who are mentioned in the plural in another decree,[6] probably constituted an annual council of the βουλή, with wide powers of independent action.[7] There is no sign at Samothrace of πρυτάνεις or a πρυτανεῖον, such as existed at Thasos and Imbros,[8] and this college may have performed the same duties, though not on a system of rotation.[9] Unfortunately there is no indication of their manner of election.

(Leipzig, 1906), I, 81, §4; K. Meisterhans, *Grammatik der attischen Inschriften* (3d edn., ed. E. Schwyzer, Berlin, 1900), pp. 102 f.

3. C. Dunant and J. Pouilloux, *Recherches sur l'histoire et les cultes de Thasos, II* (*Études Thasiennes,* V, Paris, 1958), 18–19, no. 169.

4. Michel, 352, *IG,* XII (8), p. 38, under "saec. ii in-eunte" (further bibliography in *IG,* XII, Suppl., p. 149, fin.) I. See also Vol. 1, **136**, 1.

5. Others are *IG,* XII (8), 157, 159; Dunant and Pouilloux, loc. cit., no. 169, lines 1–12. The procedure for probouleutic decrees at Samothrace is given in 158 (itself a decree of the demos), lines 1 ff.: ἡ [δ]ὲ β[ουλὴ προβεβού]|λευκεν αὐτῶι καὶ ἐγγόνοις περὶ ἐ|παίνου καὶ πολιτείας· δεδόχθαι | τῶι δήμωι τοὺς ἐπι-στάτας ἐπε|ρωτῆσαι τὴν ἐκκλησίαν κατὰ τὸν ν[ό]|μον, εἰ δοκεῖ δοῦναι πολιτείαμ, κ.τ.λ.

6. The Samothracian decree from Iasos (above, n. 4), I, line 10: τῆς δὲ ἀναρρήσεως ἐπιμεληθῆναι τοὺς προέ-δρους καὶ τὸν ἀγωνοθέτην.   7. See below, p. 28.

8. For Thasos see, e.g., *IG,* XII (8), 206; Index IV, 2, s.v. πρυτανεῖον; and J. Pouilloux, *Recherches sur l'histoire et les cultes de Thasos, I* (*Études Thasiennes,* III, Paris, 1954), Index, s.v. *prytanée.* For Imbros see *IG,* XII (8), ibid., s.v. πρυτανεία.

9. Cf. below, p. 28. The college of nine archons mentioned in *IG,* XII (8), 150 (*Syll³* 372), lines 23 ff., with reference to the ceremonies to be held at the altar of Lysimachus (ἱδρύσασθαι βωμὸν [β]ασιλέως Λυσι-μάχου εὐεργέτου [ὡ]ς κάλλιστον, καὶ θύειγ κατ' ἐνιαυτὸν [κ]αὶ πομπεύειν τοὺς ἐννέα ἄρχοντας, κ.τ.λ.), were presumably a priestly body presided over by the ἄρχων βασιλεύς, as at Athens, and not connected with the civil administration. It is worth noting that in Samothrace the term βασιλεύς survived and the term ἄρχων vanished as the title of the eponym, while at Athens the reverse occurred.

3. 38.383.

Stele consisting of five joining fragments, complete on all sides save bottom. Preserved height 1.74, width 0.40–44, thickness 0.085.

Found 7 August 1938, on the west side of the channel, lying on its side (cf. lemma to **2,** above).

Mentioned *AJA,* 43 (1939), 144.

No letters are visible on the very worn surface, and Lehmann-Hartleben said (*AJA,* above) that "it seems to have carried a painted document." The stele was with the others, is homogeneous with them, and was evidently intended to carry a decree or list of names. It seems unlikely that such a document was ever painted on stone. Possibly, it never bore writing, having been prepared for use but never inscribed. However, it would be surprising that an uninscribed stele, of the same type as the others of this group, should have survived the centuries, to be used along with them in the Roman aqueduct, and the surface is so damaged that it seems to me impossible to say that it was never inscribed. The probability is, then, that it was inscribed but that the passage of water over it has destroyed all traces.

4. 38.381. (Pl. I.)

Fragment of stele with double molding at top, broken on all sides except top right. Preserved height 0.47, preserved width 0.245, thickness 0.073. At 0.105 below top, deep profile, continued on short side.

Found 7 July 1938.

Unpublished.

The stele probably contained a decree of a foreign city, the name of which was inscribed in large letters on the wide fascia, in honor of a Samothracian. One letter, N, survives in large lettering (height 0.047), possibly the end of the genitive plural of the ethnic of the honoring city.

On the main surface of the stele the action of the water has left very few legible letters, and apart from line 1, which appears to read ———ανασσε.. , there is nothing worthy of record, though a few other isolated letters are visible.

5. 49.446. (Pl. I.)

Fragment of stele of gray marble, right edge partially preserved, otherwise broken on all sides. Preserved height 0.42, preserved width 0.33, thickness 0.065; height of letters 0.012–015, omicron 0.008. Very worn at right edge.

Brought from the church at Chora, 5 July 1949.

Unpublished.

$$\ldots\ldots\overset{ca.\ 13}{\ldots\ldots}\ldots\ \text{τον καὶ αἱ δια[νομαὶ(?)}\ \overset{2/3}{\ }]$$

[....⸬ca. 12.... ε]ὶς τὸ πλῆθος τοΥ!! .ca. 4

...⸬ca. 10...γ(ε?) καὶ ἀποδιδόναι τὴν τιμ[ὴν]

[τοῦ σίτου] το⟨ῖ⟩ς σιτοθέταις ἐν τῶι γεγρα[μ]-

5 [μένωι χρ]όνωι· ὅπως δ'ἂγ καὶ ἀδιαπτώτω[ς]

[ὑπάρχηι] χρήματα τῆι πόλει ἀεὶ εἰς τὴν ὠ-

[νὴν σίτ]ου τοὺς προεδρεύοντας ἑκάστη[ς]

[βουλῆς, Μ]αιμακτηριῶνος τῆι κα πάντα

[τὰ . .ca. 6. . κα]τατάττειν μετὰ τὰ ἱερὰ προδό-

10 [ματα ἐκ τ]ῆς προσόδου εἰς τὴν . .⸬ca. 6. .

[. . ^{ca. 7} . . το]ῦ ἀγοραζομένου τὸν [σῖτον]

. . . .^{ca. 10} . . . ὧν ἂν δεήσηι· τοὺς δὲ σιτο-

[θέτας, ἐάν τις γ]ένηται ἔκνδεια, ἀπαγ[γ]έλ-

[λειν πρὸς τὸ πλ]ῆθος, τοὺς δὲ ἀργυρολόγου[ς]

15   [διδόναι τοῖς] σιτοθέταις ὅτι ἂν αὐτο[ῖς]

[δοκῆι παραχρῆ]μα ἐξ ἁπάσης τῆς π[ρο]-

[σόδου, ὅταν συν]αχθῆι· ἐάν τε μή, ⟨εαντε⟩

[. .^{ca. 5}. ἐπελθεῖ]ν ἐπὶ τὴ[ν β]ουλ[ὴν] τοὺς

19   [. . . . .^{ca. 16}. . . . . . ἀγορ]αζ————

— — — — — — — — — — — — — — — —

For the date — second century B.C. — see below, p. 32. The marble is gray and similar in color to Lartian.

This inscription apparently contains part of a decree of the city of Samothrace authorizing the purchase and distribution of grain on behalf of the state. It is of particular interest since most of the evidence relating to the provision of grain in Greek cities[1] is concerned with the activity of individuals who gave, or sold at a reduced price, large quantities of grain in a famine or when a city was hard pressed for other reasons, and little of it relates to general laws passed to ensure adequate supplies and to remove the need for such casual benefactions. The "Samian Corn Law" is, of course, the most prominent text of this small group,[2] and another is contained in an inscription from Thuria in Messenia.[3] Rhodes, too, as we know from a rather vague phrase of Strabo, seems to have adopted a similar practice.[4] None of these parallels, however, helps us to fill up the uncertainties in the sense of the present law, the exact operation of which remains in part obscure.

The approximate length of line is given by the supplement of lines 4–5, where γεγραμ|-[μένωι χρ]όνωι is evidently sufficient. The same length of lacuna is equally satisfactory in lines 3–4, 6–7, and 12–13, in all of which the supplements are reasonably certain.

Line 1. διανομή is especially used of dole-distributions.[5]

1. See, in general, the material collected by H. Francotte, *Mélanges Nicole* (Geneva, 1905), pp. 135–57; T. Sauciuc-Săveanu, *Cultura Cerealelor in Grecia antica și politica cerealistă a Atenienilor,* Academia romănă, studii și cercetări, X (Bucharest, 1925); A. Wilhelm, *Mélanges Glotz* (Paris, 1932), II, 899 ff.; idem, *RhM,* 90 (1941), 164–67; F. Heichelheim, *RE,* Suppl., VI, s.v. *Sitos,* cols. 875 ff. A valuable discussion of the whole subject is to be found in H. Bolkestein, *Wohltätigkeit und Armenpflege im vorchristlichen Altertum* (Utrecht, 1939), pp. 251 ff.

2. *Syll*[3] 976: cf. E. Ziebarth, *ZNum,* 34 (1924), 356 ff.; Bolkestein, pp. 262 ff. W. W. Tarn, *Hellenistic Civilisation,* 3d edn., rev. G. T. Griffith (London, 1952), p. 108, gives a list (with antiquated references)

of other inscriptions which indicate the existence of a state grain supply, although for the most part reference is only incidental (in honorific decrees, etc.). In some of these only a part of the community benefits, and in others the distribution is confined to specific occasions: royal birthdays, etc.; cf. M. Rostovtzeff, *SEHHW,* II, 803–4; III, 1520, n. 73.

3. *IG,* V (1), 1379, esp. lines 11 ff., republished with improvements, and discussed, by L. Robert, *BCH,* 52 (1928), 426–32.

4. Strabo 652–53C. For the correct interpretation of this passage see Wilhelm, *RhM,* 90 (1941), 161–67.

5. J. and L. Robert, *La Carie,* II (Paris, 1954), 323, n. 3, promise a full discussion of the word. See meanwhile Bolkestein, loc. cit.

Lines 1–4. In line 4 τοὺς σιτοθέταις is clear. It seems certain that there is a lapicide's error here, and that we should read either το⟨ῖ⟩ς σιτοθέταις or τοὺς σιτοθέτα⟨ι⟩ς. The position of the words in the clause strongly suggests that they are the indirect object of ἀποδιδόναι and the sitothetai appear again in lines 13 ff. as the officials to whom payments are to be made by the ἀργυρολόγοι for the purchase of grain. I therefore take τοὺς σιτοθέταις as an error for the dative, and read το⟨ῖ⟩ς σιτοθέταις.⁶ The subject of ἀποδιδόναι in line 3 has then to be determined. The verb may refer to the payment to the sitothetai by those qualified for public alimentation of whatever sum, corresponding to the reduced price of the grain, was fixed. However, this is not a very satisfactory interpretation of the Greek, since the sentence runs more easily if πλῆθος is not the subject of ἀποδιδόναι. We may suppose rather that some other officials are to distribute the grain, and we may supply [—διανέμειν ε]ἰς τὸ πλῆθος. διανέμειν is obviously in place here, although reference to an announcement εἰς τὸ πλῆθος, as in line 14, is not impossible. After πλῆθος comes του which may be a genitive, although, since πλῆθος evidently refers to "the people," it is not easy to see what would be the substantive. More probably the upsilon forms part of some other word, of which further traces remain in the two following vertical strokes, and the reference may be to the sale of excess grain after the regular alimentations have been made: τὸ ὑπ[ερ|αῖρον σῖτον]. The letter before the kappa in line 3 is either epsilon or gamma; if the latter, σῖτο]γ is possible; if the former, one would naturally think of δ]έ or τ]ε which would not be compatible with the other supplement. Since the probability is about equal as between the two alternatives, I prefer not to insert my conjecture in the text.⁷ There is, however, every likelihood that excess grain would be sold at a low rate, rather than given away, and the money would naturally be handed over to the responsible officials — here the sitothetai — to add to the funds available for the purchases of the following year, and the first supplement suggested is thus not improbable in itself. The name of the officials who are to distribute the grain and hand the proceeds over to the sitothetai is lost. It does not seem very likely that it was the ἀργυρολόγοι, mentioned below, line 14, as responsible for payments to the sitothetai in the event of deficiencies, since these appear to be the highest financial officials, whereas the sale of excess grain was probably the responsibility of inferior magistrates, perhaps, like the sitothetai (see below, p. 32), especially appointed in connection with the new legislation.

Lines 5 ff. contain provisions aimed at ensuring a sufficiency of funds for the purchase of the grain. At the end of line 5 ἀδιαπτώτω[ς] is legible except for the final omega. The word evidently means "without a break" or "continually," and this seems to be the first epigraphic

---

6. An alternative is to leave the reading uncorrected, and to suppose that σιτοθέταις is an Aeolism for σιτοθέτας, while the article is in κοινή form. This does not seem at all likely, since there is no other Aeolic form in

the inscription, and already in the fourth century dialect forms were on the wane (see above, 1).

7. For ὑπεραῖρον in this context see the Samian Corn Law, *Syll*³ 976, line 26: τὸ δὲ ὑπεραῖρον ἀργύριον, ἐὰμ μὲν μὴ δόξηι τῶι δήμωι σιτωνεῖν, κ.τ.λ.

instance, although it appears in the sense of "without exception" in Polybius,[8] and the sense of "continual" occurs in a papyrus of the second century A.D.[9] The regular word for "continually" with reference to permanent distributions of grain, oil, etc., ἀδιαλείπτως, is not possible.

Line 7, init. ᾠ‖[νὴν αὐτ]οῦ is perhaps possible, but ᾠ‖[νὴν σίτ]ου is more explicit. The substantive to be supplied with ἑκάστης is evidently βουλῆς. The προεδρεύοντες cannot be the presidents of a body changing monthly, such as prytaneis, even if the existence of such a body was attested at Samothrace, since this would be irreconcilable with the reference to a specific month side by side with ἑκάστης.[10] At the same time the use of ἑκάστης shows that the plural προεδρεύοντες is to be understood as referring to a college of proedroi — though a college need not be of more than two persons — not to the single proedros of each successive year. There are other instances of the presidency of a council being vested in a college,[11] and that this was so at Samothrace is very strongly borne out by two other Samothracian decrees in which the προεδρεύοντες and the ἀγωνοθέτης are designated as responsible for the proclamation of honors.[12] In these two instances the proedroi are not more precisely defined, but in view of the occurrence of proedroi of the boule in the present inscription it is natural to regard both sets of proedroi as the same: [13] proedroi should not be recklessly multiplied. The fact that one probouleutic decree is introduced by ὁ πρόεδρος [14] is not in itself an argument against the collegiality of the proedroi of the boule, since it shows

8. 6.26.4: παραγίνονται δὲ πάντες ἀδιαπτώτως οἱ καταγραφέντες.

9. *PRyl*, II, 77, line 46, of the office of cosmetes in Hermopolis: ἤδη γὰρ ἡ ἀρχὴ ἀδιάπτωτός ἐστιν τῇ πόλ(ει), which the editors translate as "for the office is now secured to the city." *LS*[9], s.v., gives as the only meaning of ἀδιάπτωτος "infallible," but even if this is to be understood as meaning "without fail," it is hardly a satisfactory rendering.

10. Contrast, e.g., the expression in the Samian Corn Law, *Syll*[3] 976, lines 36–37: προτιθέτ[ω]σαν δὲ περ[ὶ]‖ τούτου καθ' ἕκαστον ἐνιαυτὸν οἱ πρυτάν[εις] ο[ἱ τὸ]ν μῆνα τὸν | ᾿Αρτεμισιῶνα πρυτανεύοντες, ποιησάμενοι προγραφήν.

11. See Busolt, *Griechische Staatskunde* (2 vols., Munich, 1920–26), I, 478. Inevitably, when a title as vague as πρόεδρος is used, and only the title is transmitted, with no definition of function, mode of election, etc., there is some uncertainty as to whether the proedroi are actually presidents of the boule, or whether they constitute a separate body such as the prytaneis. Thus H. Swoboda, *Die griechischen Volksbeschlüsse* (Leipzig, 1890), p. 96 (cf. Busolt, op. cit., p. 477) regards the proedroi at Ephesos in *Syll*[3] 742, lines 18 ff., τοὺς στρατηγοὺς καὶ τὸν γραμματέα τῆς βουλῆς καὶ τοὺς προέδρους, as equivalent to the Athenian prytaneis. However, this is not certain, and in

such circumstances it is not possible to distinguish between a college elected to serve contemporaneously with the boule, as the proedroi at Samothrace evidently were, and a prytanic body whose period of office was a fraction of that of the boule: cf. Magie, *Roman Rule in Asia Minor* (2 vols., Princeton, 1950), II, 835, n. 18.

12. *IG*, XII (8), 38 (*BMI* 444; Michel, 352), I, lines 10–11: τῆς δὲ ἀναρρήσεως ἐπιμεληθῆναι τοὺς προέδρους καὶ τὸν ἀγω[νο]θέτην; ibid. 156 (see below, p. 40), B, lines 8–9: [―― πρ]οέδρους καὶ τὸν ἀγων[ο|θέτην ἐπιμεληθῆναι τῆς ἀναγορευσέ]ως.

13. Thus they might be the presidents of the ecclesia, who were called πρόεδροι in Athens (see Busolt, op. cit., pp. 449 ff.), but there is no positive reason for the identification, while there is no doubt in any case that the boule at Samothrace was presided over by πρόεδροι (see following note). In this connection the reference to ἐπιστάται in *IG*, XII (8), 158 should be noted: δεδόχθαι τῶι δήμωι· τοὺς ἐπιστάτας ἐπερωτῆσαι τὴν ἐκκλησίαν κατὰ τὸν νόμον, κ.τ.λ. Are the ἐπιστάται the presidents of the Samothracian assembly?

14. **2**, above. In *IG*, XII (8), 159, lines 1–2 are restored by Fredrich ἔδοξεν τῆι βο[υλῆι· πρό]εδρος Πιερίω[ν..ᵇ..], but the article should no doubt be added before πρόεδρος, as in **2**.

only that the proposal was introduced by one member of the college.[15] The existence of an annual board of presidents of the boule is not unnatural in a small community such as Samothrace, in which there was probably no need for the more complicated periodic prytanic system found in many Greek states. The authority given in the present matter to the presidents of the boule reflects the authority of that body in financial matters. This is again reflected in line 18.

Maimakterion, equivalent to November-December, which is chosen as the month in which the monies should be designated, is some five or six months after the harvest. The day of the month, the twenty-first, is quite clear.

Lines 9–12. The ends of lines are very illegible, as again in lines 15 ff., and the grammatical construction is not certain. What the προεδρεύοντες are to do, that is, what funds they are to set aside, definition of which is the main purpose of this part of the decree, is not clear. The object of κατατάττειν, agreeing with πάντα, and describing the nature of the funds to be allotted, is lost, and I have no restoration to suggest (a general phrase such as τὰ δεόμενα, which would fit the lacuna, is weak, and unsatisfactory with πάντα). The normal construction after κατατάττειν is with εἰς (e.g., κατατάττειν εἰς τὰς ἱερὰς προσόδους, "to pay into the sacred funds"),[16] and εἰς τήν at the end of line 10 should therefore be taken with it. ἀπό or ἐκ τ]ῆς προσόδου is also most naturally understood as depending on κατατάττειν. It is peculiar that the πρόσοδος is apparently not further defined, since normally when reference is to the general revenues of a state either the plural is used or the singular with a descriptive adjective or phrase. Thus in Samothrace we find both αἱ πρόσοδοι,[17] and (lines 16–17 of this inscription, if the restoration is correct) ἅπασα ἡ π[ρόσοδος]. Nevertheless, the restoration here of ἐξ ἁπάσης τ]ῆς προσόδου is impossible in view of the almost inevitable restoration of the preceding phrase, which fills the lacuna at the beginning of line 10. The simple singular should signify something other than the general revenue called ἅπασα ἡ π[ρόσοδος] below, but it is difficult to see how any other source of revenue can have been mentioned in these lines. After μετὰ τὰ ἱερά the reading is difficult, but προδο corresponds to all the traces, and indeed the letters other than the doubtful delta seem fairly clear. τὰ ἱερὰ προδό[ματα], however, is not a natural phrase. If correct, it presumably means either "payments made in advance from the sacred funds to the general funds" or "payments made in advance from the general to the sacred funds," and in the context of allocations the latter seems the more probable interpretation.[18] The normal phrase τὰς ἱερὰς

---

15. As a general rule the article is omitted when a magistrate occurs as the proposer of a decree: see Swoboda (op. cit., n. 11, above), passim, for numerous examples.

16. For κατατάττειν see the references given by Robert, *Hellenica*, 9 (1950), 16, n. 3.

17. See *IG*, XII (8), 156 (below, p. 40), B, line 21, [ἵνα] ἐκ τῶμ προσόδων θυσίαι τε συντελῶνται, where the reference is apparently to general funds: cf. also below, n. 24.

18. πρόδομα seems always to be used for simple payments in advance in normal cash transactions, and I

προσόδους is not possible. Accordingly, the amount to be allocated for the purchase of grain is to be fixed after these payments to the sacred funds. Beyond this, the rest of the sentence is very obscure. In line 11 after ἀγοραζομένου tau and omicron are clear, and after that there are faint and tempting traces of other letters. τόπ[ου —] would be possible, and if this were correct the meaning would be "of the land now being bought." There is, however, no previous reference to the purchase of land in the preserved part of the text. This is not conclusive, of course, and the meaning would be that the proceeds of the land (rent, etc.) were to be devoted to the purchase of corn in the future. We would then have to suppose that some reference to the purchase of this land occurred in the lacuna at the end of line 10 and the beginning of line 11. ὧν ἂν δεήσηι would then be impersonal: "of which there should be need." Nevertheless I think it unlikely that what was, on this hypothesis, the main feature of the new regulations—the purchase of land—would be introduced in this rather tangential manner. We must therefore also consider the alternative explanation, according to which ἀγορα-ζομένου is taken in an active sense, and we read ἀγοραζομένου τὸν [σῖτον], which is paleographically no less possible. On this interpretation these measures concern the purchaser, whether private citizen or magistrate. The former alternative seems to run counter to the main provision as expressed in line 6, that the immediate aim of the legislation is to provide money for the city as such to purchase grain, and not for the citizens individually to buy the grain from the state. Consequently, it may be preferable to regard a magistrate as the purchaser and to suppose that the purchase is made on behalf of the state. This interpretation is plausible, but the reading of the last visible letter is too dubious to justify confidence in it.

With line 12 the picture becomes slightly clearer. Here we have a specific eventuality, that of the occurrence of ἔκγδεια. This normally means "deficit," and here it seems to refer to a deficit in cash available for expenditure on the purchase of grain. The word bears the meaning of "shortage" only in the Roman period,[19] and in any case the whole legislation is evidently directed to covering such eventualities as bad harvests, famine, and so on, and the possibility of such a shortage would not be added as a further contingency. Evidently, then, when the funds deriving from the sources already mentioned are insufficient, the sitothetai are to "announce" the matter, whereupon the argurologoi will transfer to them what they think necessary out of the general funds, and the purchase will then be effected as in a normal year. In line 14 ος is clear, and before that a theta seems unavoidable, while before that again are traces of a vertical stroke: [—μέγ]ε̣θος and [—πλ]ῆθος are both possible epigraphically. The former, however, could hardly be used in the sense of "amount," as would be necessary

---

know of no instance where it is used, as here, to signify an advance transfer of civic funds. However, this may be due to chance.

19. The normal word for such a shortage is, of course, ἔνδεια, but ἔκδεια occurs in a papyrus of the second century A.D. in this sense, perhaps by confusion. For the spelling ἔκγδεια cf. *Syll*[3] 135, line 17, ἐκγ Μακεδονίης; ibid. 591, line 13, ἐκγδημίαν; ibid. 972, line 74, ἐκγδ⟨ί⟩δομεν.

in this context, and can be excluded. Both meanings of πλῆθος, namely, "amount" and "citizen-body," give satisfactory sense, but in the former significance the word falls under the same ban as μέγεθος: though πλῆθος, unlike μέγεθος, can apparently be used of an "amount" of money without any reference to its size,[20] it seems most improbable that it would be used of an ἔκγδεια, while on the other hand if the reference is to the amount of money needed, that is, to a positive sum, such a phrase as πόσων δεῖται χρημάτων would be used. It is therefore more satisfactory to take it in the sense of the "citizen-body," the same sense that it bears in line 2. ἀπαγ[γ]έλ|[λειν πρὸς τὸ πλ]ῆθος fills the lacuna very well.[21] It is, however, slightly surprising to find that such a declaration is to be made *coram populo*. One would rather expect it to be made to the argurologoi, who are to supply the balance. The explanation may be simply that since the πλῆθος was the beneficiary, it was felt that the assembly should be told of the state of affairs, though it may also be a reflection of a more general authority of the assembly in financial questions.[22]

Lines 15–16. The sense is evidently that the argurologoi are to provide the sitothetai with whatever the former think necessary, ὅτι ἂν αὐτο[ῖς | δοκῆι]. This is natural, since the argurologoi are evidently the superior officials, and exercise control over the expenditure of subordinate financial officials. At the beginning of line 15 διδόναι is slightly more probable than ἀποδιδόναι, which would give a very full line, though I do not think it is impossible. In line 16 the first two visible letters may represent the termination of [————παραχρῆ]μα.[23] If the restoration in lines 16–17 is correct, the money to be transferred to the sitothetai in the event of a deficiency is to be drawn ἐξ ἁπάσης τῆς π[ρο|σόδου]. This would refer to the general revenue of the state, though the singular is unusual and one might expect ἐξ ἁπασῶν τῶν προσόδων (see above, p. 29). There seems in any case no alternative to this interpretation, and any restoration involving a word other than πρόσοδος, e.g., τῆς π[όλεως], is unconvincing. In any case, both the restoration and the phrase are justified by another Samothracian decree in which the singular is similarly used of the whole revenue, probably in exactly the same phrase.[24]

---

20. See, e.g., Tait, *Greek Ostraca in the Bodleian Library*, I (London, 1930), no. 252 (ii B.C.): εἰς τὸ παρακείμενον πλῆθος. This usage, in which τῶν χρημάτων is to be understood, seems very limited. I cannot find another instance in the papyri.

21. For ἀπαγγέλλειν πρός see *Syll³* 138 (= Tod, *GHI*, II, 117), line 15, where the stone is very worn. The usage is quite common in prose writers, as also is that with εἰς: see *LS⁹*, s.v.

22. For the financial authority of the assembly see Busolt, *Staatskunde*, I, 629 f., and below, n. 25.

23. Cf. *Syll³* 577, line 12: τοὺς δὲ ταμίας ἀποδιδόναι παραχρῆμα τοὺς ἐπὶ τῆς δημοσίας τραπέζης αἱρουμέ-

νους; *OGIS* 46, line 1: οἱ δὲ τ[α]μίαι δότω[σαν] παραχρῆμα τοῖς ἐπι[με]ληταῖς.

24. *IG*, XII (8), 153, line 13, where Fredrich has [με|ρίσαι ἐκ τῆς κοιν]ῆς προσόδου. The stone is very worn at this point (*vidi*), and nothing certain is visible to the left of the eta (itself and the following sigma barely visible). Since ἡ κοινὴ πρόσοδος, though itself a well-attested phrase, does not occur at Samothrace, we may perhaps, on the analogy of our line 16, restore [με|ρίσαι ἐξ ἁπάσης τ]ῆς προσόδου, which has the same number of letters. In any case, the singular is here used of the general revenue. For the necessary addition of ἅπασα ἡ or some similar phrase, see above on line 10.

The remaining surviving lines seem to include reference to the appearance of the sito-thetai or their representatives before the βουλή, apparently in the event of the argurologoi re-fusing to grant them enough money for their purchases. The boule here appears as the ulti-mate authority in matters of finance, as in Athens and other Greek states.[25] It is unfortunate that so much is lost here. The authority accorded to the boule here corresponds, as we have already seen, with the fact that the allotment of the funds for the purchase of grain is to be made by the presidents of the βουλή each year (see above, on line 7).

In spite of its fragmentary condition and the uncertainty of interpretation the inscription provides important information regarding the efforts of the Samothracian authorities to en-sure a regular grain supply. In an inscription of the reign of Ptolemy Euergetes,[26] Hip-pomedon, the Ptolemaic governor of Thrace and the Hellespontine areas, which included Samothrace, is praised by the Samothracians for his benevolence toward the city, which de-cides to request him to grant permission to import grain free of tax from the Pontic Chersonese and wherever else it may wish. The hand of this inscription is unmistakably earlier than that of the present decree, which both on this account and on general paleographical considera-tions should probably be dated to the early or mid-second century B.C. The present decree represents the establishment of a permanent system of state control introduced to counter the difficulties of supply experienced by a small community in the northern Aegean, wholly de-pendent on external supplies, at a time when the areas of Thrace and Macedon were among the most disturbed in the Greek world.[27] Unfortunately, at least in its present form, the decree tells us nothing as to how the corn was bought, whether it was purchased by sitonai on be-half of the government on the open foreign market, as was often the case,[28] or whether it was acquired in Samothrace from private merchants.

A further point of interest resides in the appearance of two new titles of officials, the σιτοθέται and the ἀργυρολόγοι, both hitherto unknown not only in Samothrace but else-where in the Greek world. The latter were probably the regular financial officials of the city, since we hear of no tamiai at Samothrace, such as occur in most Greek cities including the neighboring Thasos and Imbros. On the other hand it seems reasonable to assume that the sitothetai were created to administer the new system of state control, and it may be supposed that they were established by this or a closely associated decree. We may compare the ap-pointment in an identical situation of the two officials called οἱ ἐπὶ τοῦ σίτου, appointed by the Samians to administer their new system of grain supply,[29] whose functions were evi-

25. See Aristotle ᾿Αθηναίων Πολιτεία 45, 2: κρίνει δὲ τὰς ἀρχὰς ἡ βουλὴ τὰς πλείστας, ⟨καὶ⟩ μάλιστα ὅσαι χρήματα διαχειρίζουσιν; cf. Busolt, op. cit., p. 475, n. 1, and p. 625, where he refers to IG, IX (1), 694 (Corcyra), which well illustrates the authority of the boule (and also of the ecclesia) in questions of finance.
26. See above, pp. 7–8.

27. For the disturbances in this area between the second and third Macedonian wars see above, p. 12, and Walbank, *Philip V of Macedon* (Cambridge, 1940), pp. 223 ff.
28. See Durrbach, *Choix*, 48, 50, with commentary; Rostovtzeff, *SEHHW*, I, 235; III, 1469–70, n. 35.
29. *Syll*³ 976, lines 38 ff.

dently the same as those of the Samothracian sitothetai here. In Samos the ἐπὶ τοῦ σίτου were only two in number, and it would therefore be unwise to assume that the sitothetai constituted a college with several members.

The appearance of the month Μαιμακτηριών, which is found otherwise only in Ionic cities,[30] is of interest. Its presence here confirms to some extent the tradition of colonization from Samos,[31] although, as we have seen, the elements of dialect which survived into the fourth century are Aeolic.[32]

30. See Sontheimer, *RE*, s.v. *Maimakterion*, col. 560. To the places there noted—Athens, Keos, Priene (Μαιμακτήρ)—add Siphnos: *SEG*, I, 346 = *IG*, XII,

Suppl., 227.
31. See Vol. 1, pp. 19 ff.
32. See above, 1.

6. 49.447. (Pl. II.)

Top left corner of aedicula-shaped stele of island marble. Pediment with one acroterion, and Doric frieze. Preserved height 0.32; preserved width 0.32; thickness: (a) aedicula-field, 0.060, (b) pediment, 0.12. On horizontal cornice, inscription (a), height of letters 0.010; in second and third metopes inscription (b), height of letters 0.025–028; in aedicula-field inscription (c), height of letters 0.010, omicron 0.005. Underneath the horizontal cornice are two small, shallow holes, packed with stucco, which may be an ancient repair to damage caused by the lapicide in carving the first line, which is close up under the pediment.

Found, 1927, in excavations of A. Salač and F. Chapouthier.

A. Salač, *BCH*, 52 (1928), 395 ff., III.

(a) Ἐπὶ   βασιλέως   *v*   Γ̣   (Π?)————————————————————————

(b) Ψή   φισ   [μα   Ὀδη   σσ   ιτ   ῶν]·

(c) ὡς δὲ ἐν Ὀδησσῷ ἐπὶ [ἱερέω θεοῦ μεγάλου Δερζέλα(?) τοῦ δεῖνος]·
[ἔ]δοξεν τῇ βουλῇ· ἐπιμηνιεύ[οντος τοῦ δεῖνος (τοῦ δεῖνος)· ὁ δεῖνα τοῦ δεῖνος εἶπε]·
[ἐπε]⟨ι⟩δὴ τοῦ δήμου διὰ πρό[τερον θεωριῶν(?)————————————————————]
[τῶν ἐν] Σαμοθράκῃ μυστηρίῳ[ν μετέχοντος *or* μετεσχηκότος————————————]
————————————τον ἀποδιδ————————————————————————
————————————δύναμιν————————————————————————
————————————περο————————————————————————

The lettering was regarded by Salač as of the Imperial age. Certain letters, however, and the total lack of finials, suggest that an earlier date cannot be excluded: note particularly the small omicron.

The surviving left slope of the pediment is original, the right slope is broken. Consequently, in spite of the appearance to the contrary, there is no trace of the apex of the pediment above the metope bearing the letters ΦΙΣ. The original number of metopes cannot therefore be determined by reference to the dimensions of the pediment.

In fact, though a stone with more than five or six metopes is a priori unlikely, the formulae of lines 3 and 4, containing the dating by the Odessan eponymous priest and the prescript of the Odessan decree, demand a far longer line than can be restored on that basis. The dating by the Odessan eponym must have been complete with the name of the priest and his office. There are five or six instances of similar double dating in Samothracian lists of initiates, and the formulation, though the word-order varies, always contains the same elements: Samothracian eponym + ὡς δὲ ἐν + city (or ὡς δὲ οἱ + ethnic (ἄγουσιν)) + ἐπί + eponymous office + eponym's name.[1] A similar restoration seems therefore unavoidable here. We have no evidence for the eponym of Odessos in the Classic and Hellenistic periods, while in the Imperial period there is conflicting evidence as to the priesthood held by him.[2] In two documents of the third century A.D. the ἱερώμενος θεοῦ μεγάλου Δερζέλα seems to appear in this role,[3] while in another the priest of Dionysos is so named.[4] It does not seem likely that the original colonists would have chosen the priest of a non-Greek deity to serve as their eponymous deity, and Dionysos would obviously be more suitable. However, the present inscription is late Hellenistic or later, so this objection may not be valid. It thus does not seem possible to choose here between the two candidates, let alone to explain why the Odessitans should have used two different systems of eponymous dating. The restoration of the priest of the god Derzelas cannot therefore be regarded as certain. In any case we can be confident, on this ground alone, that at least half the stone, and half the line, is missing in line 3.[5] In the same way, the introductory formula of the decree can be determined within general limits.

1. See, e.g., *IG*, XII (8), 186b (now much worn in center): ἐπὶ βασ[ιλέως———], ὡς δὲ ἐν Ῥόδ[ωι ἐπὶ ἱερέ-ως] | τοῦ Ἁλίου Ἀ[ριστ]άκου; ibid., 188 (App. IV, p. 112, below): ἐπὶ βασιλέως Δίνωνος τοῦ | Ἀπολλωνίδου, | [ἀ]γορανομοῦντος Ἑρμο——|τοῦ Πυθονείκου, | [ὡ]ς δὲ Κυζικηνοὶ [ἐ]πὶ Ἑταιρίω|[ν]ος τοῦ Εὐμνήστου ἱ[ππά]ρ-[χεω], where the name of the Cyzicene eponym precedes his office. Ibid., 189 and 191 (29), the Samothracian eponym is placed after the Cyzicene eponym: [ἐπὶ———————ἱππάρχε]ω, ἐπὶ βασιλέως δὲ ἐν Σα|-[μοθράικηι τοῦ δεῖνος, κ.τ.λ.]. See also ibid., 192, 194, 195 (= Robert, *Coll. Froehner*, I, 44). Ibid., 183, the Samothracian eponym is omitted: ναυαρχοῦντος Λεοντίδος τοῦ Λεοντίδος· Ἀβυδηνῶν μύσται εὐσεβεῖς.
2. The inscriptions of Odessos are now assembled in G. Mihailov, *Inscriptiones Graecae in Bulgaria Repertae I* (Acad. litt. bulg., ser. epigr. 2, Sofia, 1956), to which I refer henceforth as "Mihailov." Where possible I have also given the reference to E. Kalinka, *Antike Denkmäler in Bulgarien* (Vienna, 1906).
3. Mihailov 47, of A.D. 215; 48 (Kalinka 114, corrected by Salač, *BCH*, 52 [1928], 394), of A.D. 238. In 49 the

same formula was no doubt employed, but the name of the god is lost. Ibid., 46, the Imperial list of priests headed οἵδε ἱέρηνται τῶι θεῶι μετὰ τὴν κάθοδον need not be of eponymous priests, and even if it is we do not learn the name of the god, though Derzelas was very popular and clearly might be referred to simply as ὁ θεός: for his cult in Odessos see Kazarow, *RE*, s.v. *Megas*, §7, col. 226, and in general Salač, loc. cit., pp. 395 ff., Danov, *JÖAI*, 30 (1937), Beibl., cols. 83–86.
4. Mihailov 50, of Imperial date.
5. In Mihailov 47, 49, and 50 (and probably 48) the eponymous priesthood is expressed by ἱερωμένου instead of by the more usual ἐπὶ (ἐφ') ἱερέω(ς). The same usage occurs at Histria (though not exclusively): see *Syll*³ 708, ἱερωμένου Ἀρισταγόρου τοῦ Ἀπατουρίου τὸ τέταρτον (for the eponymous priesthood of Apollo Ietros at Histria see J. and L. Robert, *REG*, 68 [1955], 239). The ἐπί is quite clear on our inscription, so I restore ἐπὶ [ἱερέω]. (For the genitival form of this word found at Miletos and in the Milesian colonies see *Syll*³ 495, n. 8, and 731, n. 1).

Odessan decrees contain the name of a single ἐπιμηνιεύων before the name of the proposer of the decree,[6] and therefore room must be found for both these elements: ἐπιμηνιεύ[οντος τοῦ δεῖνος (τοῦ δεῖνος)· ὁ δεῖνα τοῦ δεῖνος εἶπεν]. This, like line 3, makes an extremely long line, but I do not see that it can be avoided. In line 2 the restoration ψήφισ[μα Ὀδησσιτῶν] becomes necessary. This would occupy, at the same spacing, a space of seven metopes, that is, a total of nine metopes, including the blank metopes at either end, thus:

The Doric frieze appears to have been favored as a decorative feature of stelai carrying decrees, etc., on the west coast of the Euxine,[7] though it is rare elsewhere; this is a further reason for supposing that, as might be expected, this Odessan psephism was carved in Odessos.

The use of a title to a decree is normal when a decree of one city is erected in another.[8]

Lines 3 ff. The decree is probouleutic, the first of its kind known from Odessos.

Line 4. The ἐπιμηνιεύων was presumably the monthly president of the assembly, whose full title, as at Histria, was probably ἐπιμηνιεύων τῆς ἐκκλησίας.[9]

Line 5. The labda or delta, followed by eta, are clear as the first surviving letters, and Salač read [ἐπε]ιδή, though without attempting to indicate the sense of the passage as he understood it. ἐπειδή followed by the genitive absolute is a well-attested type of expression,[10] and it is difficult to believe that it was not intended. However, the letter before delta is unmistakably circular, therefore omicron or omega (theta can be excluded), and the corruption of iota to omicron is not easily explained. Nevertheless, the alternative assumption that the word is [γν]ώμη, indicating the introduction of the motion, would not only involve the assumption of a different corruption, since delta is clear, and leave the decree to open with the words τοῦ δήμου, which is not likely, but would also run counter to the known introductory formulae of Odessan decrees. I therefore read [ἐπε]⟨ι⟩δή.[11]

6. See Mihailov 38, 43.

7. An example at Tomis, *AEMÖ*, 11, p. 41, no. 55 (*vidi*); at Histria, *Histria*, I (1954), no. 8.

8. E.g., *IG*, XI (4), 1051–52; *Asylieurkunden aus Kos, Berl. Abh.*, 1952 (1), 4 ff.; Dittenberger and Purgold, *Die Inschriften von Olympia* (Berlin, 1896), 54; *IG*, IX, I², 176, 187, 192. The decrees of foreign states regarding the grant of ἀσυλία to Magnesia-on-Maeander are preceded by the heading παρά with the name of the city or state in the genitive (cf. Wilhelm, *Beiträge zur griechischen Inschriftenkunde* [Vienna, 1909], pp. 282–83). I have found no parallel to the arrangement of the title between the metopes of a Doric frieze as in the present inscription.

9. See *Syll³* 708, line 2, ἐπιμηνιεύοντος τῆς ἐκκλησίας, and cf. J. and L. Robert, *REG*, 68 (1955), 239. In Mihailov 36 (Kalinka 91), wrongly classed by Mihailov

as a decree, the πρυτάνεις crown two ἐπιμηνιεύσαντες and a γραμματεύς. The decrees record only one such official in the titulature, and it does not follow from this inscription that there was a college of two ἐπιμήνιοι who presided alternately: the two crowned here may have been successive. For other single ἐπιμήνιοι see Magie, *Roman Rule in Asia Minor*, II, 835, no. 18.

10. See, e.g., *Milet* (ed. T. Wiegand, Berlin, 1906—), I, 3, p. 300, 139c, line 23: ἐπειδὴ τοῦ δήμου καὶ πρότερον ἑλομένου; *Syll³* 398, lines 1–2: ἐπειδὴ τῶν βαρβάρων στρατείαν ποιησαμένων.

11. In fact, the reading which most commends itself paleographically is προ]βολή, which would involve no correction, but in addition to the major difficulty of there being no introductory conjunction, προβολή does not seem attested in the sense of γνώμη, a proposal.

Lines 5–6. The supplement after προ— is uncertain. The most likely reference here is to some previous contact between Odessos and the shrine, and my restoration expresses this. διὰ προ[γόνων] is possible, but seems to me less satisfactory in the circumstances. Salač's πρ[εσβευτῶν] is impossible, since the omicron is wholly visible.

Line 6. Σαμοθρᾴκη is also wholly visible, although Salač apparently saw none of it.

Line 8. δύναμιν is clear, but I make no attempt to restore these lines. In line 9 [——ὑ]πὲρ Ὀ[δησσ———] is possible, but leads nowhere.

Although no reference to Odessan theoroi occurs in the surviving Samothracian theoroi-lists, it is not unlikely that Odessos sent theoroi. However, since the hand is evidently later than the date of the lists of theoroi, the reference here may be to participation by individual mystae, though, if so, the city would be less naturally involved. The content and purpose of the Odessan decree cannot be determined: it may have sought the renewal of some privileges at the shrine. In any case, it may be supposed that the usual honors, for example a crown, and verbal tributes, were bestowed on the Samothracians. Such honors could hardly be bestowed on the Sanctuary as such, and the stone, if it is not originally from the city, was probably set up in the Sanctuary as being more relevant there. Shrines of the Samothracian deities are particularly common in the Thracian and Euxine regions, no doubt on account of their proximity to Samothrace,[12] and at Odessos, as in other cities of the north, provision is made for ordinary decrees to be inscribed εἰς ἱερὸν Σαμοθραικικόν.[13]

This is the only foreign decree discovered in Samothrace,[14] and it has one feature of particular interest, namely the presence of the Samothracian as well as the Odessan date. Normally when a foreign decree is set up in another city, the decree is reproduced without any additions, and if it contains any eponymous date, it is simply that of the issuing city.[15] The addition here of the Samothracian date seems in some way to assert the authority of the shrine. We may compare with this the double dates in the lists of mystae.[16] These latter documents are of course Samothracian records, and the eponymous date of the city to which the initiates belonged might be said to be added out of courtesy, but nevertheless it is possible that the latter custom led to the addition of the Samothracian date in this particular case.

---

12. See Hemberg, pp. 221 ff.

13. Odessos: Mihailov 42 (Kalinka 93); Histria: *Histria,* I (1954), 496–97 and the remarks of J. and L. Robert, op. cit. (above, nn. 5, 9), where a reference to Hemberg's detailed discussion is lacking.

14. *IG,* XII (8), 260, the Coan decree, is not from Samothrace but from the Bosporan ἱερόν: see Lehmann-Haupt, *Klio,* 18 (1923), 366 ff. (cf. *IG,* XII, Suppl., p. 149, ad num. 260).

15. I cannot at present recall an exception to this rule.

16. See above, n. 1.

7. 39.11. (Pl. II.)

Lower part of stele of Thasian marble. Preserved height 0.28, preserved width 0.22, thickness 0.09; height of letters 0.008, omicron 0.005.

Acquired 21 June 1939, from Palaeopolis (seized when being shipped to Alexandroupolis).

Unpublished.

— – – – – – – – – – –

——————————————EN . . .

. . . ^{ca. 9} . . . φιλία[. ἐπε]λθεῖν ἐς . . .

. . . ^{ca. 9} . . . βουλῆι τῆι τῶ[ν]

. . . τ̣ων πα[ρὰ τοῦ] δήμου· [ἀνα]-

5   [γρά]ψαι δὲ τόδε τὸ ψήφισμ[α]

[εἰς] στήλην καὶ ἀναθεῖ[ναι]

[εἰς] τὸ ἱερὸν τῆς Ἀθηνᾶ[ς]

raised profile.

The lettering is probably of the third century B.C. The vertical strokes have marked curvature.

Only the formula regarding publication is legible on this sadly damaged piece.

Line 4. Evidently an ethnic; the first letter is uncertain. Chi, kappa, and eta, and even alpha, all seem possible. The second letter is apparently tau and not iota. [’Ι]ητῶν is possible. Χίων would leave an unexplained space of two letters at the beginning of the line.

The stone appears uninscribed to the left of στήλην in line 5 and τό in line 6, and this suggests at first sight that the εἰς at the beginning of these lines should be retracted to the preceding line. However, there is no room for this in line 6 at all events, and the stone is so worn at the left edge that all trace of the εἰς may easily have disappeared in both lines.

Lines 4–7. The sanctuary of Athena is named in the same or similar terms as the place of exposition of other Samothracian inscriptions.[1]

1. *IG,* XII (8), 153, line 10; 158, line 15; p. 38, I, line   13; II, line 28; below, App. I, A, line 21; Dunant and Pouilloux, *Thasos, II,* no. 169, lines 22–23.

8. 50.27A and B. (Pl. II.)

Two non-joining fragments of Thasian marble. (A) Preserved height 0.060, preserved width 0.195, preserved thickness 0.040; (B) preserved height 0.075, preserved width 0.115, and preserved thickness 0.020; height of letters 0.010.

Found just west of the Central Terrace, 19 June 1950.

Mentioned Lehmann, *Hesperia,* 21 (1952), 42.

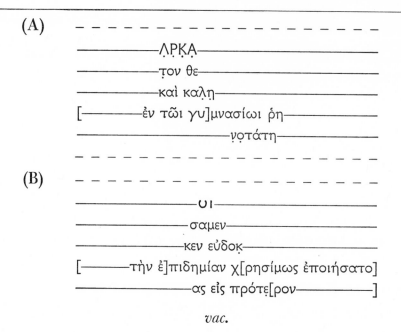

(A)

— — — — — — — — — — — — — — — — —

————————ΛΡΚΑ————————————

————————τον θε————————————

————————καὶ καλη————————————

[————ἐν τῶι γυ]μνασίωι ῥη————————

————————————νοτάτη————————

— — — — — — — — — — — — — — — —

(B)

— — — — — — — — — — — — — — — —

————————————ΟΙ————————————

————————————σαμεν————————

————————————κεν εὐδοκ————————

[————τὴν ἐ]πιδημίαν χ[ρησίμως ἐποιήσατο]

————————————ας εἰς πρότε[ρον————————]

vac.

The hand is very irregular; a date in the second century B.C. seems likely.

Below B, line 5, toward the end of the line, there is a blank space of more than 0.012, while the regular interlinear space on both fragments is 0.004–008. I therefore conclude that B is the lower fragment, with a blank space below, although the formula in lines 4–5 does not suggest that it is the end of the inscription.

A. *Line 1.* See below.

Line 3. The last but one letter is either delta or labda, and more probably the latter. The last letter is probably eta (καλέ[σαι] does not seem possible). It is this line which provided the basis for the view expressed by Lehmann.[1]

Line 5. ————MΟ is equally possible.

B. *Line 3.* εὐδοξία, εὔδοξος, εὐδόξως are not found in documentary inscriptions, and a form of either εὐδόκιμος or εὐδοκιμέω seems more likely.

It seems clear that we have an honorific decree for a foreigner (B, line 4, ἐπιδημίαν) who was a benefactor to the city and apparently in particular to the gymnasium (A, line 4). It is tempting to see in A, line 1, a reference to the nationality of the honorand: e.g., Ἀρκά[δα ————] or [————Β]αρκα[ῖον————].

1. "Among the epigraphic items, which will be published separately by Mr. Kallipolites, two fragments of a late Hellenistic votive inscription deserve a preliminary word here. Found in the area of the altar to the west of the Central Precinct, they contain, for the first time in Samothrace, part of the name of one of the divinities worshipped there and otherwise known only from scant literary references, namely Kadmilos, who was commonly identified with Hermes." (Loc. cit.) It is sufficiently clear from the surviving words that, whatever may be the true reading of A, line 3, the fragment is part of an honorific decree of some sort.

APPENDIX I

IG, XII (8), 156 = *Syll*³ 502. (Pl. III.)

This important inscription, now in the Samothrace Museum, has suffered badly since it was last studied, by Fredrich for *IG*. Much of it is now missing, and the surface is even more worn. I reprint the text, as collated by me, and underline the missing letters. A squeeze of face A, showing the whole of the face as published in *IG*, is given by L. Robert in *BCH*, 59 (1935), pl. 27. For bibliography, etc., other than that concerned with readings, see above, p. 8, n. 24.

A

─ ─ ─ ─ ─ ─ ─ ─ ─ ─ ─ ─ ─ ─

```
      [————————Ἡγ]ησίστρατος Φι[ . 4 . . εἶπεν· ἐπει]-
      [δὴ Ἱππομέδων] Ἀγησιλάου Λακεδαιμ[όνιος ὁ ταχ]-
      [θεὶς ὑπὸ τ]οῦ βασιλέως Πτολεμαίου στρατ[ηγὸς]
      [τοῦ Ἑλ]λησπόντου καὶ τῶν ἐπὶ Θράικης τόπων ε[ὐσε]-
  5   [βῶ]ς διακείμενος πρὸς τοὺς θεοὺς τιμᾶι τὸ τέμ[ενος]
      θυσίαις καὶ ἀναθήμασιν καὶ ἔσπευσεν παρα[γενό]-
      μενος εἰς τὴν νῆσον μετασχεῖν τῶμ μυστ[ηρίων],
      τῆς τε κατὰ τὸ χωρίον ἀσφαλείας πᾶσαν πρόνοιαν [ποιεῖ]-
      ται ἀποστέλλων τοὺς διαφυλάξοντας ἱππεῖς [τε καὶ]
  10  πεζοὺς στρατιώτας καὶ βέλη καὶ καταπάλτα[ς καὶ]
      τοὺς χρησομένους τούτοις, εἴς τε τοὺς μισθοὺς [τοῖς]
      Τράλλεσιν ἀξιωθεὶς προδανεῖσαι χρήματα ἔδω[κεν],
      βουλόμενος ὑπακούειν πάντα τὰ ἀξιούμενα [ἀεὶ]
      τῆι πόλει, διακείμενος δὲ καὶ πρὸς τὸν δῆμον [εὐνό]-
  15  ως πᾶσαν ἐπιμέλειαν ποιεῖται καὶ κοινῆι τῆ[ς πό]-
      λεως καὶ ἰδίαι τῶμ πρὸς αὐτὸν ἀφικνουμένω[ν, ἀκό]-
      λουθα πράττων τῆι τοῦ βασιλέως αἱρέσει, ἡ ⟨δὲ⟩ [βου]-
      λὴ προβεβούλευκεν αὐτῶι περὶ ἐπαίνου καὶ καθότ[ι]
      ἥ τε πολιτεία καὶ τὰ λοιπὰ τὰ δεδομένα παρὰ τ[ῶν πο]-
  20  λιτῶν φιλάνθρωπα ἀναγραφήσεται εἰς στήλην κ[αὶ]
      [ἀνατε]θήσεται ἐν τῶι ἱερῶι τῆς Ἀθ[ηνᾶς]· ἀγαθῆι τ[ύχηι].
```

B

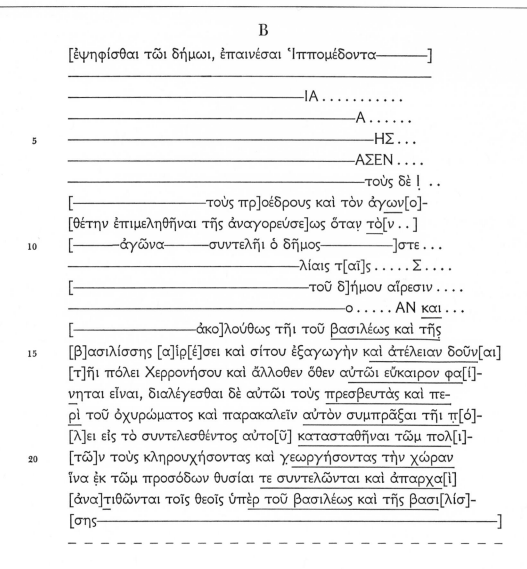

[ἐψηφίσθαι τῶι δήμωι, ἐπαινέσαι Ἱππομέδοντα————]

——————————————————————IA . . . .

——————————————————————A . . . . . .

5 ————————————————————————HΣ . . .

——————————————————————ΑΣΕΝ . . . .

————————————————————————τοὺς δὲ | . .

[————————————τοὺς πρ]οέδρους καὶ τὸν ἀγων[ο]-

[θέτην ἐπιμεληθῆναι τῆς ἀναγορεύσε]ως ὅταν τὸν [ν . .]

10 [————————ἀγῶνα————συντελῆι ὁ δῆμος————————]στε . . .

————————————————————————λίαις τ[αῖ]ς . . . . . Σ . . . .

[————————————————————τοῦ δ]ήμου αἵρεσιν . . . .

————————————————————————ο . . . . . ΑΝ καὶ . . .

[————————————ἀκο]λούθως τῆι τοῦ βασιλέως καὶ τῆς

15 [β]ασιλίσσης [α]ἱρ[έ]σει καὶ σίτου ἐξαγωγὴν καὶ ἀτέλειαν δοῦν[αι]

[τ]ῆι πόλει Χερρονήσου καὶ ἄλλοθεν ὅθεν αὐτῶι εὔκαιρον φα[ί]-

νηται εἶναι, διαλέγεσθαι δὲ αὐτῶι τοὺς πρεσβευτὰς καὶ πε-

ρὶ τοῦ ὀχυρώματος καὶ παρακαλεῖν αὐτὸν συμπρᾶξαι τῆι π[ό]-

[λ]ει εἰς τὸ συντελεσθέντος αὐτο[ῦ] κατασταθῆναι τῶμ πολ[ι]-

20 [τῶ]ν τοὺς κληρουχήσοντας καὶ γεωργήσοντας τὴν χώραν

ἵνα ἐκ τῶμ προσόδων θυσίαι τε συντελῶνται καὶ ἀπαρχα[ὶ]

[ἀνα]τιθῶνται τοῖς θεοῖς ὑπὲρ τοῦ βασιλέως καὶ τῆς βασι[λίσ]-

[σης————————————————————————]

A. *Line 2.* The lower part of the left hasta of the mu is visible.

Line 12. Τράλλεσιν, for the βραδέσιν of edd., was established by L. Robert, *BCH,* 59 (1935), 425 ff. Τράλλεις recur in the parallel Samothracian decree in honor of Epinikos, in the same role: see above, p. 8, n. 30.

B. As can be seen from the photograph, the greater part of the face is worn beyond the limits of legibility.

Line 13. Fredrich read O.....ANKAI and said, "[εὔνοι]αν non esse ectypum ostendit." I thought I read τοῦτον, but the stone is now almost smooth here, and the squeeze shows nothing definite beyond the nu, which is now on the break.

Line 14. I was able to read more of ἀκολούθως than Fredrich.

Line 16. A. Wilhelm, *GöttNachr* (1939), pp. 117–18, showed that the (ἐκ) inserted by edd. was unnecessary.

II. Dedications

---

9. No inventory numbers (except (d)). (Pls. IV, V.)
Three fragments of architrave blocks of Thasian marble. (a) broken to left, anathyrosis on right; preserved height ca. 0.64, preserved width 1.12, thickness 0.40; (b) broken to right, preserved height 0.57, preserved width 1.03, thickness 0.41; (c) broken on all sides save back, preserved height ca. 0.68, preserved width ca. 1.11, thickness 0.41. Also a fragment (d), 51.718, broken on all sides, preserved height 0.08, preserved width 0.060, preserved thickness 0.057.

Found: (a) 1951, to the north of the northwestern corner of the "Altar Court"; (b) 1952, outside the southern part of the façade of the "Altar Court"; (c) 1923, rediscovered 1951, in front of the northern part of the façade of the "Altar Court"; (d) 1951, to the south of (c).

(a) and (c), K. Lehmann, *Hesperia*, 22 (1953), 18 ff.; cf. J. and L. Robert, *REG*, 67 (1954), 158, no. 207; K. Kerényi, *Unwillkürliche Kunstreisen, Albae Vigiliae*, XIII–XIV (Zurich, 1954), p. 109; *SEG*, XII, 396.

(b) and (d), unpublished.

(c) alone: A. Salač, *BCH*, 49 (1925), 245 ff. (whence A. Schober, *JOAI*, 29 [1934–35], 1 ff.); idem, *BCH*, 70 (1946), 537–39.[1]

    (a) αδαιος κ——

    (b) ——ρραγ——

    (c) ——ων θεο——

    (d) ∠ or ⟑ (disregarded in the following reconstruction, since it may, *pace* Lehmann, be part of either a sigma or a mu and is more probably the former).[2]

The restoration of this inscription depends primarily on architectural considerations —

---

1. Salač in his original (and also subsequent) publication regarded this block as forming part of the dedicatory inscription of the "New Temple," and he restored it in the form of a Ptolemaic dedication. That it belongs to the dedicatory inscription of the "Altar Court" is quite clear from the position where it was found—see Lehmann, *Hesperia* (above), p. 19—and it is no longer necessary to consider, or refute, Salač's theory.

2. See Lehmann, p. 19: "Near by on the surface we found a fragment of the M of the missing last word [i.e., μεγάλοις]."

the length of the architrave and the disposition of the inscription on it. The architrave has been reconstructed by Mr. D. Spittle, whose co-operation I gratefully acknowledge. The restoration of the inscription in its final form derives from an observation made by him as to the position of one of the uninscribed blocks. It does not seem necessary to retrace in detail the stages by which the present restoration has been reached, or the various earlier versions which were tested and rejected for one reason or another. The restoration as now presented seems to me virtually certain, and it will suffice to justify it.

The inscription was originally thought to cover the whole of the architrave from the first intercolumniation to the last, and one large fragment (L. 41, in the diagram here, made by Mr. Spittle) was thought to form the middle block. This block was found in the river bed below the building, with the surface washed entirely away. With this block in the center, Lehmann produced a partial restoration, and I, on the same assumption, produced a different one, so as to fill the envisaged space. Spittle, however, subsequently discovered that this fragment, L. 41, was very probably either part of the last (i.e., southern) or, less probably, the first (northern) block of the architrave, of which it forms the upper part. As a result of this arrangement, which he will justify elsewhere, the two fragmentary inscribed blocks, (b) and (c), may be assigned to the central block, so that only three blocks — the central one and one on either side — were inscribed, and the total inscription is reduced by the length of two outer blocks. In other words, the central portion of my previous restoration drops out, but the essential phrases remain unchanged. This provides a satisfactory inscription, as the accompanying diagram (facing p. 45) shows.

An exact calculation of the number of letters on each block is not possible, since this will have varied according to the amount of space the individual letters occupied. The original length of the central block (3), according to the reconstruction of Mr. Spittle, was 3.78, that of (2) and (4) 2.52. The longest preserved inscribed surfaces are (a), which is 1.12, and (c), which is about the same; (b) is 1.03. (2) of which less than half the original length survives (1.12:2.52) has anathyrosis at the right end. Consequently, if fully inscribed to the left, the stone will have held approximately six or seven letters to the left of the first surviving letters, with a total of ca. 13–14 letters; since, however, it is the beginning of the inscription, it need not have been fully inscribed, and, as we shall see, in fact was not. (b) and (c) are both parts of the central architrave block (3), and their relative position is fixed by the restoration of the inscription. The block will have carried ca. 20 letters: it is half as long again as blocks (2) and (4) (3.78:2.52), and since they, if fully inscribed, would have carried ca. 14 letters (see above), (3) will have carried ca. 20–21. (b) has anathyrosis at the left end, but is broken to the right. (c) is broken to both left and right. The last block of the inscription (4), which is wholly missing, will have balanced the first inscribed block and have had approximately the same number of letters.

We may now turn to the inscription itself. First, its date. The architectural style according to Lehmann points to the period 340–330.[3] This seems rather early for the lettering of the inscription, for which, judged independently, a later date, even in the earlier part of the third century, would be possible.[4] If both conflicting dates are correct, one might suppose that the building was a good many years in construction, and that the inscription represents the final date. However, where our knowledge is so scanty any very great precision would be dangerous, and we may rest content with the knowledge that the building in its completed form is of the earliest Hellenistic age.

Lehmann proposed to restore the partially preserved inscription on (a) as [Ἀρρ]ιδαῖος, whom he identified with Philip Arrhidaios, the half-brother of Alexander the Great. He restored the center of the inscription with the aid of **65**, which he believed to contain a duplicate of our inscription (see the commentary on **65**) as follows:

$$[Ἀρρ]ιδαῖος ἱ[δρύσατο ἀπὸ λαφύρ]ων θεο[ῖς] Μ[εγάλοις —]ρρᾶι.^5$$

This restoration preserved the sequence of the stones according to the position in which they were found, from north to south. In particular, it observed the position of (a) and (b) as the outside blocks, a sequence which Lehmann regarded, and still regards, as axiomatic.[6]

The fact that Arrhidaios, when king, was known not as Arrhidaios but as Philip, Lehmann overcame by assuming that he made the dedication shortly before he became king.[7] On the basis of this restoration he outlined a far-reaching reassessment of the character

3. Lehmann, p. 18, originally dated the building, on the basis of the very considerable material (pottery, coins, etc.) found in the extensive fill in the interior of the building after the published report was written, to between 330 and 300 B.C., with a preference for the period 330–310. Subsequent investigation, the results of which will be given in the final publication of the "Altar Court" by Lehmann and Spittle in Vol. 4, pt. II, of this publication, has led him to prefer the slightly earlier date indicated in the text.

4. The hand is clearly more rigid than that of the dedicatory inscription of the "Arsinoeion" (**10**; Pl. V), and slightly more so than that of the inscription of the "Ptolemaieion" (**11**; Pls. VI, VII), but this would not be a conclusive argument that it was earlier than both or one of these. On the other hand, the dedication of Alexander the Great at Priene and that of Idrieus at Labraunda (before 344 B.C.) appear somewhat earlier. See, respectively, Hiller von Gaertringen, *Inschriften von Priene* (Berlin, 1906), 156 (O. Kern, *Inscriptiones Graecae* [Bonn, 1913], 21, top) and *Labraunda* I, 1 (*The Propylaea*, by K. Jeppesen [*Acta Inst.*

Athen. regn. Suec., 4⁰, V, 1:1]), p. 26, fig. 18 (section only). Dated monumental hands of the end of the fourth century are, unfortunately, very rare.

5. Lehmann did not publish any restoration of the latter part of the inscription.

6. See Lehmann, p. 18. He states (*per ep.*) that block (2), containing fragment (b) (——ρραχ——) was discovered in an undisturbed area of the late antique destruction, as it had fallen in the collapse of the building, presumably in an earthquake of the sixth century A.D., and that it should therefore belong rather to the end than to the beginning of the text. He feels that this argument could be countered only by very cogent reasons of epigraphy. In spite of the inconvenience caused to readers, we have therefore agreed to differ on this important point, which unavoidably affects the restoration of the entire inscription.

7. Lehmann did not touch on this point in his discussion in *Hesperia* (above). However, in *Guide*, p. 68, he says, "The architrave bore the dedicatory inscription, probably of Arrhidaios, half brother of Alexander the Great, who dedicated the structure to the Great Gods

and achievements of Arrhidaios, seeing in the inscription testimony for a more direct intervention by him in affairs than had previously been suspected.[8] He rejected the possibility of an identification with Arrhidaios the satrap,[9] though he tells me that he now regards this as possible, since the dedications of Idrieus at Labraunda (see n. 4, above) offer an analogy to a dedication of a large structure within a sanctuary by a satrap.

Quite apart from the lack of conviction this restoration in general carries, Lehmann's publication of the fragments contains some incorrect readings of partially preserved letters, of which we must now establish the correct reading. The following points call for attention: (1) On (a) the first surviving stroke was taken by Lehmann as the remains of an iota.[10] However, as Kerényi [11] and others, including myself, have seen by independent observation, and as is plainly visible on the photograph (Pl. IV), the surviving apex is of the following form: ➘, while that of the undoubted iota on the same fragment is ⟍. The first apex at the same time closely resembles that of the terminal of the nearest alpha, and I think there is no doubt that we must take it as a part of an alpha or a labda (see below). (2) Lehmann [12] regarded the final letter of (a) as iota, whence came ἱ[δρύσατο]. It is, however, clear that the stroke is differently formed from the preserved iota in (a). The curvature which on the iota is visible only immediately above the apex, is here observable through almost the entire preserved length, and the difference in shape and lie of the two apices is evident. I thus thought first of a mu, nu, or pi. A revision of the stone, however, convinced me that the letter is a kappa. This seemed to me to be established by the faint traces of the bed of the oblique strokes, particularly of the lower one, which apparently determined the precise direction of the break at this point. The reading Ḳ is therefore fully justified in my opinion. I have since learned with satisfaction that Mr. W. G. Forrest and Mr. Spittle independently recorded the possibility of the same reading. Traces of both oblique strokes are faintly visible on the photograph, Pl. IV*a*. (3) The final stroke of (b), also taken by Lehmann as an iota,[13] is evidently too oblique for that letter, and we must prefer other letters, such as gamma, kappa, or mu. We thus reach the readings as recorded above:

from war booty, very likely shortly before he was called upon to succeed Alexander after his sudden death in 323 b.c." Lehmann's reference to war booty derives from the earlier restoration of the inscription, based on the hypothesis of a longer dedication, in which he had restored ἀπὸ λαφύρ]ων from the —ύρων of **65**, below. In any case the supposed identity between **9** and **65**, now impossible since the lacuna in **9** is too short for the restoration, was subject from the beginning to fatal difficulties: see on **65**. See Addendum.

8. See Lehmann, *Hesperia*, p. 20.

9. See ibid., n. 100: "His [i.e., Philip Arrhidaios'] namesake, who was in charge of the bearing of Alexander's body to Egypt and later satrap of Bithynia on the Hellespont, never assumed royal dignity, and can hardly be credited with any such dedication."

10. Ibid., p. 19: "One recognizes before the delta the lower end of a vertical hasta, in position and shape seemingly another iota." In fact the hasta is not vertical but acute and splayed out.

11. See *Unwillkürliche Kunstreisen*, p. 109: "der Name kommt zweimal gleich verstümmelt vor, als . . . ΔΑΙΟΣ, über der Altar-Vorhalle zudem noch so, dass davor eher das äusserste Fussende eines Alpha oder Lambda als eines Iota sichtbar ist. Also ein . . . ΑΔΑΙΟΣ oder . . . ΛΔΑΙΟΣ kein Arrhidaios?"

12. Loc. cit., p. 19.

13. See the restoration quoted above, p. 43.

(a) ạδαιος Ḳ   (b) ρραγ   (c)————ων θεọ————.

These then are the data at our disposal, but we are now faced with another difficulty. If we follow Lehmann, we must preserve the order of the blocks as he employed them in his restoration, which he maintains was that in which the stones fell in antiquity and which has not been disturbed since. Full weight must be given here to the observations of the excavator, whose detailed observations supporting this view will be found elsewhere.[14] With great reluctance I find myself compelled to disagree, for two reasons—one positive, and one negative and born of despair. In regard to the position of the blocks, it may well be that they have not been moved since antiquity (for this Lehmann's detailed observations are of the greatest importance and must be carefully considered), but, whatever may have been the cause of their fall, *how* they fell—that is, whether one rolled farther than another, or in a different direction—can unfortunately only be a matter of conjecture. It is in fact certain that (2), when it fell, fell backward and sideways, in a totally different direction from the rest of the blocks, and block (1), according to the new position assigned to it by Spittle, will also have fallen away from its original position. Alongside this must be set the second, negative fact, regarding the validity of which opinions may differ. After continual experiment I am unable to restore any reasonable type of dedicatory formula with the blocks in this order. It will not be denied that such architectural dedicatory inscriptions offer a restricted number of formulae in regard to their general style, and moreover, sufficient of this inscription is preserved for the general formula to be evident. Yet with the blocks in the sequence postulated by Lehmann I can find no normal epigraphical formula.

With a change in the order of the blocks, the inscription falls immediately into place as a normal dedicatory text. This change is in the juxtaposition of fragments (a) and (b), which provides the dedicant with a patronymic. The number of letters on each of the two side-blocks was ca. 7–8, or, if they were fully inscribed, 13–14, while that on the main block was considerably more, ca. 20–21. This gives the following simple dedication:

(a)   (b)   (c)
'Ạδαῖος Ḳ[ο]ρράγ[ου Μακεδ]ὼν θεọ[ῖς | μεγάλοις].
(2)   (3)   (4)

Although the formula itself is normal, the restorations call for a few observations.

(a) Although labda is as possible as alpha as the first letter, personal names in -λδαῖος are very rare, and one may, I think, be fairly confident that the letter was alpha. This being so, at first sight two possible names suggest themselves, both Macedonian, and each including, among individuals so called, persons of rank and distinction, namely 'Αδαῖος and 'Αρραδαῖος. Other names in -δαῖος[15] are not epigraphically possible. Between these two

14. Cf. above, n. 6.   15. E.g., Κλεοδαῖος, Θρασυδαῖος, Μενεδαῖος, Συνδαῖος.

names there is little to choose epigraphically. Both are approximately symmetrical to the μεγάλοις of the end of the inscription, but if anything the former gives a more precise symmetry than the latter. However, ['Αρρ]αδαῖος can in all probability be excluded on other grounds. The name 'Αρριδαῖος is of frequent occurrence in Hellenistic inscriptions,[16] but there does not seem to be any instance in which it is spelled 'Αρραδαῖος. It is true that the name 'Αρραβαῖος occurs in the literary tradition in the form 'Αρριβαῖος,[17] although 'Αρραβαῖος is usual in inscriptions,[18] but this does not justify the reading ['Αρρ]αδαῖος, since in the case of 'Αρραβαῖος there is no epigraphic instance of 'Αρριβαῖος, whereas 'Αρριδαῖος (with one or two rhos) is the regular spelling in inscriptions and literary texts alike, and there are no grounds for introducing the spelling with alpha.[19] We are accordingly left with 'Ạδαῖος as an inevitable reading.

(b) Ḳ[ο]ρράγ̣[ου] is the natural supplement of the patronymic. It is also paleographically almost certain. Among the other numerous words in Κορρ- only Ḳ[ο]ρράμ̣[ου] is possible per se,[20] and this is epigraphically impossible, since the surface of the block is preserved where the second leg of the mu would fall, and there is no trace of it. Κορράγ[ου] may then be accepted without hesitation.

(c) Μακεδ]ών is a natural supplement after two conspicuously Macedonian names. It is of precisely the right length, and fixes the position of the other fragment (c) beyond cavil. Such phrases as ἀπὸ λαφύρ]ων or ἀπὸ πολεμί]ων are too long for the lacuna and

16. *Syll*[3] 135 (389–383 b.c.), 'Ερριδαῖος; ibid., 157 (ca. 370), 'Αρριδαῖος; *OGIS* 225 (Welles, *Royal Correspondence*, 18), (254 b.c.), line 24, etc., 'Αρριδαῖος; *OGIS* 301 (Eumenes II), 'Αρριδαῖος; *PPetr*, II, 30b, lines 16, 49 (iii b.c.), 'Αρριδαῖος; *BMI* 451 (302 b.c.?), 'Αρ(?)]ριδαῖος; *IG*, XII (9), 212 (ca. 250 b.c.); *PRyl*, II, 72, line 73 (99–98 b.c.), 'Αρριδαῖος. For further details see Russu, *EphDac*, 8 (1938), 174, s.v. 'Αρριδαῖος. The satrap of Hellespontine Phrygia, Arrhidaios (H. Berve, *Das Alexanderreich* [2 vols., Munich, 1926], II, no. 145) is of course ruled out along with all other persons of that name (cf. p. 44). The identification of the satrap with the honorand of *BMI* 451, suggested by Kaerst, *RE*, s.v. *Arrhidaios* (5), and A. Wilhelm, *AM*, 22 (1897), 196, has nothing to recommend it, since Arrhidaios the satrap is not recorded in our sources after 319, and the name, as we see, is very common. Haussoullier's suggestion, *Études sur l'histoire de Milet*, p. 88, to identify the Arrhidaios of *BMI* 451 and the homonym of *OGIS* 225, has equally little to commend it, though it serves to emphasize the uncertainty of the date of the former inscription. It may also be noted that Droysen's suggestion, adopted by Kaerst, loc. cit., that we should identify the satrap with the Arrhabaios of *OGIS* 4 (see below, n. 18) is undoubtedly wrong: see Wilhelm, op. cit., p. 196;

Dittenberger, *OGIS* 4, n. 16. Thus the satrap is known epigraphically only from *Marmor Parium* (*FGrHist* II B 239), B. 12.
17. See Thucydides, lib. IV, passim, with Classen-Steup's note on 4.79.2; and Polyaenus 7.30 (cf. Wilhelm, loc. cit., n. 2). Russu, op. cit., s.v. 'Αρραβαῖος, wrongly records the Thucydides passages as giving the form in alpha.
18. See the numerous instances given by Russu, op. cit., s.v. 'Αρραβαῖος.
19. The spelling with alpha would, in any case, be very unlikely if the derivation of 'Αρριδαῖος from ἀρ(ρ)ι- and -δαῖος is correct: see Hoffmann, *Die Makedonen* (Göttingen, 1906), p. 135. 'Αριδαῖος occurs in *Mar. Par.*, B. 12, as Hoffmann, ibid., n. 4 (cf. Wilhelm, op. cit.) pointed out. Lehmann, *Hesperia*, 22 (1953), 20, n. 100, "the spelling of Arrhidaios with only one *rho* occurs in some literary sources," thus needs modification.
20. See G. Lefebvre and P. Perdrizet, *Les Graffites grecs du Memnonion d'Abydos* (Nancy, 1919), no. 89; cf. Perdrizet, *BCH*, 46 (1922), 50. For Κορρ- names in general see also L. Robert, *Études Épigraphiques et Philologiques* (Paris, 1938), pp. 203 ff. Κορραίου (*BCH*, loc. cit.) is, of course, not possible here, in view of the iota.

need not be further considered.[21] In θεο[ῖς——] the omicron is certain since the small surviving arc of the curve is far too small for an omega, by comparison with the omega on the same block. θεο[ῖς——] is therefore inevitable. θεο[ῖς——] is in turn necessarily followed by μεγάλοις on the last block (4), which provides a symmetrical balance to Ἀδαῖος. This completes the inscription according to the reconstruction of the architrave by Mr. Spittle.

I do not think we can hope to identify this Adaios at present. There are various distinguished Macedonians of this name in the later fourth century and the age of the Diadochi, to say nothing of others in the third century, but by an ill chance not one patronymic survives.[22] In particular, one thinks of the tyrant of the Thracian city of Kypsela, up-river from Ainos and thus relatively close to Samothrace, who appears to have ruled there in the third century, possibly about the middle of it.[23] Unfortunately, unless the date of Adaios could be shown to be earlier than is commonly supposed, this identification seems to founder hopelessly on the chronological limits within the third quarter of the fourth century imposed by Lehmann on the archaeological evidence.[24] In any case, the name is so common that all attempts at identification must at present be resisted. Of no less importance than the actual identification of Adaios is the fact that his dedication adds one more piece of evidence to that already discussed,[25] to the effect that the shrine lay at this time firmly within the orbit of

21. Cf. above, n. 7, and below, **65**.
22. For instances of Ἀδαῖος see in particular Hoffmann, p. 190. Two distinguished persons of this name of the fourth century are the general of Philip II, for whom see Theopompus, *FGrHist*, 115 F 249, and the chiliarch of Alexander killed in the siege of Halikarnassos (Berve, *Das Alexanderreich*, II, no. 22). The first is certainly too early for our dedication, and the second improbable on account of both his early death and his comparatively humble position.
23. There is a basic discussion of Adaios by Niese, *Hermes*, 35 (1900), 69 f., who identified the person named in the fragment of Damoxenos (Athenaeus 11.469a = Kock, III, 348, frg. 1), προὔπιεν δέ μοί ποτε | ἐν Κυψέλοις Ἀδαῖος, with the *Adaeus* apparently mentioned by Trogus *Prol.* 27 as having been defeated at some point in history by a Ptolemy, probably Ptolemy III. The Trogus passage is noted for its obscurity, and nothing positive can be based on it, but it suggests a date in the middle of the century for the suppression of Adaios, if it be he: see Fraser, *Gnomon*, 28 (1956), 583. Niese attributed to this same Adaios the copper coinage with legend Ἀδαίου (*Die antiken Münzen Nord-Griechenlands* [Berlin, 1906, 1935], 3, No. 2, 147–48, nos. 17–21), but Gaebler, ibid., says that this Adaios is to be assigned at the earliest to a date "towards the end of the third century." Add to this the fact that the date assigned to Damoxenos by Niese, mid-third century B.C., is based solely on the fact that he mentions Epicurus (Kock, III, 349, frg. 2,

lines 12 ff.), and it will be observed that though Niese was probably right in maintaining that the Adaios of Damoxenos could not be identical with the general of Philip II, ὁ Ἀλεκτρύων (see n. 22), little else is certain. Niese argued that Adaios probably in some way acquired control of this area of Thrace, including the region of Maroneia, when Seleucid power in Thrace declined, and held it until deprived of it by Egypt. Seleucid power in Thrace is shadowy indeed—see B. Niese, *Gesch. der gr. u. mak. Staaten*, II, 22–23, 74, 137 ff., 777 (on p. 138)—but it is surely more than a coincidence that Antiochus II(?) captured, or at least sacked, Kypsela (Polyaenus 4.16), though the link with Adaios is obscure. Beloch, *GG²*, IV, 1, 672, n. 4, points out that Ἀντίοχος Ἀντιόχου in the passage of Polyaenus might refer to Antiochus Hierax, which would make a connection with Adaios difficult to explain. I cannot help wondering myself whether there are not two homonyms involved here, both distinct from the Ἀλεκτρύων and both members of the same dynasty: (1), the Adaios of the Damoxenos fragment, who, if Damoxenos wrote when Epicurus was alive and active in Athens (306–270 B.C.), might well be a figure of twenty or so years earlier: προὔπιεν δέ μοί ποτε, as Kock points out ad loc., suggests that Adaios was no longer alive. This Adaios could be identical with the Adaios of our dedication. (2), the Adaios of Trogus and the coins. But this is evidently very speculative.
24. See above, n. 3.
25. See above, p. 13.

Macedonia and Macedonian Thrace. The nature of the building dedicated by Adaios does not emerge from the inscription itself, as restored, but Lehmann has published a preliminary discussion of this, to which reference may be made.[26]

26. *Hesperia,* 22 (1953), 16–22; *Guide,* pp. 68 f.

10. (Pl. V.)

Several new fragments of *OGIS* 15 = *IG,* XII (8) 227,[1] the dedicatory inscription of the "Arsinoeion," have come to light. Unfortunately they add very little of substance to the text, but I take the opportunity of republishing the dedication and of giving photographs of this very beautiful inscription.

Newly discovered fragments:

(a) 49.983. Preserved height 0.14, preserved width 0.17, preserved thickness 0.37. Found 30 July 1949, near right bank terrace wall: *Hesperia,* 20 (1951), 11.

ευ   or   γυ

Kallipolites, in *Hesperia,* loc. cit., assumed this was ευ, and took it to be part of the ευ of εὐχήν supplied by Conze in the lacuna. I prefer to regard it as the γυ of γυνή: paleographically there is nothing to choose between them, but I consider εὐχήν an unlikely supplement (see below), while γυνή may be regarded as reasonably certain.

(b) 49.495. Preserved height 0.15, preserved width 0.13, preserved thickness 0.22. Found 7 July 1949 in debris of lime-kiln near "Arsinoeion": *Hesperia,* ibid.

∠   or   ∖

Lehmann, *Hesperia,* ibid., records this as "part of an A or M." It is probably one or other of these letters, but it could also conceivably be part of a sigma (though I think this less likely), and I have consequently not noted this fragment in the text given below.

(c) 49.769. Preserved height 0.15, preserved width, 0.15, preserved thickness 0.24. Height of letter 0.125. Found 19 July 1949, in debris of lime-kiln, near the "Arsinoeion": *Hesperia,* ibid.

α

This might be from any of six places in the text, and I therefore omit it also.

(d) 49.494 and 51.146. Two joining pieces, left edge preserved. Preserved height 0.40, preserved width 0.27, preserved thickness 0.22. Height of letter 0.130. Found: (i) 8 July 1949, close to lime-kiln near "Arsinoeion"; (ii) 1951, in the southern section of the same area as (a) above: *Hesperia,* loc. cit.

1. In the lemma to *IG* Fredrich omits the reference to *OGIS;* in *Hesperia,* 20 (1951), 11, Lehmann wrongly gives the number in *IG* as 277 instead of 227.

ηρ

I print here the text as it may now be reconstructed (omitting (b) and (c)) in the light of the following discussion. A diagram is given facing p. 45.

	A			B	(d)
[βα	σ]ίλισσα 'Αρ	[σινόη βασιλ	έως Πτολε]μ	αίου θυγά[τ]	ηρ
	βασιλέω[ς Λ	υσιμάχου] γυ	[νή, ———θ]	εοῖς μεγάλ[ο	ις]
1	2	3 (a)	4	5	6

The history of the text has been recorded by the earlier editors.[2] It was engraved on six blocks of which two, the second and the fifth, those marked A and B above, survived in 1840. A has never been seen again, while B remained in the neighborhood of the building and has been copied several times. Our (d) constitutes the first known fragment from the sixth block.

In line 2 I have rejected the supplement εὐχήν, due originally to Conze and accepted since then. Conze's only comment on it was that one might expect it at the end of the dedication, after θεοῖς μεγάλοις, but he was able to parallel this by reference to other inscriptions and was satisfied. He rejected the supplement τὸν οἶκον and any other supplement naming the building, on grounds of lack of room. The formula εὐχήν, however, is not frequent (though it does occur) in dedicatory inscriptions of buildings, etc., and is usually confined to those dedications to deities in which the inscription itself or rather the stone on which it is inscribed — most frequently a plaque — is the object dedicated.[3] Usually, in dedications of buildings, either the building itself is named or no grammatical object is included.[4] In the present instance an object is necessary for reasons of space.

Conze's restoration seems to have been based in part on false calculations. Although his restoration of the first line (and the corresponding division of the inscription over six blocks, based on the surviving block, B, which is complete to the left, and nearly so to the right) is undoubtedly correct in general, he did not observe that, to judge from B, there is not an absolute correspondence between the letters in the two lines on each block. B, line 1, has nine letters, while line 2 (almost certainly) has ten. On the other hand, in Conze's restoration

2. See Conze, *S,I*, pp. 15–16.
3. For a few examples: E. Breccia, *Iscrizioni greche e latine* (Cairo, 1911), no. 105; *OGIS* 69; *SB* 8297, all from Ptolemaic Egypt; *Inscr. Délos* 2141, 2149, 2151, 2173, 2177–78; *OGIS* 330.
4. I cannot give all the evidence here. For an example of the normal dedication with object named, see *OGIS* 61: βασιλεὺς Πτολεμαῖος βασιλέως Πτολεμαίου καὶ | 'Αρσινόης, θεῶν ἀδελφῶν, καὶ βασίλισσα Βερενίκη | ἡ βασιλέως Πτολεμαίου ἀδελφὴ καὶ γυνὴ καὶ | τὰ τούτων τέκνα τὸν ναὸν Ἴσει καὶ ʿΑρποχράτει; for one in which no object is named, see the architraval inscription,

OGIS 167: βασίλισσα Κλεοπάτρα καὶ βασιλεὺς Πτολεμαῖος, θεοὶ μεγάλοι Φιλομήτορες | [καὶ Σωτῆρ]ες καὶ τὰ τέκνα 'Αροήρει θεῶι μεγίστωι καὶ τοῖς συννάοις θεοῖς. Instances with εὐχήν are rare, but do occur, at least in private dedications on behalf of the royal house: e.g., the twin inscriptions, *SB* 6252–53: ὑπὲρ βασιλέως Πτολεμαίου | καὶ βασιλίσσης Κλεοπάτρας τῆς ἀδελφῆς | καὶ βασιλίσσης Κλεοπάτρας τῆς γυναικός, | θεῶν εὐεργετῶν, καὶ τῶν τέκνων αὐτῶν | 'Αγαθόδωρος 'Αγαθοδώρου 'Αλεξανδρεὺς | τῆς β̄ (ἱππαρχίας) καὶ 'Ισιδώρα Διονυσίου ἡ γυνὴ καὶ τὰ τέκνα | τὸ πρόπυλον καὶ τὸν λίθινον δρόμον Πνεφερῶι θεῶι μεγά|λωι μεγάλωι *vvv* εὐχήν *vvvv* Ⳑ λδ, Θῶθ θ̄.

of the lost third block, line 1 has ten letters and line 2 nine. This can hardly be right. There are undoubted differences in the distances between the letters in the two lines of B. In line 1, between iota and omicron there is a space of 0.065, while in line 2 there is only 0.041 between the same letters. Again, between the vertical stroke of the gamma and the bottom of the left oblique stroke of the alpha in line 1 there is a space of 0.072, while the space between the same points of the same pair of letters in line 2 is 0.060. It is indeed evident to the eye (see Pl. V) that the letters of line 2 are more crowded than those of line 1, and this can only have been to enable more letters to be inscribed throughout on the former line. We should therefore restore the upsilon of γυνή as inscribed on the third block, and a supplement about two letters longer than εὐχήν must be supplied in line 2, giving ten letters on the fourth block in that line and nine in line 1. That there was no object at all expressed, as in **11**, is, it will be clear, not possible in view of the evident crowding of the letters. The actual supplement cannot be established since we do not know the ancient name of the "Arsinoeion." Conze's rejected τὸν οἶκον will probably still be too long. τὸν ναόν would fit the space well, but, as Lehmann points out to me, this building could probably not be so designated. τὸ ἱερόν is equally suitable in length, but again there is no reason to suppose that the building was so called. The same disqualification applies also to τὴν θόλον.[5]

The interpretation of the text hinges on the supplement [———— Λυσιμάχου] γυ[νή ————] in line 2. This, proposed by Wilamowitz,[6] was accepted by Conze and all subsequent editors, and is evidently correct. It provides the necessary contrast to the [— βασιλέως Πτολε]μαίου θυγά[τ]ηρ of line 1: and βασιλέω[ς Πτολεμαίου] γυνή, the original supplement, referring to Philadelphus, is not possible since Soter is evidently regarded as still living. The dedication can then only belong to the period when Arsinoe was married to Lysimachus, from 299 to 281 B.C., and very probably to the years 287–281, when Lysimachus was king of Macedon.[7] I make therefore no attempt to disturb this restoration.

5. Suggested to me by Lehmann who argues against the possibility of τὸ ἱερόν that the use of the word at a later date to designate the neighboring "New Temple" would lead to confusion if the "Arsinoeion" was already so named. No doubt: but I do not think that the "New Temple" was called the "Hieron" (see my comments on **62**), nor is there any reason to suppose that the "Arsinoeion" was either. Although the true word cannot be established, it is difficult to see what other type of phrase could have stood here.

6. *AZ*, 33 (1876), 174; cf. Conze, *S,II*, p. 111.

7. Conze, ibid., rightly points out that the short period of Arsinoe's marriage to Ptolemy Keraunos need hardly be considered: see above, p. 5, for the events of that time.

11. 56.1. (Pls. VI, VII.)

One new fragment of *OGIS* 23 = *IG*, XII (8), 228, has been discovered. As with **10** I take the opportunity of publishing the whole inscription in so far as it is preserved and of giving photographs of it. The stones have been damaged since their last publication. They are badly weathered.

Fragment of architrave block with egg-and-bead molding, left edge preserved (with clamp hole near edge), broken at right. Preserved height 0.51, preserved width 0.51, preserved thickness 0.83–67 (below); height of letters: omega 0.105, nu 0.12.

Found 18 July 1952, in river bed to northwest of the "Ptolemaieion."

ων

The inscription was engraved, in identical terms, on the east and west sides of the "Ptolemaieion." On the eastern side the last block carried the letters |ήρων. The new fragment bears only the letters ων. Faint traces of the original anathyrosis on the left edge, and the presence of the clamp hole, prove this is the full extent of the block on this side.

No systematic publication of the inscription was provided by the Austrian excavators, who described the discovery (S,II, pp. 11, 45), and gave a reconstruction of the building with the inscription (ibid., pl. XXXV).

The inscription of the eastern epistyle is given (pl. XXXV) thus (in majuscules):

1	2	3	4	5
[————]ψς	Πτολεμαῖος Π	τολεμαίου καὶ	Βερενίκης Σωτ	ήρων
		θεοῖς μεγάλοις		

Block 2 is now damaged, the left edge containing the first three letters having been broken off; of block 3 the right edge has been broken; the fifth block has not reappeared. It should also be noted that, contrary to the drawing in pl. XXXV and the diagram in IG, the division of block 2/3 is across the pi. The present state of the inscription is therefore:

1	2	3	4	5
[————]ψς	Πτολεμαῖος	ͲͲτολεμαίου καὶ	Βερενίκης Σωτ	ήρων
		θεοῖς μεγάλοις		

The inscription of the western epistyle is given in S,II, pl. XXXV, thus:

βασιλεψς Πτολεμαῖος Π|————.

Both these blocks have been rediscovered near the "Ptolemaieion" on different occasions, when the area was being cleared, and are now propped up on the eastern bank of the river. The new fragment, constituting block 5 of the west face, involves a different distribution of letters on the architrave from the east face. The change has to be distributed between blocks 3 and 4, though its precise form is uncertain.

The present state of the western inscription therefore is:

βασιλεψς Πτολεμαῖος Π[τολεμαίου καὶ Βερενίκης Σωτήρ]|ων
|[θεοῖς μεγάλοις]

For the date of the dedication see above, p. 6.

12. 53.72. (Pl. VII.)

Fragmentary block of Thasian marble with molding above, broken on all sides. Preserved height 0.23, preserved width 0.51, thickness ca. 0.25; height of letters 0.060.

From the church of Hagios Demetrios, Halonia, 30 June 1953.

Mentioned, *Guide,* p. 99; *Guide²,* p. 104.

The measurements indicate that the stone was not part of the architrave of a temple, but rather belonged to an altar. The monumental nature of the inscription seems to show that the reference is not to the Samothracian eponymous βασιλεύς. The letters are evidently of the third century B.C., and Lehmann has suggested that the structure should be identified with the βωμός erected to Lysimachus at some time between 288 and 281, at which annual festivals were to be held.[1] But the fragment may equally well commemorate a later and different ruler; the letters would permit a date fifty or more years later than Lysimachus, and no doubt Philadelphus was shown some mark of gratitude for his liberality toward the shrine, while sacrifices were offered to the gods "on behalf of" Euergetes I and Berenike, ca. 228–225.[2]

Since the stone comes from Halonia, on the far side of the island, it cannot be determined whether the altar stood originally in the city or in the Sanctuary.[3]

1. See *BCH,* 78 (1954), 145 ("Chronique des Fouilles"); *Guide,* loc. cit.; for the βωμός see *IG,* XII (8), 150 = *Syll³* 372 (cf. above, p. 5).

2. Below, p. 40, B, lines 21–22.
3. It is not stated in the preserved part of *Syll³,* loc. cit., where the altar of Lysimachus was to be erected.

13. 39.914. (Pl. VIII.)

Round altar of Thasian(?) marble. Height 0.18, maximum diameter 0.135; height of letters 0.005–010.

Found 1939, outside the central entrance door of the "Anaktoron."

Lehmann-Hartleben, *AJA,* 44 (1940), 355–56, and fig. 37 (misread); mentioned, *Guide,* pp. 82–83; *Guide²,* p. 86 (corrected from true reading supplied by myself).

> Παρίων θεωροί·
> Χαιρίτης
> Τιμοδώρου,
> Χαῖρις
> 5 Κρίτωνος
> θεοῖς
> μεγάλοις.

The lettering suggests a date in the second century B.C. Parian θεωροί do not occur in the theoric lists.

The name Χαῖρις, a hypocoristic form of longer names in Χαιρ- (e.g., Χαιρίτης) is not uncommon at Paros.[1] A thymiaterion from Chersonesos in Crete[2] bears a striking resemblance to this altar, and it is noteworthy that the dedication is also by a Parian: Μνησίθεος Πάριος Σαράπιδι; the very irregularly sized lettering with exaggerated finials is also strikingly similar to that of the present inscription. One would conjecture that both objects were manufactured and engraved in Paros at about the same date: the specimen from Crete is said to be of Parian marble while the Samothracian altar is said to be Thasian, but one may wonder whether it is not in fact also Parian.

1. See *IG*, XII (5), 461; *HN²*, p. 490 (Χαιρι) (cf. Chantraine, *La Formation des noms en grec ancien* [Paris, 1933], p. 338). It is, however, quite widely spread elsewhere (Athens, Megara, Laconia).
2. *Inscriptiones Creticae* (Rome, 1935—), I, 35, no. 3.

14. 56.6. (Pl. VIII.)

Fragment of lower part of block of Thasian marble, broken to left and right, on back and above. Preserved height 0.062, preserved width 0.125, preserved thickness 0.11; height of letters 0.010–013.

Found May 1956 between the "Ruinenviereck" and the Stoa.

Unpublished.

_ _ _ _ _ _ _ _ _ _ _ _ _ _ _ _
_____·_____
_____αοσοιεπια_____
[———θεοῖς μ]εγάλοις χ[αριστήριον ?].

The hand is probably of the second or first century B.C.

Line 1. There are traces of two finials above the first omicron of line 2. The interspace between the traces and line 2 is the same as that between lines 2 and 3.

The fragment is evidently part of a dedicatory inscription, and χαριστήριον is an obvious restoration. Line 2, however, is difficult to restore, and it is quite uncertain how much is missing. Line 3 was probably placed symmetrically in the center and thus gives no clue to the length of the preceding line. αοσ in line 2 is a difficult group—the servile name Δᾶος (which occurs in *IG*, XII [8], 177a, line 5, as that of a μύστης εὐσεβής) can hardly be what is required since it gives no sense to what follows. We should perhaps read α ὅσοι ἐπι α —. ἐπι cannot be part of the Samothracian eponymous date, since the letter after iota cannot be beta, and the ἀγορανόμος who often occurs alongside the βασιλεύς was not eponymous and therefore has no ἐπί —. I have no solution to offer to this difficulty. A dedicatory formula such as [τὸ ἄγαλμ]α or [τὸ ἀνάθεμ]α may have preceded this.

15. 50.379. (Pl. VIII.)

Fragment of base of Thasian marble, broken to left and right. Height 0.046, preserved width 0.125, preserved thickness 0.090; height of letters 0.008–010, omicron 0.006.

Found 9 July 1950, on top of the south slope of the Theater.

Unpublished.

Λύσων(?)
[Μέ]δοντο[ς]
[θεοῖς με]γάλοις *vac.*

The inscription is roughly cut and the lines unevenly spread. Line 1 is very faint, and the reading far from certain. In any case, line 1 presumably carried the name of the dedicant, and line 2 the patronymic. The block is the upper part of a statue base. The surface has preserved a part of a clearly tooled bedding (0.028 deep) for insertion of the plinth of a marble statue, or statuette, placed 0.055 from the face of the base. The underside is carefully tooled, for placing the stone on a lower block.

The hand appears to be Hellenistic.

16. 52.1. (Pl. VIII.)

Two joining fragments of plaque of Thasian marble, broken at right. Preserved height 0.445, preserved width 0.96, thickness 0.105; height of letters 0.04.

Found 1951, near the southern end of the "Hall of Votive Gifts."

Lehmann, *Hesperia*, 22 (1953), 12, and pl. 6.

M. A[u]fidius ▪ M ▪ l ▪ de ▪ suo

Expanded by Lehmann to *M(arcus) A(l)fidius M(arci) l(ibertus) de suo. A(l)fidius* was suggested by F. Brown, and Lehmann said, "The restoration A(u)fidius seems excluded by the preserved surface." However, neither on the stone nor on squeeze or photograph have I been able to detect any trace of the original surface on either side of the break. I restore *A[u]fidius* for reasons indicated below.

The symbol between *l* and *e*, CI, corresponds to no known letter-form, and H. Bloch and N. Lewis plausibly regarded it as an attempt by a Greek lapicide to render a Latin cursive *d. De suo* is a complete formula of dedication by itself and it is not necessary to assume, as Lehmann does in his majuscule text, that a word is missing.[1]

The hand suggests a date in the late second or early first century B.C.[2] If *A[l]fidius* is

1. For the various possibilities—*de suo, de suo dedit, de suo dono dedit*, etc.—see *ILS*, Index xv, p. 766, s.vv.
2. Cf. Diehl, *Inscriptiones Latinae* (Bonn, 1912), pls. 6b (106 B.C.), 7a (early i B.C.; see *ILS* 862, n. 1 for the date), 8a–d (early i B.C.). The rectangular outlined punctuation marks on our stone recur also, ibid., 7b (= Durrbach, *Choix*, 116 = *Inscr. Délos* 1753; 113 B.C.), and on 8d (= Durrbach, *Choix*, 141 = *Inscr.*

correct, the dedicant was presumably a freedman of Livia's grandfather, M. Alfidius Lurco, as Lehmann supposed, since the name Alfidius is not known outside this family. It is, of course, not impossible that a retainer of this obscure family should appear at Samothrace in the Republican period, but it seems most improbable. On the other hand, members of the *gens* Aufidia are not uncommon in the Aegean in the period to which this inscription is to be assigned. They occur at Delos, and later at Tenos.[3] I therefore regard *A[u]fidius* as preferable.

Délos 1712; cf. comment on ibid., 140, for the attribution to the father of Julius Caesar), cf. E. Hübner, *Exempla Scripturae Epigraphicae Latinae* (Berlin, 1885), p. LXXV, who shows that it is an early form (and cf. also now J. S. and A. E. Gordon, *Contributions to Palaeography of Latin Inscriptions* [University of California Publications in Classical Archaeology 3, 3, 1957], pp. 183, 185.)

3. For Delos see *Inscr. Délos* 1728–29, of the late second or early first century B.C.; for Tenos, *IG*, XII

(5), 860, and the commentary of Hatzfeld, *BCH*, 37 (1910), 398, n. 44, reproduced in *Inscr. Délos*, on 1728; in *IG*, XII, Suppl., p. 195, ad num. 931, Ziebarth reads "Ἀφύδιος (Aufidius)." For Aufidii in Pontus in the Imperial period see *Studia Pontica* (3 vols., Brussels, 1903–10), III, no. 72a; cf. L. Robert, *Hellenica*, 10 (1955), 241 ff.; in Egypt, *CIG* 5117 (*IGRR*, I, 1373; *SB* 8541). It may be noted that in Suetonius *Caligula* 23, M. Alfidius Lurco is called Aufidius, perhaps through confusion of a rare *nomen* with a common one.

17. 50.632. (Pl. VIII.)

Fragment of base of Thasian marble, inscribed (a) on front, and (b), later, on right face, broken above, to left and behind. Preserved height 0.22, preserved width 0.515, preserved thickness 0.395; height of letters: (a) lines 1–4, 0.030; line 5, 0.015; (b) lines 1–2, 0.025; line 3, 0.030.

Found in the ancient town, above the upper spring, near the Roman aqueduct. Unpublished.

(a)
> [Σα]μο[θράικων]
> ὁ δῆμος *vac.*
> Πυθοκλῆν
> ['Απ]ολλοφάνους
> [ὁ δεῖνα ἐ]ποίη[σεν]

(b)
> ————Atelli[us—f. (*or* 1.), mys]-
> [tes] pius . . . nio.ni—
>   epo⟨p⟩tes.

(a) The lettering seems to be of good Hellenistic date. The phi of line 4, Φ, is already found in the third century B.C.[1] The inscription appears to be complete to the left in lines 2–3, and the whole was apparently engraved close to the left edge, and not centered symmetrically, which is unusual.

1. See, e.g., *FdDelphes*, III, 1, 104.

Line 1. The restoration is paleographically not wholly satisfactory, and is not the only possibility (for instance, ηθ is possible).

Line 5. The reading is far from certain, particularly the first two letters, on which the rest depend. However, the letters πρ are certainly possible, and in view of their markedly smaller size, the restoration of a sculptor's signature seems reasonable.

(b) To judge by the lettering, notably the wide open *p*, a date before the middle of the first century B.C. is probable.

Line 1. The first visible stroke is oblique, and should be *A*. [*V*]*iṭelḷi*[*us*] is therefore out of the question. *Aṭelḷi*[*us*] and [*S*]*aṭelḷi*[*us*] are both possible. Atilius, the name of the *inlustris adulescens* who addressed the Samothracian ἐκκλησία in 168 (Livy 45.5.2) is not possible.

Lines 2–3. The word after *pius* is very difficult to read. It appears to be .²*.nio.nị*. The lettering differs considerably from that of the word *pius*. In line 3 the stone has *epontes*. However, since the initial *e* is clear, there can be no doubt as to the reading, though the cause of the mistake is not obvious. It is surprising that the *mystes* occurs before the *epoptes*. There is apparently no other instance of this.

The base was found in the ancient city, and (a), which is a dedication by the demos, would normally have stood there and not in the Sanctuary. However, (b) relates to the Sanctuary, and it is not likely that a used base would be transferred from the city to the Sanctuary to be re-used there. The dedication therefore was probably originally erected in the Sanctuary and re-used on the spot, and transferred to the site of the city at a somewhat later date.

18. 39.108. (Pl. IX.)

Two non-joining pieces of Thasian marble, (a) front and left edges preserved, (b) front and right edges and back ((c)) preserved. Both broken at top. (a) Preserved height 0.14, preserved width 0.41, preserved thickness 0.37; (b) preserved height 0.13, preserved width 0.34, thickness (with (c)) 0.66; height of letters: (a) and (b) 0.030–035, (c) (later date) 0.050. (c), which originally formed one piece with (b) (see *IG*, loc. cit., below) is now broken.

(a) From the walls of the church of Hagios Demetrios in Chora, 1939.

(b) and (c) first seen in Chora by Conze (*S,I*, p. 42, no. 18).[1]

(c) only, Conze, loc. cit. (who apparently did not notice (b)).

(b) and (c) Kern, *AM*, 18 (1893), 377, no. 28; *IG*, XII (8), 242.

(a), (b), and (c) (mentioned *AJA*, 44 [1940], 355); H. Bloch, *AJA*, 44 (1940), 485 ff.: cf. J. and L. Robert, *REG*, 57 (1944), 222, no. 151b.

---

1. H. Bloch, loc. cit., p. 485, says of this piece that it was "found in the Austrian excavations," but adds, "All the three fragments were found in Chora." The latter statement is correct and, of course, incompatible with the first.

[ἡ βουλὴ καὶ ὁ δῆμος Λεύκιον Καλπόρνιον]

(a)   (b)

Λεύκιον υ[ἱὸν Πείσ]ωνα
τὸν αὐτοκράτορ[α καὶ πά]τρωνα τῆς πόλεως.

(c) of later date

[————θεῶν] μεγάλων

This inscription has been the subject of a careful study by H. Bloch, and I content myself in the main with accepting his supplements and conclusions, according to which the honorand was L. Calpurnius Piso, governor of Macedonia 57–55 B.C.[2] The dedication was made when he was governor (αὐτοκράτωρ). Cicero mentions the visit of Piso to Samothrace.[3]

Bloch's assumption (see n. 1, above) that the dedication is from the Sanctuary leads him to say, "It is significant that Piso occurs as *patronus* of the town, because this institution then was still of relatively small importance; the patronate alone would be sufficient proof of Piso's initiation." But I doubt very much whether such weight can be put on a term the use of which becomes common at just this time.[4] The stone came from Chora, and there is thus no a priori probability that it originally stood in the Sanctuary rather than in the town. Furthermore, Piso is called *patronus* of the city, and nothing is said of his relations with the Sanctuary. A distinction is usually made between benefactions toward one and the other, and when both were involved it is so stated.[5] In favor of Bloch's interpretation might be urged the later reference to the θεοὶ μεγάλοι on the reverse of the stone. But, granted that it is unlikely that the stone would have been transferred from the city to the Sanctuary in antiquity (cf. above, p. 56), there is no reason why a statue of a ἱερεὺς θεῶν μεγάλων should not be erected in the city.

Therefore, though Piso may have been at some time initiated (in contrast though this would be with his behavior in Rome, where, according to his contemporary, Varro,[6] he suppressed the Egyptian cults), this inscription does not afford any direct proof of it. It is a simple dedication by a city to a Roman magistrate.

2. T. R. S. Broughton, *The Magistrates of the Roman Republic* (2 vols., New York, 1951–52), II, 193.

3. Cicero *In Pisonem* 89: "Quid quod . . . cum sustentare vix posses maerorem tuum doloremque decessionis, Samothraciam te primum, post inde Thasum cum tuis teneris saltatoribus . . . contulisti." See above, Vol. 1, **199**.

4. See the old but valuable discussion of T. Eckinger, *Die Orthographie lateinischer Wörter in griechischen Inschriften* (Munich, 1892), pp. 135–36. He emphasizes that the title "Patron" of a city is almost exclusively pre-Imperial.

5. *IG*, XII (8), 150, lines 2–3: πᾶσαν ἐπιμέλειαμ τοι[ού]μενος τοῦ ἱεροῦ καὶ τῆς πόλεως; ibid., p. 38

(*BMI* 444, Michel 352), I, lines 3–4: ἀγαθὸν διατελεῖ ὑπὲρ τοῦ ἱεροῦ καὶ τῆς πόλε[ως | κ]αὶ τῶν πολιτῶν; cf. ibid., 152, line 5: [————εὐεργέ]τας τῆς πόλεως, and 156A, where the distinction is made between (lines 4–5) ε[ὐσεβῶ]ς διακείμενος πρὸς τοὺς θεούς, and (line 4) διακείμενος δὲ πρὸς τὸν δῆμον. For the distinction between Sanctuary and city in an honorific dedication or decree, such as might be expected here, if Piso had been specifically benefactor of the shrine as a result of initiation, cf. the honors paid by the Delphians in 207–206 B.C. (*Syll*[3] 555–56 = *FdDelphes*, III, 4, 21–23), καὶ εἶμεν Μεσσανίους εὐεργέτας τοῦ ἱεροῦ καὶ τᾶς πόλιος (556, lines 7–8).

6. See the references given by Bloch, loc. cit., p. 489, n. 24.

19. 49.441. (Pl. IX.)

Fragment of marble stele, left and bottom edges preserved, molding along lower edge. Preserved height 0.246, preserved width 0.019, thickness 0.09; height of letters: lines 1–3, 0.023; lines 3–7, 0.015–017.

From Chora, 5 July 1949.

Unpublished.

> [ἀνέθηκαν(?)]
> τὸ τέμ[ενος οἱ]
> ἐν πλοίῳ, Δι . .⁴/⁵ .
> β̅ τοῦ Εἰσιδ[ώρου *or* -ότου]
> καὶ σὺν α[ὐτῷ]
> 5   Θήρων β̅ τοῦ Μ[ενάνδ]-
> ρου,
> Εὔνους.

raised molding.

The top edge of the stone is not preserved, and there may have been another line containing a main verb. A verb, however, is not absolutely necessary, and the indentation of the first preserved line suggests that there was nothing above it.

The absence of καί after [–οἱ] ἐν πλοίῳ shows that Δι— and Θήρων are in apposition to this phrase. There is obviously no room for more than the patronymic in line 3, and the length of the other lines can thus be approximately determined by the word Εἰσιδ[ώρου/ότου] in line 3.

In line 1 tau seems preferable to iota, and τέμ[ενος] gives the right length. ἱερ[όν] in any case makes a short line.

In line 4 σὺν α[ὐτῷ], an obvious supplement, is slightly illogical after [–οἱ] ἐν πλοίῳ and probably reflects the superior status of Δι—.

Line 6 is written in a different style (Є not E), but the cutting is very similar, and the lapicide may have been the same. A Θήρων Περίνθιος occurs in the list of ναῦται initiated in *IG*, XII (8), 186 *b*, line 25, which is of a considerably earlier date (*vidi*).

The inscription is apparently of the second or third century A.D. The provenance of the stone is not known, but to my mind there can be little doubt that it comes originally from the Sanctuary. The Samothracian gods were, of course, particularly regarded as patrons of seafarers.[1] The quality of the inscription suggests that the shrine dedicated by the crew was probably very simple.

1. See Hemberg, pp. 100 ff., esp. p. 101, n. 3. See also above, Vol. 1, Index 4, s.v. *sailors*.

20. 48.286. (Pl. IX.)

Plaque of Thasian marble, broken to right and left, upper and lower moldings preserved. Height 0.372, preserved width 0.61, thickness 0.055–070; height of letters 0.038.

From Halonia, 18 July 1948.

G. Downey, *Hesperia,* 19 (1950), 21 ff. (from squeeze and field drawing), and pl. 14 (drawing made from squeeze by P. A. Underwood): cf. J. and L. Robert, *REG,* 64 (1951), 183, no. 170; referred to, *Guide,* p. 17.

> [τ]οῦτο λοετρὸν τ———————
> [τ]ὸ μέγα πρὸ ἐτῶν β———————
> .. ἀνανεοῦτε εὐτ———————
> ['Ιο]υστινιανοῦ ἔτους———————

There is much that is puzzling in this piece, and no satisfactory restoration is possible. The left end is very worn, and the edge can only be estimated by the reading [τ]οῦτο in line 1. Of this, the first omicron and the upsilon are just visible; before the omicron the stone is broken. It seems likely that the inscription began with the word [τ]οῦτο, and I therefore assume that very little is missing to the left in the following lines: see further below. To the right there is no indication of how much is missing. Downey, the first editor, regarded the inscription as almost complete, but I see no reason for this assumption. On the contrary, the text as it stands seems incomprehensible, and I should suppose a good deal was missing.

Line 1. If the reading [τ]οῦτο is correct, as I believe, τό may have been omitted by haplography, but its absence is attested at this period and is probably intentional.[1] The tau at the end of the line is clear.

Line 2. The omicron at the beginning of the line, before the mu, is clear. Presumably we should supply [τ]ό, for τ|ό, which is in any case an unlikely division of the word, would leave the omicron inset. After omicron, μέγα, written ΜΕΓΑ, is clear.[2] Downey's reading [...θεομη]νείᾳ, which he understood to refer to the earthquake of A.D. 543 that destroyed Cyzicus, is impossible.[3] πρὸ ἐτῶν β is difficult. It can most easily be taken, with Downey, as an indication of time, "two years ago," though it is rather surprising that so brief a lapse of time as two years should be specifically indicated. A possible alternative is to regard πρὸ ἐτῶν as incorrectly inscribed for πρὸ———ἐτῶν (the phrase as it stands could hardly be equivalent to πρὸ πολλῶν ἐτῶν) and the β as part of another word. The first alternative is perhaps preferable.

1. See the instances given by L. Radermacher, *Neutestamentliche Grammatik*[2] (Tübingen, 1925), p. 113.
2. Cf. J. Keil and A. von Premerstein, *Dritte Reise in Lydien* (*DenkschrWien,* 57 [1], 1914), 116, lines 16 ff. (A.D. 206 / 7), recording subscriptions εἰς τὴν ἐπισκευὴν τοῦ μεγάλου βαλανείου.

3. This view appears in Lehmann's reports, *Hesperia,* 20 (1951), 12; 21 (1952), 41; 22 (1953), 13. He tells me *per ep.* that while he accepts my reading for line 2, nevertheless "a tremendous earthquake caused the ruin of the major buildings of the Sanctuary at about that time."

Line 3, init. The same considerations of space apply here as in line 2. There is room for one letter or perhaps two before the first alpha. The form ἀνανεοῦτε was taken by Downey as a degenerate form of ἀνενεώθη. J. and L. Robert pointed out that it is in fact simply a form of ἀνανεοῦται. From the point of view of orthography this is no doubt correct, but there remains to explain the use of the present middle tense, which can hardly be regarded as equivalent to an aorist passive, or indeed be given a past sense at all, such as would be required here. However, in view of the state of the inscription, there is no case for "correcting" the form. ευτ was taken by Downey as part of either εὐτυχῶς or εὐτέχνως, and this seems likely, since these adverbs (particularly the former) are found in late building-inscriptions in such phrases as, for example, ἐκτίσθη εὐτυχῶς.

Line 4. Downey read the date formula as [...ἐπὶ ᾽Ιου]στινιανοῦ, but apart from the probability that there is no room even for ἐπί on this line, the formula itself seems insufficient; at this period one would expect some such introductory word as βασιλείας and probably an indictional date. This is but one of several reasons for supposing that the stone is very incomplete to the right.

For the scanty remains of the bath see *Hesperia* (above), quoting the Expedition diary. Dedications and repairs of bathing establishments are frequent in inscriptions of the Imperial and Byzantine periods, more particularly, as might be expected, in Syria and in a Christian context.[4]

4. See, for pagan baths, L. Robert, *Études Épigraphiques,* pp. 128 ff. (*IGRR,* IV, 946); for the importance of baths in the early church see F. Cabrol and H. Leclercq, *Dictionnaire d'archéologie chrétienne et de liturgie* (15 vols., Paris, 1903–53), s.v. *bains;* and J. Zellinger, *Bad und Bäder in der altchristlichen Kirche* (Munich, 1928), pp. 115–28. For the baths at Corycus in Cilicia see S. Guyer in *Monumenta Asiae Minoris Antiqua* (London and Manchester, 1928—), II, 82–87. For Syrian baths see Prentice, *Greek and Latin Inscriptions in Syria* (New York, 1908), 217; *IGLS* 333A (*corrigenda,* p. 382), ibid., no. 1685: cf. J. and L. Robert, *REG,* 68 (1955), no. 234. *Anth. Pal.,* IX, 606–40 contains a collection of late poems on baths. J. and L. Robert (loc. cit. in lemma) explain the form λοετρόν in line 1 of our inscription as derived from such verse.

21. 49.448. (Pl. X.)

Fragment of (revetment block of?) base of Thasian marble, upper molding preserved, broken to left and right (and at bottom). Preserved (?) height 0.50, preserved width 0.31, thickness 0.10; height of letters 0.023–024.

From Chora, 5 July 1949.

Unpublished.

[ἡ πόλ]ις Εὐβούλωι
[Θρ]ασυδαίου τοῦ Γ̅
[κα]τὰ ψήφισμα.

vac.

I think nothing was inscribed after line 3, although one might expect βουλῆς καὶ δήμου (see below). The stone is very worn, and it is only too easy to imagine traces of letters, but I cannot convince myself that there really are any.

The hand is evidently of the third century B.C., and closely resembles that of *IG*, XII (8), 247.[1]

The block is too thin for an ordinary honorific base and therefore may be, as Lehmann suggests, a revetment slab of a built-up core.

The dedication probably came from the city. It is the only Samothracian dedication bearing the words κατὰ ψήφισμα, though the formula is common enough elsewhere, particularly in the Imperial period — in decrees and dedications and in the formulae of tombstones, either in the simple formula used here or in the more complex κατὰ ψήφισμα βουλῆς καὶ δήμου, or in the form of initials Ψ.Β.Δ.[2] The present inscription must be among the earliest instances of the usage in a dedication, though it is noteworthy that it occurs at about this date or earlier as a formula in decrees at Thasos.[3]

1. See *S,II*, p. 102, no. 15 for a line-drawing. The temptation to restore and read that inscription as ['Αρισ]τοβούλη [Θρασυδα]ίου, and to regard 'Αριστοβούλη as the sister of the Euboulos of the present inscription must be resisted, since the mu is wholly preserved in the drawing in *S,II*, and even though the iota is not as clear as one could wish in our inscription,

for reasons of space it is not possible to read a mu.
2. See in general Larfeld, *Griechische Epigraphik*[3] (Munich, 1914), pp. 445–46.
3. *IG*, XII (8), 267–68, and *IG*, XII, Suppl., 355, ἀνέγραψαν κατὰ ψήφισμα βουλῆς καὶ δήμου; cf. Pouilloux, *Thasos, I* (*Études Thasiennes*, III, Paris, 1954), 396.

III. Lists of Theoroi

THE main principles to be followed in the publication of the Samothracian theoroi-lists were laid down by Benndorf, *S,II,* pp. 97–101, and accepted by Fredrich, *IG,* XII (8), p. 47.[1] These were that the oldest group was that in which the name of the city which the theoroi represented stood in ethnic form in the nominative, *IG,* XII (8), 160–69; this group was followed by that in which the name of the city appeared in the genitive, ibid., 170–72; while the most recent group was that in which the μύσται εὐσεβεῖς were added to the theoroi (173–76). The chronological limits of the theoroi-lists were given by Fredrich thus: "Omnes autem theororum tituli aetate minores decretis sunt inde a saec. ii a. Chr. n. ineunte usque ad saec. 1 p. Chr. initium orti." Benndorf also assumed that all the blocks containing the inscriptions had formed part of the wall of a single building, which he thought might be the "Old Temple" – that is, the building called by Lehmann the "Temenos." There is still no indication as to which building they were exposed in, but the new theoroi blocks, **23** and **24**, confirm the observation that they all belonged to a single building, since they are of the same height (ca. 0.34) as those on which Benndorf based his conclusions.

The new list, **22**, involves some expansion of both aspects of this reconstruction. As we have seen, this list of theoroi is apparently earlier than any of the preserved lists of theoroi-proxenoi, and it is inscribed on a stele. Moreover, the list is one of theoroi only – that is, there is no suggestion that they were made proxenoi. It is tempting to think that the stele represents the earlier form of record, before it had become the custom to bestow the privilege of proxeny on all theoroi, and that at this time the lists were inscribed on individual stelai. But *IG,* XII (8), 172, which was obviously of the same form, seems to be of a considerably later date, and we should therefore probably conclude that simple lists of theoroi existed concurrently with the list of theoroi-proxenoi. One other point is clear: in this early list the names are in the genitive. "Benndorf's rule," if so it may be called, thus evidently did not apply here; and this perhaps weakens the force of its application, as a general rule, to the other lists. The list of theoroi published below, p. 69, as Appendix III A, may, it is suggested there, also offend the rule.

1. Cf. also Hemberg, p. 126, n. 5.

22. 38.376. (Pl. X.)

Two fragments of stele, broken above, once making complete join, now broken, a piece having been broken off the bottom right corner of the top fragment, (a), during the war of 1939–45. Combined height 1.74, width 0.40–45, thickness 0.085–10; height of letters 0.015. The whole stone is very worn and largely illegible. The first line appears to be outset by about three letters to the left, and to continue right across the stone; the remainder apparently are placed centrally; the ethnics are inset still further. Pl. X gives a photograph of the stone in its entirety when found, and shows the two halves as they now are.

Found **7** August 1938, in Roman aqueduct: See above, on **2–4**.

Mentioned *AJA*, 43 (1939), 144.

                    ἐπὶ βασιλέως ᾿Α[θ]ανοδώρου τοῦ Αἰγ[*or* π]————·
                         Τηΐων·
                    Πολυμ———— ————————
                    ᾿Απολλώνιος .³. ιπίδου.
        5   Κνιδιων·
                    ᾿Αγαθοφῶν ᾿Αγαθονίκου
                    ῾Αμέτερος Παντακλέος
                    Δαμόπολις ῾Αγησιδάμου.
                         Μηλίων·
        10   Διόδοτος Πρωτοφίλου
                    Πύθων Πυθοκρίτου
                    Νικόστρατος ᾿Αριστοβούλου.
                         Μηθυμναίων·
                    Θυμητᾶς Δεινα[γόρ]ου
        15   ————ν Μίνδρου
                    [Πρ]ύτανι[ς]   ————————
                    Πι...⁶...ων   ————————
                    Α————   ————————
                    ————————   ————————

        20   Σα[μί]ων·

                    ————————   ————————

                    ————άτιο[ς]   ————φου

                    ————————   ————————

                         [Κολο]φων[ίων]·
        25   ———— ῾Ηροδ————
                    ————ώνιος .³. π .². ίου
                         ————ίων·
                    Παυσανίας Πλειστίου
                    Πλειστοκράτης ᾿Αρίστωνος
        30   ᾿Αγησίας Στρα————

```
            ———ηνου
        ————Θεοφίλου
   ῾Ερμοπείθης ᾿Αριστόλα
   Εὔμηλος Στρατωνύμ[ου]
35      ————᾿Αθηναγόρα
       ———— Διονυσίου
   Παλλάντης Σκαμανδρ[ίου].
       Κλαζομενίων·
   ῾Ηραγίτων Δημητρίου
40  Τηλεφάνης Μητροδώρου
   ᾿Αρτεμῶ[ν]  ———φάνου[ς].
       Καυνίων·
       ————ίων Βοΐσκου
   Λυ . .⁴. . Πανταλέοντος.
45      ᾿Αβδηριτῶν·
   Εὐκράτης ῾Ηρακλείδου
   ᾿Απολλόδωρο[ς] Πυθόδ———
   ————————  ————————
   ————————  ————————
50  ————————  ————————
        Παριανῶν
   ————᾿Απολλωνίου
   ————  ———— ου
   Πολυδ . .⁵. . . ᾿Επιγόνου
55  ———λλ.π———  ————νος
   ————————  ———ν————
   —π————  .υ . . μένου
   —υ————  ————μο[υ]
   ———υ————
60  ————————  ————————
   ————————  ———λ————
   ————————  ———ν————
   Πολύδωρος Διονυσοδότου
   Στράτηγος . .⁵. . οθέου·
65      Καλχηδονίων·
   ————————  ————————
   Αμ————  ————ωνος
   Φιλοφάνης [Μυ]ρρίνου
            ————ς
70  Διογένης Μεγύλλου ῾Ρόδιος
   Πισικράτης Εὐτίμου .². ἴδιος.
```

vac.

This stone is extremely difficult to read. I collated it in 1954, 1956, and 1957, and also read from time to time a few more letters on the squeeze: Bean also made some contributions to readings from the squeeze in 1956. He succeeded in particular in demolishing my reading ἐπίδο[σ]ι[ν] in line 4, on the basis of which I had originally supposed that the stone contained the names of theoroi, by states, who had contributed to an ἐπίδοσις. The establishment of a patronymic in line 4 showed that the stele in fact contains a simple list of theoroi. Finally in 1957, I recovered the ethnic in line 2, Τηΐων. It is, of course, possible to suppose that the list records the names not of theoroi, but of some other representatives, or members, of foreign states, such as proxenoi, but there is no analogy to such lists at Samothrace, and I think it is safe to assume that the names are those of theoroi.

The type of theoroi-list which emerges is that of an inscribed stele containing simply the Samothracian eponymous dating, followed immediately by the first ethnic in the genitive. This has an exact parallel in a list seen by Cyriac, *IG*, XII (8), 172, apparently of the last century B.C., which probably also, to judge by the general form of the inscription, was inscribed on a stele. The present inscription is evidently of the middle or later third century B.C., and probably the earliest surviving list of theoroi. It is perhaps significant that the list contains some ethnics which do not recur later. The absence of any descriptive heading suggests that the stone may have been one of a series.

I have not attempted the impossible task of recording the varying degrees of paleographical uncertainty throughout, and confine myself mainly to noting parallels from other lists.

Line 2. Teian theoroi occur in *IG*, XII (8), 163, line 30, and 171, line 30.

Line 5. Κνιδίων is not certain. Knidian theoroi do not occur elsewhere in the theoroi-lists, and Bean prefers to read the word as Μηλίων, though this seems to me more probable in line 9.

Line 9. Melians are not found elsewhere in the lists.

Line 13. Methymnians also do not occur elsewhere.

Line 20. Samian theoroi occur in *IG*, XII (8), 165, line 8 and 170, line 55.

Line 24. Kolophonian theoroi occur in *IG*, XII (8), 163, line 24; 164, line 7; 166.

Lines 27 ff. This group of theoroi consists of ten names, which seems rather many. Perhaps another ethnic should be read in line 31 in place of the uncertain —ηνου: for example, —ηνῶν.

Line 38. Klazomenian theoroi occur in *IG*, XII (8), 161, line 8; 168, line 4.

Line 42. Kaunian theoroi occur in *IG*, XII (8), 160, line 7; 170, line 45: *b*, line 10 (restored): below, p. 69 (restored).

Line 45. Abderite theoroi occur in *IG*, XII (8), 161, line 15; 170, line 52.

Line 51. Theoroi from Parion occur in *IG*, XII (8), 170, line 81; 175.

Lines 56 ff. Perhaps one of these lines (56, 59, 60) should be understood as forming a new ethnic heading: cf. on lines 27 ff., above.

Line 65. Kalchedonian theoroi appear here for the first time. A Kalchedonian is honored in *IG*, XII (8), 152.

Lines 70–71. Two names with ethnics are placed at the end. The reading in line 71 may be [Κν]ίδιος, in which case he was presumably omitted from the Κνίδιοι in lines 5 ff. (See the note on that line.) The stone is uninscribed after line 71.

23. 52.779. (Pl. XI.)

Block of Thasian marble, top, lower left, and bottom edges preserved. Right front face battered. One rectangular dowel hole (0.045 wide, 0.035 deep) preserved in upper surface. Preserved height 0.35, preserved width 0.44, thickness 0.24; height of letters: lines 1–2, 0.018; lines 3 ff., 0.015.

Found 3 August 1952, near the Genoese Towers.
Unpublished.

[ἐπὶ β]ασιλέως Θεοδώρου [(τοῦ δεῖνος)· οἵδε πρόξενοι ἐγένοντο τῆς πόλεως],
[τῶνδε] τῶν πόλεων θεωροὶ πα[ραγενόμενοι]·

(a)	(b)	[(c)]
Λαρισαιοι·	Ἐφέσιοι·	
.. τίας Ἀριστομένους	Ἡράκλειτος———	
5　[Εὔ]δημος Εὐδήμου	Ἰσόδικος Σα———	
[Ἀ]ντίγονος Θερσίππου　15	Ἑρμαγόρας———	
[Δ]ημήτριος Νικολάου.	– – – – – – – – –	
Κυμαῖοι·		
Φαέννης Ἱκεσίου		
10　[Φ]αέννης Φαέννου τοῦ Ἱκεσίου		
. ε . . . . . ν		
– – – – – – – – – – –		

The hand suggests a date in the late third or early second century B.C.

Line 1. The βασιλεύς is not attested elsewhere.

Lines 1–2. A normal document of this type contains a record of award of proxeny to the θεωροί in the following phrase: οἵδε πρόξενοι (τῆς πόλεως) ἐγένοντο, θεωροὶ παραγενόμενοι, and a reference to proxeny is likely here.

Probably the title was spread over three or more columns, as in *IG*, XII (8), 170–71. Line 1 will be much longer than line 2, as in 170. In addition, τῶν πόλεων seems to need further definition, and I have added [τῶνδε]. The phrase does not occur elsewhere in these opening formulae.[1]

1. In the formula οἵδε πρόξενοι ἐγένοντο τῆς πόλεως θεωροὶ παραγενόμενοι, τῆς πόλεως is naturally taken

(a) *Line 3.* Λαρισαῖοι, Bean: Larisan theoroi occur here for the first time. They are presumably from Larisa-on-Hermos.

Line 8. Κυμαῖοι: other Kymaian theoroi appear in *IG*, XII (8), 163, *c*, lines 27–29; 170, *b*, lines 24–27.

(b) *Line 1.* Ἐφέσιοι: other Ephesian theoroi appear in *IG*, XII (8), 164, lines 10–12; 170, *f*, lines 85–88.

with πρόξενοι ἐγένοντο (in *IG*, XII [8], 171, the formula as restored, [οἵδε πρόξενοι τῆς πόλεω]ς ἐγένοντο, shows this). *IG*, XII (8), 168, lines 1–2 (Inv. 54.49) are restored thus: [ἐπὶ βασιλέως....?....]α [οἵ]δ[ε πρόξενοι ἐγένοντο τῆς πόλεως | θεωροὶ τοῦ δή]μου παραγενηθέντες. [θεωροὶ τοῦ δή]μου introduces an otherwise unrecorded formula, but it is difficult to avoid, since the theoroi must have been mentioned.

24. 39.1131. (Pl. XI.)

Block of Thasian marble, used as altar-top (?), cut on all sides, left side beveled. Preserved height 0.35, preserved width 0.45, preserved thickness 0.19; height of letters 0.010–015.

From Chora, 15 August 1939.

Unpublished.

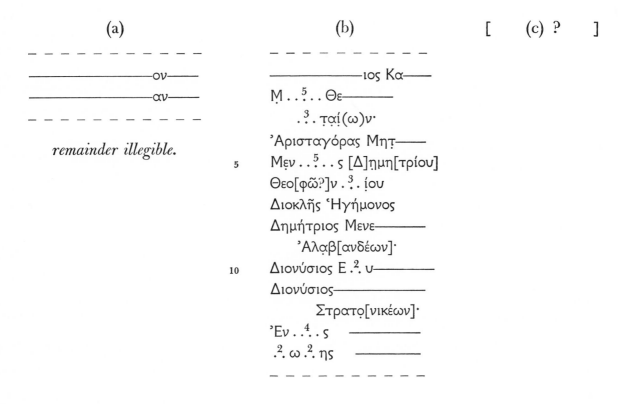

<table>
<tr><td align="center">(a)</td><td align="center">(b)</td><td align="center">[(c) ?]</td></tr>
</table>

The hand is probably of the second century B.C.

This very worn inscription is clearly part of a list of theoroi: the characteristic layout can be detected in (b), but the stone is barely legible. The larger letters in lines 1–2 probably belong to the heading embracing columns 1–2, and we have here the beginning of two columns. How far the stone extended to the left and right, and how many columns there originally were, cannot be determined. The photograph reveals more than the stone itself or the squeeze.

(b) *Line 3.* Well indented and clearly part of an ethnic. The nu at the end shows that it was in the genitive plural.

Line 11. Στρατο[νικέων], Bean. Stratonikean theoroi occur also in *IG*, XII (8), 170, line 72. There is no indication either here or in 170 of which city is meant. In 170, the Stratonikeans are recorded between the Iasians and some envoys of King Attalus.

APPENDIX III A

The following fragment of a list of theoroi was discovered in the storerooms of the Istanbul Museum and identified as Samothracian by Professor L. Robert, who has kindly waived his rights of publication. I have not seen the stone and publish it from Professor Robert's squeeze. Measurements and other details I owe to Professor Bean.

Fragment of block of Thasian marble, part of top edge preserved. Preserved height 0.17, preserved width 0.24, preserved thickness 0.105; height of letters 0.008–010. Pl. XI (squeeze).

Now in the Istanbul Museum.

Unpublished.

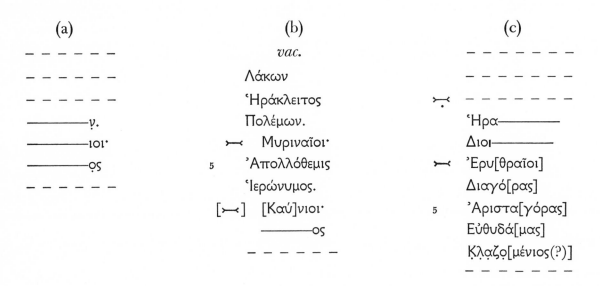

(a)	(b)	(c)
– – – – – –	*vac.*	– – – – – –
– – – – – –	Λάκων	– – – – – –
– – – – – –	Ἡράκλειτος	⊱⊰ – – – – – –
————ν.	Πολέμων.	Ἡρα————
————ιοι·	⊱⊰ Μυριναῖοι·	Διοι————
————ος	5 ’Απολλόθεμις	⊱⊰ ’Ερυ[θραῖοι]
– – – – – –	Ἱερώνυμος.	Διαγό[ρας]
	[⊱⊰] [Καύ]νιοι·	5 ’Αριστα[γόρας]
	————ος	Εὐθυδά[μας]
	– – – – – –	Κλαζο[μένιος(?)]
		– – – – – –

The identification of this stone as Samothracian seems certain in spite of some peculiar features which distinguish this list from the known lists of theoroi (see below). The stone is Thasian marble and it is hardly possible that there should be another cult-center in the area from which it could have come.

The list, consisting of three columns, is exceptional in that the names of the θεωροί

69

were evidently not accompanied by the patronymic. This may be deduced from a comparison with the other theoroi-lists in all of which the ethnic group-name is centrally placed above the name and patronymic, whereas here Μυρινᾶιοι in column 2 and ᾿Ερυ[θραῖοι] in column 3 are placed above the single name. Again it is clear from the successive nominative terminations in (b) that the patronymic, had it been used, could only have been on the same line as the name, and not below it. However, quite apart from the very clear spacing between columns 2 and 3 (which is not decisive in itself),[1] the word in column 3 alongside Apollothemis ((b) line 8) is an ethnic, since a comparison with (b) line 7 shows that it is ethnics which are preceded by the paragraphus. It may be noted in passing that this is the only Samothracian list with a paragraphus.[2]

The lettering of the inscription is far more carefully and elaborately executed than that of the other theoroi-lists (some of which, notably the right half of *IG*, XII [8], 170 (see below), are inscribed in a very rough manner) and could be of later date: (note the Ƴ (five times), the ⲭΩⲭ, and the highly developed terminals throughout). As has been noted above,[3] the other lists (except **22**) conform to the rule enunciated by Benndorf, according to which it is the earliest theoroi-lists, of the earlier part of the second century, which have the ethnics of the theoroi in the nominative. It is an open question whether this inscription offends that rule, or whether the hand, in spite of appearances, is of the early second century B.C.; for this there would be analogies, though not in Samothrace.[4] One must in this connection also bear in mind the idiosyncrasy of the inscription in not recording the patronymic. In view of the contrast between this hand and that of the other lists, my feeling is that the inscription is of later date.

The theoroi themselves call for no comment. Μυρινᾶιοι, line **7**, are known as theoroi from *IG*, XII (8), 162, line 11, and 171, line 3; the restoration [Καύ]νιοι in line 10 is not certain, but a short ethnic is necessary to judge by the alignment of the left margin, and Kaunians occur elsewhere in the lists: ibid., 160, lines 7–9; 170, lines 45 ff.; and above, **22**, lines 43 ff. Lines 14 ff., ᾿Ερυ[θραῖοι], do not occur elsewhere in the lists, but there is no alternative. Line 18, Κ̣λ̣α̣ζ[ομένιοι], seems certain at first sight; they occur in *IG*, XII (8), 161, lines 9–11, and 168, lines 4–6; also above, **22**, lines 39 ff. However, the letters are not indented and preceded by a paragraphus as are the other ethnics, so we should perhaps read

---

1. Wide gaps are often left between name and patronymics in the theoroi-lists: see, e.g., *IG*, XII (8), 170; there are many other instances.
2. The same sign occurs, for example, at Delos, *Inscr. Délos* 313, I (λ), line 14; 316, lines 62, 111, 113 ff.
3. See above, p. 62.
4. Thus it resembles the hand of the letter of Antiochus III to Magnesia-on-Maeander (inscribed in Mag-

nesia), Kern, *Die Inschriften von Magnesia am Maeander* (Berlin, 1900), 18 (Welles, *Royal Correspondence*, 31) and pl. III, 2 (though the Ƴ of the Samothracian inscription is not paralleled there); and certain inscriptions of the second century at Delos (e.g., *Inscr. Délos* 1518); but the extent of decoration is certainly unusual.

Κλαζο[μένιος], as Bean suggested to me. This is not an improbable name for a citizen of Erythrai.

In (b) lines 1–3 there are three names without ethnic; since the top edge of the block is preserved at this point, the names must form part of the last group in the previous column, as is not infrequently the case. The names are common and give no indication of their city of origin.

APPENDIX III B

In July 1954 I visited the ruined church of Ἅγιος Χριστός about one hour east of Palaeo-polis, and was able to collate the texts of most of the theoroi-lists which are there, either built into the various lintels of the church or else on loose blocks lying outside. Time, Bulgarians, and Greeks have sadly defaced the latter. I give a brief description of the present condition of the blocks here, together with the few corrections I have been able to make. Where I have a squeeze, I note the fact, should anyone wish to consult it. The corrections are from readings of the squeezes, since (2), (3), and (5) are no longer legible on the stone.

(1) *IG*, XII (8), 160. This I was unable to collate, either by reading from the stone or by taking a squeeze, since the inscribed face is downward on the underside of the very low lintel of the inner door.

(2) Ibid., 161. Now outside the church among the fallen blocks on the left side as you approach from Palaeopolis. It was badly defaced across the inscribed surface in 1938 (the new inscription is conveniently dated, as is an earlier one of 1758). The inscription (par-ticularly the first pair of names in each line) is now worn almost beyond legibility, and it is barely possible to follow the text as printed in *IG*, let alone correct it. Squeeze.

(3) Ibid., 162. Outside the church on the right side leaning half vertically, with in-scribed face now inward. This is very weathered, particularly in the left column, but still legible, though any correction on the text in *IG* would be most unwise. Squeeze.

(4) Ibid., 170. The most legible of all the stones. Above the inner door of the church. The difference in hand noticed by previous editors is very clear on the photograph of the squeeze. Columns (a) and (b) are in a very strange angular slanting hand which unex-pectedly recalls the Greek graffiti of Egypt. In line 22 the second letter appears to be rho rather than alpha. I know no other instances of the name Πριώνιος, so if the letter is indeed a rho we should perhaps read Π⟨α⟩ιώνιος. In (c), line 37, βασιλέως. In (d), line 41, Fredrich correctly gave Μητροδότου in his majuscule copy, but by an oversight transcribed this as Μητροδώρου. It was corrected by Salač, *Niederlův Sborník* (*Mélanges Niederle*), p. 159 (= *SEG*, III, 754). Line 50: Salač already read Σωσ[αν]δρίδου for Fredrich's Σωσ[ικ]λείδο[υ]. Salač's reading is correct; the alpha is also visible on the squeeze: read Σωσα[ν]δρίδου. Line

65: Ῥ[οδί]ων. (e), line 73: not Ματροκλεί⟨ου⟩ς but Ἰατροκλεί⟨ου⟩ς, as already Salač (above). Squeeze.

(5) Ibid., 173 (= *CIL*, I², 667 = Degrassi, *Inscr. Lat. Lib. Rei Publ.*, I [1957], 211). Outside the church to the left. The date of the inscription, 66 B.C., should make the Latin part of it of considerable value in dating other inscriptions, but unfortunately much, but not all, of the Latin text is illegible. (Thus, in line 2, the squeeze does not support the *mystae* of Dessau, followed by Degrassi, against the *mistae* of Fredrich: the *i* is clear.) The Greek is still fairly well preserved. In (b), line 13, not Ἰσοκλῆς but Σωκλῆς. On line 10 Fredrich says of Πάττικος, "Nomen certum est; exspectes Πατί[σ]κος vel Πάτ[αι]κος." I read Πάτριχος tentatively: the rho seems clear to me. In line 20 I read Εὔδωρος: two names without patronymic are obviously necessary after ἀκόλουθοι. I suspect Εὐημέρου was a bad guess. Squeeze.

IV. Lists of Initiates

THE main features of the lists of initiates may be briefly summarized: (1) they are mostly of Imperial date, and thus barely overlap with the Hellenistic theoroi-lists; (2) Latin and Greek lists, in the material published here, appear almost equally (22 Greek, 19 Latin); (3) some of the Latin texts are among the earliest.

The lists of mystae exhibit greater range in regard to the form of stone used for inscribing than do the lists of theoroi-proxenoi. Several were found during the excavation of the "Sacristy" lying within that building, and Lehmann plausibly concluded from this and from the fact that many of the stones have been smoothed at the edges and provided with slightly receding edges, that the initiatory records were fitted into its walls.[1] Others were evidently free-standing.[2]

I have arranged the material in so far as possible chronologically, Latin and Greek together. Except, however, for the few dated Latin documents, the only criterion is that of the lettering; so a considerable margin of error must be allowed.

1. See Lehmann-Hartleben, *AJA*, 44 (1940), 345: cf. *Guide*, p. 48; Hemberg, p. 126, n. 5. Stones thus treated are, e.g., **35**, **42**. Such inserted stones were apparently called πίνακες ἔμβλητοι: see *Inscr. Délos* 1403, B, *b*, ɪɪ, 18; ibid., 1417, A, ɪɪ, 36; cf. Vallois, *CRAI*, 1929, 37.

2. E.g., below, **27**, **31**, **33**, **37**, **45**. Cf. the similar variety of types of lists of theoroi, above, p. 62.

25. 53.2. (Pl. XII.)

Fragment of plaque of Thasian marble, broken to right. Height 0.150, preserved width 0.225, thickness 0.030; height of letters 0.025–030.

From the region of the Genoese Towers, early 1953.

Unpublished.

> Ḷ. Iuentius · Ṃ[·fil.]
> Thalna · m[ystes]
> pius *vac.*

Line 1. The lapicide presumably intended to write *Iuventius*, but omitted one *u*. [*fil.*] rather than [*f.*] seems necessary to fill the line and preserve symmetry, since *mystes* must have been written in full in line 2.

The letter-forms suggest that the inscription belongs to the second century B.C. but do not permit further precision. The family of the Iuventii Thalnae was most active at this time,[1] and it is tempting to identify the initiate with the L. Iuventius Thalna, who was active in 185 / 184.[2] Such an early date is, however, unlikely, though not impossible.[3] At a slightly later date, after the battle of Pydna and Perseus' flight to Samothrace, the island was visited by numerous Roman officials,[4] and Thalna may well have been among them.

The nature of the inscription is not clear. It may be a dedication, or else a simple record of a single initiation. Such single records—which presumably correspond to single ceremonies of initiation—are rare as compared with lists inscribed after a collective ceremony, but there are other instances.[5] The line between a dedication and a record is obviously very thin in such cases, and I have therefore included the inscription in the catalogue of mystae.

1. See *RE,* s.v. *Iuventius* (25) ff.
2. Known only from Livy 39.31.4; ibid., 38.4.
3. The earliest Latin text from Delos is *Inscr. Délos* 1731, of ca. 140. I think no photograph of this has been published.
4. See above, p. 12.
5. See *IG,* XII (8), 197*b*, 200, 202.

26. 49.444. (Pl. XII.)

Fragment of Thasian marble broken to left and below (see below). Preserved height 0.19, preserved width 0.275, thickness 0.07–055; height of letters ca. 0.007.

From Chora, 5 July 1949.

Unpublished.

(a)

```
– – – – – – –
– – – – – – –
– – – – – – –
– – – – – – – –
– – – – – – –
      Ἐ      π      ό      π      τ      α      ι
————υπ————
——επ . . ca. 7 . . α
————όδοτος
5   [Ἀ]πολλόδωρος β
– – – – – – –
————ε . ν————
– – – – – – –
```

(b)

```
– – – – – –
– – – – – –
Πο————
Μίνναρος
Φιλοκτα
Θεύδο[το]ς
Διοφάνης
Κόνων
Διον————
Α . . ————
Ἀσκληπ————
– – – – – –
```

This list of initiates is probably of the second or first century B.C., and is thus among the earliest. There is insufficient space in (b) for patronymics to have been on the same lines as the names of the initiates, and there is no suggestion—except perhaps in line 3, where the possible sigma of Φιλοκτᾶ is lacking but the stone is very worn — that the patronymics were on the lines below the personal names. In column (a) ['Α]πολλόδωρος B is on one line, but there is no evidence for the other names.

In line 4 ἐπόπται is spread across both columns, and presumably refers to all names beneath it. Θεύδο[το]ς, inscribed on the same line as ἐπόπται and immediately after it, is presumably also an epoptes.

27. 49.442. (Pl. XII.)

Fragment of pedimental stele of Thasian marble, complete to right. Preserved height 0.21, preserved width 0.12, thickness 0.070; height of letters: line 1, 0.008; lines 2–3, 0.010; lines 4–9, 0.015. Traces of object in center of tympanum?

From Chora, 5 July 1949.

Unpublished.

(a) *on cornice:* [ἐπὶ βασιλέως τοῦ δεῖνος τοῦ ——]κου,

(b) *in field:* [ὡς δὲ ἐν———————, ἐπὶ ἱερομ]νάμονος
　　　　　　　　[τοῦ δεῖνος ————]ωνίου·
　　　　　　　　[μύσται εὐσε]βεῖς·
　　　　[————————Βε]νδιδώρο[υ]
　　　　————————   ————ου
　　　　————————   ————ους

It is clear from the necessary restoration of line 4 that a considerable portion of the stone is missing to the left. Thus, in spite of appearances, the apex of the pediment is not preserved.

Line 1. Evidently contained the Samothracian date.

Lines 2–3. The reading and restoration in line 2 seem quite certain, and constitute the non-Samothracian eponymous date. Ἱερομνάμονες are most familiar as the eponyms of Byzantium,[1] but other cities must be considered, notably Perinthos and Kalchedon.[2] Perinthians outnumber Byzantines in Samothracian documents,[3] but I leave the city name open.

Line 5. [————Βε]νδιδώρο[υ], Bean, is clearly right. Names in Βενδι- are especially common in Macedonia, Thrace, and Thasos.[4]

1. For the Byzantine hieromnamones see K. Hanell, *Megarische Studien* (Lund, 1934), pp. 156 ff.; L. Robert, *Hellenica*, 7 (1949), 38–40; ibid., 10 (1955), 18 ff.
2. For Perinthos see *IGRR*, I, 787 (cf. Robert, *Hellenica*, 10 [1955], 19, n. 1); and for Kalchedon, Michel 540; cf. Hanell, op. cit., pp. 150–51; L. Robert,

RevPhil, 13 (1939), 187–88.
3. *IG*, XII (8), 186, line 25; 203, line 1.
4. See E. Sittig, *De Graecorum Nominibus Theophoris* (Halle, 1912), pp. 151–52; J. and L. Robert, *REG*, 71 (1958), 300, no. 395.

28. 53.560. (Pl. XIII.)

Block of white marble inscribed on three faces. Large piece missing from front surface on left and right. On upper and under surfaces square dowel holes. Behind dowel hole of upper surface pi-shaped clamp hole. Height 0.66, width 0.28–32, thickness 0.19; height of letters: front face 0.020–025, left and right faces 0.015–020.

From Hagios Demetrios, 1953.

Unpublished.

(a)	(b)	(c)
– – – – – – – –	– – – – – – –	– – – – – – – –
i̯ . . a . oe	. . . OΛI	[Δ]ιον[ύσιος]
. . . id . Iunieis . epop[ta]	[M]ύσται εὐσ[εβεῖς]	[Δ]ιονυσ[ίου]
[.]Cornelius·L·f·Lent[ulus]	[Σ]ώστρατο[ς]	['Η]ρακλῆ[ς]
leg·pro·pr· vac.	Προκλείο[υ]	['Η]ρακλέ[ους]
⁵ mustae piei,	⁵ . . θόδημο[ς]	[Γ]λαυκί[ας] ⁵
[L·C]ornelius·L·l·Phil[o]	['I]ερόμαχο[ς]	. όλωνος
[C·] Mutius·C·l·Erun—	Ἀτ[τ]άλου	[Π]τολλᾶ[ς]
[. M]anius Demetr[ius]	[K]ροῖσος	['Ηρ]ακλέο[υς]
[P·M]allius·P·l·Lict[avius?]	[Λ]υκόφρον[ος]	[Ἀπ]ολλὼ[ς]
¹⁰ . . . Cor . . Matrod[orus]	¹⁰ ἀκόλου[θοι]·	[Δι]οδότ[ου] ¹⁰
. . . . c . . . . . νμ	'Ηλιόδωρ[ος]	ἐφόπται· (0.010 m.)
. . . . us Cornel[ius—·l·]	[Π]τολεμᾶ[ς]	[Ἀ]ρίδαμος
. . . . . . r. Muti (us) ·C·[l·] . . .	[Ἀ]μφί⟨λ⟩οχο[ς]	[Ἀ]ριδάμο[υ]
. . . . . o. Corne[lius—·l·]	Σώσαρχος	[Λ]έων
¹⁵ ——————n——————	– – – – – – –	[Βο]σπορίχο[υ] ¹⁵
– – – – – – – – – –	vac.	[Γλα]υκίας
		[Λέο]ντος
		[. . σ]θένης
		[Φα]έννο[υ]
		. . . ειο . . . ²⁰
		– – – – – – – –

(a) *Lines 1–2.* Presumably contained the consular, and perhaps the Samothracian, date, though this may have been only on (b).

Lines 2–3. There is no room for *pius* after *epop[ta]*. Its absence is paralleled.[1] As Lehmann points out to me, the absence of *"mystes pius et"* before *epop[ta]* is striking. Lentulus' origi-

1. See **17**; *IG*, XII (8), 215.

nal initiation was probably recorded elsewhere. The same feature occurs also on *IG*, XII (8), 205, also a Roman *epoptes*.

Lines 3–4. The *nt* of *Lentulus* are in ligature, N; evidently space ·was running out.

Line 9. Not *lict[ores]* (cf. **53** bis, line 2), for the name of the *libertus* must have been recorded.

Line 10. The *tr* of *Maṭrodorus* are perhaps in ligature.

(b) The Samothracian date presumably stood at the head of this list. There is a difficulty regarding the distribution of patronymics. That patronymics were employed in at least some cases is clear from lines **7** and **9**, where the termination is not in doubt. There are, however, only three names above ['I]ερόμαχο[ς] 'Ατ[τ]άλου, so it would at first sight appear that a patronymic is missing. This may be so; and since Προκλειο is inset, it seems likely that this is a patronymic, and I have so regarded it. Line 5 reads .ηθοδημο, and evidently is a nominative: ..θόδημο[ς]; but the opening of the word is uncertain. The first visible letter looks like an eta; neither [Π]ει̣θόδημο[ς] nor [Π]υθόδημο[ς] is satisfactory; Π̣ι̣θόδημο[ς] is more likely. Evidently not more than two letters are missing.

Lines 10 ff. The ἀκόλουθοι are presumably slaves, or persons of very humble origin, associated with the previous persons. I have therefore assumed that they did not have patronymics.

Line 12. [Π]τολεμα[ῖος] would be the natural restoration here, but the space is rather short and I have preferred [Π]τολεμᾶ[ς], a suitable form for a servant.

Line 13. Δ was apparently carved by error for Λ in ['Α]μφίλοχο[ς].

(c) The surviving terminations in lines **4, 6, 8,** and **17** show that patronymics were given. The names call for no particular comment.

The architecture of the block is interesting. There is barely room for more than one line on each of the three faces above the surviving first lines, and yet the inscriptions themselves if complete on these blocks need more than one line. Thus on the front face, (a), there are traces of one line of Latin characters above the month-date, and this presumably held part of the consular date, but it cannot have held it all. Similarly, on the left side-face, (b), the first preserved line contains the rubric but there seems to be no room for either a date-formula or any other heading above it. Again, on (c) one, or at the most two lines are missing. Evidently then, either the block carried one inscription only, with a simple Latin date (a), or else it did not contain the complete inscription. The latter alternative is borne out by the presence of dowel and clamp holes in the upper and lower surfaces. These must have served to join the block to other blocks, and the block above, whatever form it took, may well have been inscribed. We may thus regard our block as one of a vertical series: probably — the dimensions would encourage the supposition — part of an architectural member such as an *anta*. Lehmann points out to me that the slight tapering of the sides supports this.

Clearly if the blocks form part of a vertical series on three faces of a large monument it is not probable that the names all belong to one occasion: a list of such dimensions would be unusual. Moreover, (b), which ends halfway down the stone, is obviously the end of one list. Consequently, if (c) was part of the same list it must have preceded it. However it is clear that (c) is in a different (and probably earlier) hand. It seems then reasonable to suppose that we have here three separate lists or fragments of lists. The front face was probably the first inscribed, even though the hand of the right face (c) would not be surprising at an earlier date. (c) and (b) probably were inscribed in that order.

(a) The main interest here resides in the epopta, Cornelius Lentulus, *leg. pro. pr.* Unfortunately, it does not seem possible to identify this person with certainty. The inscription is probably of the later second or first century B.C. and possibility of identification is naturally very small.

The initiates are all *liberti* of different persons, and presumably formed part of Lentulus' suite. Lentulus was made epopta on the same day as the freedmen were initiated. For a rather fuller picture of a combined ceremony of this sort see **36**, with commentary.

29. (a) 39.16 (= *IG*, XII [8], 191, 211) and (b), *IG*, XII (8), 192, 212. (Pls. XIV, XV.)

Two non-joining fragments of a decorated relief, representing a round building: (a$^{1-2}$) left edge preserved, (b^2) small part of right edge preserved. (a) Preserved height 0.33, preserved width 0.28, preserved thickness 0.08; (b) preserved height 0.20, preserved width 0.23, thickness, 0.13; height of letters: (a) lines 1–4, 0.013; line 5, 0.018; (a) lines 6 ff. and (b) 0.016.

(a^1) (MS: Cod. Ambr. A.55); Muratori, *Thesaurus*, III, p. MDCXXXVI, no. 16 (without line 5) = *CIG* 5926a (without line 5) = *CIL*, III, 719 = *IG*, XII (8), 211.

(a$^{2-3}$) Muratori, *Thesaurus*, I, p. CLXXVI, no. 1 ("Romae, e schedis meis") = *CIG* 2157 (with numerous corrections by Boeckh) = Rubensohn, p. 172 = Kern, *AM*, 18 (1893), 364 = Michel 1141; (Hamburg, MS 253), E. Ziebarth, *Programm des Wilhelm-Gymnasiums* (1903 [9]), "Eine Inschriftenhandschrift der Hamburger Stadtbibliothek," p. 9, no. 18 (cf. id., *AM*, 31 [1906], 414, no. 10); *IG*, XII (8), 191.

(b^1) (MS: Cod. Ambr. A.55); Muratori, *Thesaurus*, III, p. MDCLXX, no. 1 = *CIG* 5926B (without lines 8–9) = *CIL*, III, 718 = *IG*, XII (8), 212.

(b^2) = right half of (a^2), lines 6–10, with (b^1), line 9; stone rediscovered, Kern, *AM*, 18 (1893), 363, no. 7 = *IG*, XII (8), 192.

(a$^{1-2}$) stone rediscovered, (a^3) MS Cod. Ambr. A.55, Ashmole MS f.140r (cf. Saxl, *Journal of the Warburg Institute*, 4 [1940], pl. 5d and p. 44), (b^1) MS as for (a^3), (b^2) stone, as above: Lehmann-Hartleben, *Hesperia*, 12 (1943), 115–34 (with reconstruction of whole monument by S. M. Shaw, pl. Vc): cf. J. and L. Robert, *REG*, 57 (1944), 222, no. 151; K. Kerényi, *Symbolae Osloenses*, 31 (1955), 151, esp. n. 1.

The two fragments here republished form part of the monument seen by Cyriac of Ancona on his visit to Samothrace. (b²) was recognized by Fredrich (*IG*, XII [8,] ad loc.) to be part of (a), though (a) was at that time known only in manuscript tradition. The discovery of (a¹⁻²) shows that (b²) does in fact belong. (a¹) and (b¹), at that time also preserved only in manuscript, were conjectured by Ziebarth (*AM*, 31 [1906], 414, no. 10; cf. lemma to *IG*, XII [8], 191) to belong to the same monument. The discovery of (a¹⁻²) shows that this conjecture was also correct. The lower part of the inscription, (a³), and the right upper part, (b¹), as recorded by Cyriac, are still wholly missing. Lehmann-Hartleben has discussed the inscription, and its transmission in three copies, at length, loc. cit., and I confine myself here to printing a reliable text, underlining those letters known only from manuscript and commenting on epigraphical points.

<table>
<tr><td align="center">(a)</td><td align="center">(b)</td></tr>
<tr><td>(¹) (in left wreath)</td><td>(¹) (in right wreath)</td></tr>
<tr><td align="center">Ἀνδρό-</td><td align="center">Ἐφό[π]της</td></tr>
<tr><td align="center">μαχος</td><td align="center">Θεο⟨ζ⟩ᾶ⟨ς⟩</td></tr>
<tr><td align="center">Δημητρί-</td><td align="center">Μοιρα⟨γ⟩ό⟨ρ⟩ο⟨υ⟩</td></tr>
<tr><td align="center">ου vac.</td><td align="center">Ζή⟨λω ?⟩τος</td></tr>
<tr><td align="center">(below wreath)</td><td align="center">Ῥοδοκλήου,   5</td></tr>
<tr><td align="center">5   Q. Visellius L·f.</td><td align="center">Ῥόδω-</td></tr>
<tr><td></td><td align="center"><u>ν.</u></td></tr>
<tr><td></td><td align="center">(below wreath)</td></tr>
<tr><td></td><td align="center"><u>prece</u> (?)</td></tr>
<tr><td></td><td align="center"><u>pius</u></td></tr>
</table>

(²) [Κ] υ ζ ι κ η ν ῶ ν ἱ ε ρ ο π ο ι ο ὶ κ α ὶ μ ύ σ τ α ι (²)

    εὐσεβεῖς, ἐπ' Ἀντι|<u>γένου</u>

    τοῦ Ἑρμαγόρου ἱ|<u>ππάρχεω</u>

    [ὡς δὲ] Σαμοθρᾷκες ἐπὶ βασιλέω|ς Ἀριδήλου

10   (³) [τοῦ . . .]ίχου· Παρμενίσκος Ἀριστέω[ς]

      [Φιλό]ξενος Φιλοξένου· <i>vac.</i>

        ⟨μύσ⟩ται εὐσεβεῖς·Ἀσκληπιάδης Ἀ⟨ττ⟩άλου

        Θέρσων Ἡρογείτονος, κυβερνήτης Μηνόφιλο⟨ς⟩.

In the following notes I do not quote readings in the manuscript tradition where the stone survives. The line divisions of the Ambrosian and Ashmole copies of Cyriac's drawings at (a²), lines 7–8, are wrong (see the reproductions in Lehmann-Hartleben, op. cit., pl. IIIa, and pl. IV), and there can be no guarantee as to the true line divisions of lines 10–13: the

MSS all agree, while the reconstruction of Shaw is divergent. I give the line divisions of the MSS.

(a³) *Line 10.* ——ἴχου is given by Muratori as ιχος.

Line 11. ΣΕΝΟΣ Ashm.: the Ƨ of Ambr. is obviously right. Two Cyzicene theoroi Παρμενίσκος 'Αριστέως and Φιλόξενος Φιλοξένου occur side by side in *IG*, XII (8), 163.[1] They are probably the same persons.

Line 12, init. ΑΙΤΑΙ Murat.Ambr., Ashm. ΑΙΤΕΑΙ Hamb. ⟨μύσ⟩ται is naturally to be read.

Line 12, fin. ΑΓΑΛΟΥ Murat.Ambr., ΑΓΑΔΟΥ Ashm. These readings are hardly possible, and in any case the Cyzicene 'Ασκληπιάδης 'Αττάλου occurs, as Boeckh saw, in *IG*, XII (8), 188 (below, p. 112), line 9. Evidently there is nothing missing at the beginning of the line, as there is in lines 10–11.

Line 13. The MSS have ΗΡΟΓΕΙΤΗΣ; corrected by Boeckh to 'Ηρογείτ⟨ονο⟩ς.

Line 13, fin. The MSS have ΜΗΝΟΦΙΛΟΥ. Fredrich in his note wrote "Μηνόφιλο[ς]? cf. n. 206, 12," and I have no hesitation in writing Μηνόφιλο⟨ς⟩. Κυβερνήτης, as a proper name, is not likely, and the κυβερνήτης of the ship would naturally appear at the end of the list.[2]

(b¹) *Line 1.* The MSS have ἐφό[π]της on one line, and the division between two lines, ἐφ|όπτης, which appears on Shaw's reconstruction, seems to lack authority.

Line 2. The MSS have ΘΕΟΣΑΣ, which has been emended to Θεο[λ]ᾶ[ς] (Mommsen); Θεο[φ]ᾶ[ς] was suggested as a possibility by Fredrich, Θε⟨ωτ⟩ᾶ[ς] by Boeckh. The central letter, Σ, can hardly stand, and could be emended to, e.g., Θεο⟨λ⟩ᾶς, Θεο⟨φ⟩ᾶς, Θεο⟨δ⟩ᾶς, but the nearest would be Θεο⟨ζ⟩ᾶς, a hypocoristic form of Θεόζοτος. It is difficult to see how, if any of the original letter was visible at all, Λ could be read as Σ.[3]

Line 3. The MSS have ΜΟΙΡΑΠΟΙΟΣ. Μοιρ⟨ο⟩ποιός (i.e., Μυροποιός), Boeckh. Mommsen suggested ἱεραποιός — cf. (a²), line 6. Μοιρα⟨γ⟩ό⟨ρ⟩ου, Hiller, followed by Fredrich and Lehmann-Hartleben. A patronymic may be necessary, as in (a¹), but this leaves lines 4 ff. unexplained. Lehmann-Hartleben's suggestion (p. 123), that the inscription originally contained only the name of the ἐφόπτης and that the rest was added later, is attractive.

Line 4. The MSS have ΖΗΓΙΝΤΟΣ. Ζ⟨ακυ⟩ντος (i.e., Ζ⟨ακυ⟩νθος), Boeckh. Ζή⟨λω⟩τος, Fredrich (who also suggested Ζη⟨νόφα⟩ντος), followed by Lehmann-Hartleben. None of these corrections appears satisfactorily to explain the gamma.

Line 5. The MSS have ΡΟΔΟΚΛΗΟΥ which it is unnecessary to alter. This line is omitted from Shaw's restoration.

1. This was pointed out by F. Bechtel, *Die Inschriften des ionischen Dialekts* (Göttingen, 1887), ad 236.
2. Cf. *IG*, XII (8), 206, line 12.
3. The matter has been slightly complicated by the fact that Mommsen in *CIL* gave the last letter as a lunate sigma, though neither Ambr. nor Muratori's copy of it does so. I am inclined to regard this as an oversight on Mommsen's part.

Lines 8–9. The MSS have *Prege pius. pre⟨c⟩e,* Mommsen. Lehmann read the traces of the Latin on the stone as *pṛẹ,* and restored the line thus: *Pre(c)⟨e pius⟩.* If this were correct, Cyriac would have divided between two lines an inscription in fact inscribed on one line, which would not be beyond his powers. In fact, however, the surviving marks on the stone are clearly *pịụs,* the tail of the *S* being unmistakable. There is hardly any trace of the *U.* Cyriac is thus vindicated in this particular.

The monument as a whole is among the most complex pieces known from Samothrace. The connection between the main body of the inscription (a²), (b²), (a³), and the upper part is not clear. Lehmann-Hartleben's suggestion (pp. 122–23) that the names of the epoptae (presumably (a) is also an epoptes) in the wreaths, or, as he regards them, "the purple scarf which the initiated wore around the abdomen for protection from evil," are contemporary with the lower inscription, which contains the names of ἱεροποιοί and μύσται only, seems likely. It is evident that the whole monument coheres and that the first Greek names enclosed are organic parts of it. The μύσται εὐσεβεῖς of lines 12–13 were probably inscribed separately because they were not ἱεροποιοί — i.e., Cyzicene cult-officials — but simply citizens of Cyzicus who were also initiated; one of them, Ἀσκληπιάδης Ἀ⟨ττ⟩άλου, occurs as a Cyzicene envoy in another inscription (below, p. 112). The persons in (a¹) and (b¹) are presumably not Cyzicene.

The lettering of the surviving Greek text suggests a date in the late second century B.C.[4] Lehmann-Hartleben suggested (p. 120) that the Latin text is probably of a later date, like the lower part of the Greek inscription in the right circle, and suggested that Q. Visellius L. f. might be a son of the cos. of A.D. 24. An earlier date seems to me not impossible and indeed preferable. Visellii of Brundisium were, as Mr. L. Benaki points out to me, active as winegrowers and exporters in the first century B.C.,[5] and it may well be a member of this family who visited Samothrace in the late Republican period. In that case the Latin and Greek texts may be of about the same date. For the interpretation of the monument as transmitted in MSS, I refer to Lehmann-Hartleben's article.

4. The lettering of *IG,* XII (8), 163, in which the same Cyzicenes appear (see above), is dated by Fredrich, ad loc., to the first century B.C. That on our monument is similar but more careful. I should be inclined to date both slightly earlier than Fredrich does.

5. See *CIL,* X, 545: L · Visellius · **L·Ɔ·Ɔ·L** | felix | Mercator · vinar | vix · ann · LV.

30. 49.4. (Pl. XV.)

Fragment of blue-gray (Thasian?) marble, broken on all sides. Preserved height 0.16, preserved width 0.08, thickness 0.05; height of letters: line 1, 0.030; line 2, 0.015; lines 3–7, 0.005.

Found 17 June 1949, in the "Ruinenviereck," north of the Stoa.

Unpublished.

— — — — — — —

———.ṭius

[ep]optes piu[s]

vac.

—oṇiṇi C·Mari·

—çẹḷạçị *vac.*(?)

5   —(.?) aminantẹs

————ari————

— — — — — — —

This is a fragment of more than usual interest, owing to the presence of *C. Mari* — in line 3, a name which it is difficult, in a Republican inscription such as this clearly is (for the hand cf. **31**), not to connect with the great figure of C. Marius Cn. fil.[1] Its interpretation, however, is more than usually obscure, and it would be rash to do more than associate it with his eastern trip in 98 / 97 B.C.

Line 1. t seems certain. Therefore not [*C. Ma*]*rius.*

Line 3. It is possible that the space between lines 2 and 3 contained, to the left of the now preserved edge, some such word as [*servi*]. Alternatively, line 3, —*oṇiṇi C. Mari.*, may describe the names that follow. The reading is very uncertain. None of the normal words found in this context, *servi, pedesequi, ministri,* seems possible.

Line 4 init. çẹ, rather than *çị.* There is perhaps a stop after the *l,* but the stone is damaged at this point.

Line 5. Presumably this word is (wholly or almost) complete, though what it is, is not clear. It might be a cognomen or (more probably, from its form) an ethnic. [*D*]*aminantes* might derive from Δαμινὸν or Δαύνιον τεῖχος, a site on the Propontis which is mentioned under various slightly differing names from the fifth century B.C. onward.[2]

1. Cf. the bilingual dedication at Delos to Marius and the Italian merchants resident in Alexandria, *Inscr.* *Délos* 1699 (and to the bibliography there given add Passerini, *Athenaeum,* 27 [1939], 70 ff.).

2. See *ATL,* I, s.v. Δαυνιοτειχῖται.

31. 49.442. (Pl. XVI.)

Fragment of stele of Thasian marble, left edge preserved. Preserved height 0.38, preserved width 0.19, thickness 0.060; height of letters: Greek, illegible; Latin: line 1, 0.030; lines 2–3, 0.015–020; line 4, 0.020–025; lines 4–7, 0.010–015.

From Chora, 5 July 1949.

F. Chapouthier, *BCH,* 49 (1925), 256 ff. (with photo) = *AEp* (1926), 34 = *CIL* I², 2505 = Degrassi, *Inscr. Lat. Lib. Rei Publ.,* I, 209.

9 or 10 lines of Greek illegible.

M.Anton[io] [A.Postumio *or* P. Dolabella]
                                                    cos.A.D.iv———   [*99 or 44 B.C.?*]
                                                    epoptes p[ius]
                                                    Q·Luccius·Q[·f·]
5   mystae·piei
                                                    P.Antonius·Cn·f·V———
                                                    M.Antonius·Cn·f·———
                                                    Antonia·M·l·————
                                                    ——ised————

— — — — — — — — — —

Line 1. Anton (*io*), Chapouthier, but I could not identify satisfactorily the central point after the *n; Ant* (*onio*), wrongly, Degrassi. Chapouthier correctly pointed out that the possible consuls named M. Antonius are M. Antonius, cos. 99, with A. Postumius and his grandson, the triumvir, whose only lasting consulship fell in 44 B.C., when he had as colleagues first Julius Caesar and then P. Dolabella. Paleographically it does not seem possible to decide between the two dates, and the question must be left open. As Degrassi (loc. cit.) indicated, in the year 44 the name of Caesar always precedes that of Antony, so if the later date be correct the second consul will be Dolabella.

Line 4. Lucius, Chapouthier: corrected in *AEp*. Degrassi supplies "[*f*. vel *l*]," but since the mystae are Roman citizens by birth the epoptes probably was one also.

Lines 5 ff. The initiates are evidently of one household, those in lines 6–7 probably being brothers, but the identity of family names with that of the consul is presumably fortuitous. The same feature occurs in **40**. In line 6 Chapouthier, followed by other editors, read nothing after *Antonius*. In line 7 Chapouthier read *Q.* [*f.*] and Degrassi *C. f. Cn. f.* is clear.

Chapouthier[1] connected the tree in the surviving portion of the stone with the vegetable nature of the Cabiri attested at Lemnos and Samothrace,[2] and suggested that it might be due to the connection of the Cabiri with Dionysos, who had the cult epithet ἔνδενδρος.[3] Lehmann suggests (*per ep.*) that "it may be just a setting, not uncommon in votive and grave reliefs."

1. Op. cit., pp. 261–62.
2. Fredrich, *AM*, 31 (1906), 80–81.
3. For the cult of Dionysos ἔνδενδρος see Hesychius, s.v. ἔνδενδρος· παρὰ ʿΡοδίοις Ζεὺς καὶ Διόνυσος ἐν Βοι-

ωτίᾳ. Perhaps also at Paros: *IG*, XII (5), 1027 (but cf. *SEG*, XIII, 449a). For the connection between Dionysos and the Cabiri see Hemberg, pp. 41 ff. (Imbros).

32. 57.856. (Pl. XV.)

Top left fragment of Thasian marble, with molding along top. Preserved height 0.27, preserved width 0.22, thickness 0.75; height of letters: line 1, 0.010; lines 2–6, 0.020–025; lines 7–9, 0.020. Traces (original?) of red in lettering and on face.

Found near the Genoese Towers.

Unpublished.

(a) *on molding:* [ἐ]πὶ βασιλ[έως τοῦ δεῖνος (τοῦ δεῖνος)]

(b) *in field:*   Cn.Oc[tavio M·f·]

                 C.Scrib[onio C·f· cos]   [*76 B.C.*]

                 A.D.x———

5   mustae [piei]

                 Q.Minuc[ius —?]

                 The[rmus]

                 P.Magul[nius]

                 [..]aberi[us———]

                 – – – – – – – – –

The lettering of line 1 is much smaller than that of the rest, so there was probably room for the patronymic. The following lines indicate that the original right edge of the stone was little, if at all, beyond the existing right edge at the rear. Which of the Minucii Thermi active at this time is here referred to is uncertain.[1] If he be the later governor of Asia, in 51 / 50, and correspondent of Cicero,[2] this will be his earliest appearance, although he was already in 73 B.C. a member of the *consilium* which decided the dispute between Oropus and the Roman tax-gatherers.[3]

Line 8. A certain M. Magulnius M. f. occurs at about the same time at Delos among the dedicants of the Agora of the Italians.[4]

Line 9. [.L]*aberius* and [.F]*aberius* are both possible. It seems possible that the persons whose names are here preserved held government posts in Macedonia.

1. See Münzer, *RE*, s.v. *Minucius* (60), (66), (67).   4. *Inscr. Délos* 1687 (cf. J. Hatzfeld, *BCH*, 45 [1921],
2. Ibid. (67).   3. *Syll*³ 747.   483 ff.).

33. 39.548. (Pl. XVI.)

Two joining fragments of stele of Thasian marble, broken at top only. At bottom rough projection for insertion into base. Back smooth. Preserved height 0.62, width 0.38–39, thickness 0.070; height of letters: Greek 0.010, Latin 0.010–015. Inscribed on both faces ((b), back, very slightly).

From Chora, 20 June 1939.

Mentioned, and lines 13–15 quoted, *AJA*, 44 (1940), 358 (misread).

(a)

I	II	
– – – – – –	– – – – – – – –	
. . . ωνεως	– – – – – – – –	
Ὠπηνεὺ[ς]	– – – – – – – –	
Ἀριστοκλείους	Φιλ―――――	
Πυθίων	Δημ―――――	
5 Ἀριστοκλείους	Ε[ὐ]μέν[ης](?)	
Θεόξενος	Σι̣ . . τας	
Μητροδώρου	Πρόκλος	5
Μηνόφιλος	――――Λι――――	
Φιλίππου	Ἕλενος	
10 Διονυσοκλῆς	―――――κου	
Μητροδώρου	―――――λε――	
Διζάσσκος	―――――one	10
Ἀρίστων	[C.] I[ul]io Caesare	
Ἀριστοθε̣[ί]ου	M.Lepido·cos·A.D.	[18 Oct.
15 Λεύκιος Ἀ̣κ̣αι[ο]ς	XV·K·Nov. musta	a.u.c. 708 =
Διοφάνου̣ς̣	pius M.Paccius P·f·	46 B.C.]
Περιγένης	Fal·Rufus·C·Pacciu[s]	15
Φιλοχάρους	C·l·Apollonides	
Διονύσιος	Philodamus Pac[ci]	
20 Διοδότου	Antiochus Pac[ci]	
Δίναρχος	―――――my―――――	
Ἀγαθ̣――	– – – – – – – – –	
Ἐπιγένη̣ς̣		
– – – – – – –		

(b)

– – – – – – –

―――――――iiv

―――――――onia――

– – – – – –

vac.?

(a) *Line 1, col. 1.* The termination of this name is uncertain, perhaps -εως. ωνε seems certain.

Line 2. This name eludes me. Names in -εύς, other than heroic names, are usually of ethnics standing as proper names,[1] but I cannot find one to fit here.

1. For the termination in -εύς common in the Homeric poems (Ἀχιλλεύς, Ἰδομενεύς, etc.) see Pape-Benseler, p. xviii (2), (a)–(b); E. Schwyzer, *Griechische Grammatik* (Munich, 1939), I, 477. For ethnics in -εύς serving as proper names see Bechtel, *Die historischen* *Personennamen des Griechischen bis zur Kaiserzeit* (Halle, 1917), pp. 53 ff.; cf. E. Bosshardt, *Die Nomina auf* -εύς (Zurich, 1942), pp. 87–143, with ibid., pp. 166–75, a useful list of words.

Line 12. A Thracian,[2] he is the only person whose father's name is not recorded.

Line 15. The name after Λεύκιος is not clear. Ἄπαιος and Ἄκαιος are both possible, but neither very attractive. The second letter involves a vertical stroke. For the kappa for chi in Ἄκαιος, if correctly read, there are numerous parallels (see above, p. 23, n. 2).

(a) *col. 2.* Whether these names were alternately inset is not clear, and, in addition, the patronymic does not seem to have been regularly recorded. There is an evident patronymic in line 8 but not in line 5, where it might be expected.

(b) probably the end of the Latin inscription of (a) col. 2.

This inscription consists of two separate lists of mystae. The first inscribed was a list in one and a half columns of Greek initiates, all except one — (a) line 12, in col. 1 — with patronymics; in col. 2 the disposition of the names is uncertain. The Latin inscription, dated by the consulate of C. Julius Caesar and M. Lepidus to 46 B.C., was evidently inscribed in the blank space left at the end of the Greek list. The traces of later letters on the reverse, (b), probably represent the end of the list. The Greek inscription is not, to judge from the lettering, much earlier than the Latin: note also, in line 15, the name Λεύκιος. The stele was apparently free-standing, in a base of some sort, unlike most of the lists of mystae.

The Greeks may all have been from one city, the name of which was inscribed at the top, though their names give no clue to their origin. The authorities of the Sanctuary, and the pilgrims themselves, seem to have attached considerable importance to the place of origin, at least for persons of Greek origin, and it is not likely that no indication of origin was given.[3]

The Latin inscription of 18 October 46 B.C.[4] evidently contains a list of initiates all belonging to one household, that of M. Paccius P. f., Fal. Rufus. The *gens* Paccia (a member of which may appear at Samos a generation later[5]) is frequent in Campania and particularly at Formiae and Minturnae, and it seems likely that it is in fact the household of the present inscription which we encounter at Formiae where Q. Paccius M. f. occurs as an aedile[6] and where we meet the *libertus* Philodamus.[7] The same family occurs at the neighboring Minturnae, where six slaves of a M. Paccius are recorded.[8] In lines 19–20 Philodamus Pacci and Antiochus Pacci are slaves.[9] Philodamus, then, was liberated before death. The heading *musta pius* refers only to the first-named person, and consequently the status of the remainder is uncertain.

2. Διζάσσκος: for Thracian names in Διζ- see Tomaschek, *SBWien*, 131 (1), pp. 32–33.

3. The city of origin of the persons in *IG*, XII (8), 180–82, is similarly uncertain. In 181 Metronax and Sokles are both common Samothracian names, and the recorded persons may be Samothracians.

4. Lehmann read the date as *a.d.v.k. Nov.:* i.e., Oct. 28.

5. In *IGRR*, IV, 991, 46 ff. Ross read νεωποίης εὐσεβὴς Λεύκιος Πάκιος Δέκμου υἱός (and so also J. Hatzfeld, *Les Trafiquants* [Paris, 1919], p. 98), but Stamatakis, Σαμιακά (Hermopolis, 1862), Συλλογή no. 45 (*non vidi;* followed by *IGRR*) read Λεύκιος Πάπιος Δέκμου

υἱός.

6. *CIL*, X, 6105, "litteris vetustis."

7. Ibid., 6148: M. Paccius M. l. Philodamus.

8. See *Excavations at Minturnae*, ed. J. Johnson (2 vols., Rome, 1933–35), II, pt. I, p. 66: *RM*, 50 (1935), 328; Münzer, *RE*, s.v. *Paccius* (10). Note also Cicero's acquaintance M. Paccius (*Ad Atticum* 4.16.1, Münzer, op. cit. (8)). On the name in general see now R. Syme, *Historia*, 4 (1955), 65; for Paccii in Pisidian Antioch see also B. Levick, *JRS*, 48 (1958), 77–78.

9. On the form of the simple genitive of the *dominus* to express the slave's name see A. Oxé, *RhM*, 59 (1904), 120 f.

34. 51.98. (Pl. XVI.)

Top part of left edge of pedimental stele of Thasian marble. Preserved height 0.226, preserved width 0.225, thickness 0.074; height of letters: line 1, 0.010–012; line 2, 0.008; lines 3–4, 0.015; lines 5 ff., 0.008–010.

From the neighborhood of the Genoese Towers, 17 June 1951.

Lehmann, *Hesperia*, 22 (1953), 12–13, and pl. 6*d*.

    (a) *in pediment:* Hilarus Prim[us]

    (b) *on horizontal cornice:* [ἀγ]ορανομοῦντος Χ——

    (c) *in field:* L.Cornuficio[1]·Sex·Po[mpeio]   *[20 June*

                cos·A·D·XII·K·Iul(ias)   *35 B.C.]*

   5   mustae p[i]ei

        [M.S]ervilius M.l.Philo

        [M.S]e[rvilius?] M.l.Pamp[hilus]

        ————————————l————

      – – – – – – – – – – – – –

(a) *Hilar(i)o*, Lehmann. The reading of (b) seems quite certain; (a) should therefore contain the name and title of the βασιλεύς. But one would expect it in Greek, and in the genitive with ἐπί.

    (c) *Line 3. Sext[o]*, Lehmann.

Line 5. Mystae, Lehmann.

Line 6. Ru(tili)us, Lehmann. *M. Servilius* is clear.

1. For L. Cornificius see Münzer, *RE,* s.v. *Cornificius* (5); Broughton, *Magistrates,* II, under 35 B.C. The name of the consul is spelled Cornuficius in *CIL,* VI, 4305; see *PIR,* II[2], 373, no. 1503.

35. 39.12. (Pl. XII.)

Fragment of Thasian marble, broken on all sides. Preserved height 0.23, preserved width 0.14, thickness 0.07; height of letters 0.006–018; line 8, 0.013.

Found 21 June 1939, near the Genoese Towers.

        – – – – – – –

        ————————ου

        [*e.g.,* Διόδ]οτος

        [*e.g.,* Ἀριστοδ]άμου

        ————————ω[?]

   5   [μύσται εὐσε]βεῖς

        ———— ————ου

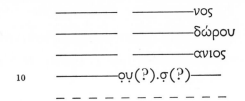

———— ————νος
———— ————δώρου
———— ————ανιος
10 ————ου(?).σ(?)————
- - - - - - - - - -

This very illegible fragment appears to be of the late Hellenistic age. The reading ——βεῖς in line 5 is quite certain and determines the nature of the list.

Lines 1–4. Possibly contained the dating formula, but the obvious nominative -οτος is hard to reconcile with this. Probably, as in *IG*, XII (8), 205, an ἐφόπτης was included, here [e.g., Διόδ]οτος [e.g., Ἀριστοδ]άμου, and the dating formula is completely lost. In line 1, ΟΥ is too uncertain to be used as evidence.

Line 8. Inscribed in larger letters than the rest (with the possible exception of line 9), and may have contained the title and name of the ἀγορανόμος. If so, then line 10 was probably the last of the inscription.[1]

1. Cf., e.g., *IG*, XII (8), 184–87.

36. 39.1072. (Pl. XVI.)

Plaque of limestone, broken at right and to bottom. Preserved height 0.32, preserved width 0.32, thickness 0.08; height of letters: lines 2–4, 0.014; line 4, 0.012; lines 5–16, 0.008; line 17, 0.014; lines 18–19, 0.008.

Purchased from Kamariotissa, where it was used as a step, 30 July 1939.

Lehmann-Hartleben, *AJA*, 44 (1940), 356 ff., no. 2; *AÉp* (1947), 3.

[ἐ]π[ὶ βασιλέως ^{ca. 4}.]ου τοῦ			
Μητρώνακτος·			
M·Iunio Silano·L·Norbano Bal[bo cos.]		[*6 June*	
viii.Idus Iunias, mystae pii		*A.D. 19*]	
5	C·Marius L·f·Ste·Schinas	servi Schinae	
	[R]upilia Q·f·Quinta	Cedrus	An——
	Symmust[ae]·pii	Laetus	*vac.* 20
	L·Iulius·Sp·f·Pap·Niger	[Her]mas	Opt[atus]
	————aisidius Stephaniu[s]	Clenas	Sc——
10	————Marius Fructus	Eoc——	To——
	————y.rus Pergamenus	Pho[e]bus	————
	[Me]nander Chius	Paneros	———— 25
	[——?] l.usius	Epaphus	————

		Paideros	Sp——
vac.		Tarula	Pa——
	Epoptae	Felix	Xy[stus]
15	[C·] Marius L·f·Ste·Schinas		
	[Rupili]a·Q·f·Quinta		
	——Marius Fructus		

30   [ἀγοραν]ομοῦντος Ἀπολλ[οδώρου (*e.g.,*) τοῦ]
          Διοδότου.

Line 6. Iulia, L-H (above); line 9, *Clodius,* L-H; line 11, ——*lus,* L-H; line 20, *Lectus,* L-H; line 22, *Cap....* , L-H; line 23, *Loc[rius],* L-H; line 28, *Sarula,* L-H; line 29, *Xo[uthos],* L-H.

Line 2. Μητρώνακτος is evidently the patronymic, since the agoranomos occurs in lines 30–31.

Line 3. For the coss. see Degrassi, *Fasti Consolari, sub ann.*

Line 6. [*R*]*upilia* seems quite clear.

Line 9. aisidius suggests either [*C*]*aisidius* or [*P*]*aisidius.* But *Misidius* is also possible. *Lisidius* and *Disidius* are not possible.

Line 10. Marius Fructus is taken by L-H to be a Roman citizen on account of his name, and because he, like Schinas and his wife, received ἐποπτεία. But he lacks tribal denomination (unlike Schinas and, line 8, Niger) and Fructus may be a translation of the common Greek name Κάρπος.

Line 13. l.usius. There is space for a letter between the *l* and the *u,* but no clear sign of one. There may have been a punctuation mark or stop. On the whole *L. Usius* seems to me the most likely reading. *Vo*]*lusius* would be possible only if the space between the *l* and the *u* was uninscribed, which I doubt. The position of the name here, after the Pergamene and the Chian, raises the possibility that the individual may be a Greek, and L-H suggested that it was possibly an ethnic termination, *lusius* = —λούσιος. But it does not seem likely that there was both a personal name and an ethnic on this line; there is room for two or three letters to the left of *l,* but there can hardly have been another name farther to the left, though unfortunately nothing can be made out on the stone.

Lines 18–29. The names of the slaves are all common. Tarula (line 28) is a familiar Illyrian name.[1]

The list, in its general lines—eponym and agoranomos in Greek, the rest in Latin—is analogous to *IG,* XII (8), 207, but it is more developed.

---

1. For Tar- names see Krahe, *Lexicon Altillyrischer Personnennamen* (Heidelberg, 1929), pp. 110–11; Perdrizet and Lefebvre, *Les Graffites grecs du Memnonion d'Abydos* (Nancy, 1919), nos. 81 (Ταρόλλας) and 93 (Ταρούλας) and Index (p. 121) where the name is listed under "Noms Thraces"; *IG,* IX (2), 1228, line 64 (Τάρουλα); and other instances given by L. Robert, *Hellenica,* 9 (1950), 72, n. 4.

The inscription presents a fairly complete picture of how a (presumably) wealthy Roman of the early Imperial age would visit Samothrace. He arrived with his entire household: his wife, about twenty-one slaves, and half a dozen people whose names are given but whose status can only be guessed (lines 8–13). The *paterfamilias* C. Marius Schinas and his wife are described first as *mystae pii,* and then, farther down, as *epoptae.* Together with them (*symmustae*) were initiated half a dozen others: L. Iulius Niger, – Marius Fructus, ——ạisidius Stephanius, a Roman citizen or a freedman (?), and two Greeks – one a Pergamene, the other a Chiot. One may wonder whether these symmustae were directly connected with Schinas. The inscription is presumably a record of all who were initiated on one day, but it does not necessarily follow that the names inscribed represent one party. The second stage, the epopteia, was attained only by Schinas and his wife, and by one other of the symmustae, and it could be argued that if the persons named were all of one party, all of them would have proceeded together. It might, however, be maintained with equal probability that all were of one party, but that for some reason only the *paterfamilias,* his wife, and one other proceeded to the stage of ἐποπτεία.

The status of the two (or three) Greeks is obscure. They preserve their Greek ethnics and were therefore free persons. There is no explicit indication of any connection with Schinas, though Lehmann's suggestion that they were the officers of the crew of the ship carrying Schinas, while the slaves were the crew, is attractive. Why their names were inscribed in Latin rather than Greek is, on any explanation of their status, a problem, since the Samothracian lapicides were familiar with inscribing in both languages. Lehmann (*per ep.*) sees in the use of Latin throughout a further indication that the persons recorded were all of one party. As he puts it, "Schinas paid the bill for all his party." This is certainly another point to be borne in mind, but in any case the whole question must be left open.

Schinas, his wife, and M. Fructus seem to have been received into μύησις and ἐποπτεία on one and the same day.[2] That such a rapid performance of the rites was usual seems unlikely in itself,[3] and particularly so since nearly all the other lists contain references to μύσται only, suggesting that the epopteia occurred later. The comparative rarity of references to ἐπόπται in the inscriptions, as contrasted with the frequency of the primary initiates, suggests that in any case by no means all advanced to the second stage.[4]

---

2. That the epoptae were added to the stone on a later occasion seems unlikely in view of the uniformity of writing and the absence of a second date.

3. Thus Lehmann, loc. cit., says only that it was "possible"; cf. A. D. Nock, *AJA,* 45 (1941), 577, n. 4.
4. Cf. Lehmann, *AJA,* loc. cit.; *Guide,* p. 29; Hemberg, p. 116, n. 2.

37. 53.7. (Pl. XII.)

Fragment of Thasian marble, broken on all sides. Preserved height 0.185, preserved width 0.15, preserved thickness 0.25; height of letters 0.010–015.

Found 27 June 1953, west of the "Arsinoeion."

Unpublished.

$$
\begin{array}{l}
\text{------} \text{I . } \Lambda \text{L} \text{------}\\
\text{------} \upsilon\pi o\gamma\iota\sigma \ldots \\
 \text{’} A\nu\tau\iota\pi\alpha\tau\langle\rho\rangle o\varsigma \\
 [\text{’}A\lambda\epsilon]\xi\alpha\nu\delta\rho o\upsilon \\
\text{5} \sigma\iota\alpha\nu\acute{o}\varsigma \\
\nu o\rho\acute{\epsilon}\omega\varsigma
\end{array}
$$

The hand is crude and unformed, and evidently of Imperial date.

Line 2. Between the omicron and the sigma the most likely letters are gamma and iota, but they make a difficult group. The final sigma seems clear. [ἐ]πόπτης is not possible.

Line 6. Evidently a patronymic. At the beginning, iota, mu, nu, and pi are all possible but nu seems most likely. The genitive in -έως implies a nominative in -εύς, for which see above, note on **33**, (a), line 2.

38. 53.148. (Pl. XVII.)

Bottom(?) right fragment of Thasian(?) marble, tang at bottom(?). Preserved height 0.20, preserved width 0.16, preserved thickness 0.008; height of letters: lines 1–4, 0.010; lines 5 ff., 0.015.

From Chora, 1 July 1953.

Unpublished.

$$
\begin{array}{l}
\text{------} \text{us} \ldots \ldots \text{i}\underset{.}{\text{s}} \text{------} \\
\text{------} \text{vs Vincun} \text{/} \mathcal{T} \ vac. \\
\text{------} \text{s}\underset{.}{\text{o}} \text{(?)---Ovinio} \ vac. \text{(?)} \\
\text{------} \text{All[i]a Paro.nilici} \\
 (spat.?) \\
\text{5} \text{------Varro II} \ldots \ldots \\
 (spat.) \\
 \text{vi I .. us------}
\end{array}
$$

[—]rsus———— ———

———urus————————

– – – – – – – – – – –

I have been unable to reach any positive conclusions about this text. At the bottom of the
stone there is a tang-shaped projection which may be original — but is not necessarily so [1] —
while the top is rough. Thus the original dimensions are uncertain. The inscription is probably lacking only a letter to the left, since lines 4 and 6 at least suggest that only the praenomi-
nal initials are here missing.

A much more serious difficulty lies in the fact that while lines 5 ff. are inscribed in a
normal late Republican hand, the cursive of lines 1–4 appears to be considerably later: note
particularly *n* (if such it be), and the final ligature of line 2 and the ligature of line 3. Possibly we have here two lists of mystae of which the second (later) one was inscribed in the
blank space originally left above the first inscription: there are parallels in some lists for this
rather illogical procedure.[2]

1. If it is original, the stone is probably one of the few 2. E.g., *IG*, XII (8), 190, 209(?), 215 (lines 12–17
free-standing catalogues of mystae (cf. above, p. 74).   added later).

39. 49.437. (Pl. XVII.)

Upper left corner of pedimental stele of gray marble. Preserved height 0.21, preserved width
0.155, thickness 0.070–085; height of letters: lines 1–2, 0.015; lines 3–4, 0.015–020.

From Chora, 5 July 1949.

Unpublished.

> (a) *on horizontal cornice:* ἀγαθ[ῆ τύχη]
> (b) *on molding:* mist[es pius *or* -ae pii]
> (c) *in field:*
>> . Afini[us (?) — (?)]
>> Maur[us (?)]
>> Ṭ.ụ————
>
>> – – – – – –

The Latin lettering suggests an early Imperial date.

Line 2. The etacism in *mistes* occurs also in *IG*, XII (8), 173, line 2 (cf. above, p. 73).

Lines 3–4. There are very faint traces of the initial of a praenomen before *Afinius*, perhaps
P. The restoration of the lines is quite uncertain. The fact that half, or a little more, of the
line is missing suggests that we should regard the names in these two lines as belonging to two
separate persons. Line 4 may read *M. Aur[el —]*.

40. 39.1071. (Pl. XVII.)

Fragment of stele of Thasian marble, left edge and left acroterion preserved. Preserved height 0.33, preserved width 0.145, thickness 0.080; height of letters: line 1, 0.020; line 2, 0.027; line 3, 0.025; line 4, 0.030; line 5, 0.020; lines 6–7, 0.017–018.

From Chora, 13 August 1939.

Lehmann-Hartleben, *AJA,* 44 (1940), 356, no. 1. *AEp* (1947), 2.

[ἐπὶ]
βασι[λέως τοῦ δεῖνος (τοῦ δεῖνος?)]
L·Non[io————————]
M·Arru[ntio——cos. (?)]
K.Sept·M[ystae pii]
5   L·Arrunti[us————magister,]
pro mag[istris]
Ti·Claudius D————
Ti.Cl[audius————]

– – – – – – – – – – – – –

The hand closely resembles that of **39** and is probably of the first century A.D. M. Arruntii occur as consuls in A.D. 66 and 77 (?),[1] and the inscription should probably be assigned to one of these two years.

Line 1. [ἐπί]; correctly, L-H, ἐπί, *AEp.*

Lines 3–4. L-H assumed the existence of a line between 3 and 4 containing the word *cos.* But there is no room, and analogy does not require it (see **32, 33** where *cos.* is on the same line as the name of the second consul). This supplement of L-H occurs in *AEp* as a reading: *cos.*

L-H assumed that the list is dated to the kalends of September, but A.D. followed by a numeral may possibly have been inscribed on the preceding line. The date "1 sett." in Degrassi, *Fasti Consolari,* p. 130, is thus a *terminus ante quem.*

Line 4. M[*ystae pii*]. This is a natural supplement. All lists of initiates have (so far as we can tell) the title.

Lines 5–6. L-H, followed by *AEp,* reads *L. Arrunti*[*us——*] *promag*[*ister*] (rather, *pro mag*[*istro*]). However, the normal custom in these lists is for such a series of names to be preceded by a descriptive title (see the present work and *IG,* XII [8], passim); consequently *pro mag*[*istris*] seems preferable. Correspondingly L. Arruntius becomes *magister.* As in **31**, the chief initiate by chance belongs to the same *gens* as the consul.

1. See PIR², A, nos. 1134, 1139.

Line 8. L-H, followed by *AEp,* reads *le*[*gatus*], referring presumably to Ti. Claudius of line 7. The reading appears to be *Ṭị Çḷ*[*audius*].

The *magister* and *pro mag*[*istris*] of this inscription, if the words are correctly restored, may be of the type found at the head of Roman and Italian communities in the East, whose functions have been much discussed.[2] Apart from the abundant Delian evidence[3] we know them also from Salona, Narona, Samos, Ephesos, Alexandria, and perhaps Thespiae.[4] It is not likely that there was an Italian community at Samothrace, and, if the officials are of this type, they doubtless came from elsewhere.

2. See Hatzfeld, *Les Trafiquants,* pp. 257 ff.
3. See ibid., pp. 263 ff.
4. I take these instances from Hatzfeld. Salona: *CIL,* III, 8795; Narona, ibid., 1820; Samos, ibid., 458; Ephesos, *Forschungen in Ephesos* (Vienna and Baden, 1906—), II, 182, no. 74; Alexandria, *CIL,* III, 12047; and perhaps Thespiae, ibid., 7301.

41. 56.2. (Pl. XVII.)

Fragment of stele of Thasian marble, broken on left and at bottom, and perhaps above. Preserved height 0.040, preserved width 0.24, thickness 0.09; height of letters 0.015–020.

Provenance unknown.

Unpublished.

```
         — — — — — — — —
         [ἐπ]όπ[——— εὐσεβ———]
         ———ΛΗ . . . . ΗΣΥ
         ———Σόσσιος———
         Μύσται εὐσεβ[ε]ῖ[ς]·
     5   [Λ]ούκιος .θ(?)———
            'Αθηνίων,
         [Κόϊν]τος Φλάουιος
         ['Ρ]οῦφος Έρμ . . . ιας·
            δοῦλοι 'Αθηνίων[ος]·
    10   [Χ]ρήσιμος, ———.ληϙϙ———·
         [ἐπὶ β]αϙιλέως 'Απολλο-
         [δώρ(e.g.)]ου τοῦ Εὐ———
         [ἀγοραν]ομοῦντος
         [τοῦ δεῖνος] τοῦ———.
```

The names and the lettering suggest a date in the first century A.D. The eponym does not appear elsewhere. The right-hand part of the stone is very difficult to read.

Line 1. [ἐπ]όπ[τ —] is uncertain, though it comes where the word might be expected.

The apparent circle round the left-hand stroke of the second letter, which makes one take it as a phi at first, is, I think, accidental. To the left, part of a circular letter is visible, but it is a long way from the pi. However, the latter is large, and the word may have been spaced. If [ἐπ]όπ[τ –] is correct, there were evidently two epoptae above the mystae.[1]

Lines 7–8. Ἑρμ[αγό]ρας is possible, but uncertain.

Line 9. For other δοῦλοι see **47, 58, 59**; ᾿Αθηνίω[νος] seems certain; the first two letters in particular are clear.

1. Cf. *IG*, XII (8), 205 (*Syll*[3] 1053), which closely resembles this inscription in style (though it is of an earlier date), and where there are two epoptae above the mystae.

42. 53.84. (Pl. XVIII.)

Fragment of stele of Thasian marble, broken to right. At top, double molding. Dowel hole 0.065 from right end of upper surface. Height 0.475, preserved width 0.17, thickness 0.10; height of letters: lines 1–5, 0.015–018; line 6, 0.025; line 7, 0.020; line 9, 0.015.

Found 30 June 1953, in the neighborhood of the "Anaktoron."

Unpublished.

> [ἐπὶ βασιλέω]ς Φρυνίχου
> [τοῦ Δι]οδώρου·
> [μύσται εὐσ]εβεῖς Αἴνιοι,
> [ὁ δεῖνα Φ]ιλώτου
> 5 [ὁ δεῖνα Δ]ημητρίο[υ]
> [ὁ δεῖνα——]ηνος
> ————ΙΟΣ *vac.*
> (*spat.0.050*)
> ————υλος—
> – – – – – – – – – – (?)

The lettering suggests an early Imperial date. The inscription adds to the number of the lists of Ainian mystae.[1]

Line 1. The eponym Phrynichus is not recorded elsewhere.

Line 5. —ηνος probably represents the genitive of the father's name in -ήν,[2] since there is no reason to suppose that the person is not an Αἴνιος (i.e., to regard —ηνος as an ethnic termination such as ᾿Αβυδηνός).

Below the uninscribed space of 0.050 the end of a further line is visible. In this position one might expect the name of the agoranomos, but this is otherwise always in the genitive.

1. *IG*, XII (8), 217, 218, 221 (218, μυστίδες Αἴνιαι).
2. For such names see Fraser and Rönne, *Boeotian and West Greek Tombstones* (Lund [*Acta Inst. Athen. regn. Suec.*, 4°, VI], 1957), pp. 167 ff.

In the lower right-hand part of the stone is a design which may be contemporary with the inscription, and is possibly a symbol. It is of the following shape: ⬤.

43. 39.545.
Stele of Thasian marble, broken below. Preserved height 0.70, width 0.49, thickness 0.08; height of letters 0.025.

From Chora, 20 June 1939.

Unpublished.

ἐπὶ [βα]σιλέως 'Αντι[γ]-
όνο[υ τοῦ Μν]ησικλέου[ς]
[μύσται] εὐσεβεῖ[ς]
Ἐπτ(?) . . . . . [Κρί]σπος
5 —————————M(N?)—
vac.?

The lettering, which is very full and round (though now very faint) suggests an early Imperial date.

Lines 1–2. The βασιλεύς is otherwise unknown.

If the stone was inscribed beyond line 5, no trace now remains.

44. 56.4. (Pl. XVIII.)
Fragment of Thasian marble broken on all sides. Preserved height 0.13, preserved width 0.13, thickness 0.040; height of letters: left column 0.012, right column 0.015, between pairs of ruled lines 0.027–030 apart.[1]

Provenance unknown.

Unpublished.

```
  — — — — — — — — — — — — — —
  — — — — — — —    I——————
  —————ienus       Ia—————————
  —————der         Pha——————
  —————imus        Arch—————
5 ——————————————ius Chre (stus or -simus)
  — — — — — — — — — — — — — —
```

1. The letters do not fill the vertical space between the lines, and it is not certain what relation if any the lines bear to the inscription. Lehmann suggests that they may have been drawn for an inscription in much larger letters which was never inscribed. Lines 2–4 are carefully inscribed between two such pairs of lines.

The hand suggests a date in the first century A.D. The names in both columns seem to be those of slaves. The name in the left column, line 4, was evidently long. It projects across the gap between the two columns.

45. No number. (Pl. XIX.)

Fragment of building block, left edge with molding preserved. Preserved height 0.71, preserved width 0.33, preserved thickness 0.50; inscribed 0.59 from bottom; height of letters 0.030–033.

Found in excavations, southwest of the "Arsinoeion." Now ibid.
Unpublished.

> Ἀγαθῇ τύ[χη]·
> (*spat.0.060*)
> [μύστ]α[ι εὐσεβεῖς]
> – – – – – – – –

Imperial.

This I include among the lists of initiates, since ἀγαθῇ τύχη followed by μύσται εὐσεβεῖς is found on **46, 49, 54, 59**, and does not appear to be found in other contexts in Samothrace.

The stone (but not the inscription) may cohere with **57**, q.v.

46. 39.83. (Pl. XVIII.)

Re-used building block of Thasian marble, with raised edge at right side, broken below. Originally the stone had been in a horizontal position, as anathyrosis on its back shows. In second use it was put upright, and again included in a structure (clamp hole on upper surface) before the inscription was carved. Preserved height 0.060, preserved width 0.19, thickness 0.25; height of letters: lines 1–6, 0.020; line 7, 0.030; lines 8–10, 0.025–030.

From Chora, 25 June 1939.
AJA, 44 (1940), 358, no. 4.

> [ἀγ]αθῆ[ι]
> τύχηι·
> ἐπὶ βασι-
> λέως Κλ.
> 5   Διονυσίου·
> μύστης
> εὐσεβὴς
> Παράμονος

Ζωίλου

10   Cιρραῖος.

vac.

The lettering is probably of the second century A.D.

Lines 3 ff. The βασιλεύς does not occur elsewhere.

Lines 5, 9. ου is in ligature.

The initiate is presumably from Sirra, or Seres, the city in the plain of the Strymon, between forty and fifty kilometers north of Amphipolis, in Odomantike. There is considerable confusion about the form of the name of this city and its ethnic, and ancient authorities give various places of the same name, some of which probably result from variations in spelling.[1] Σέρρειον, described by Stephanus as πόλις Σαμοθρᾴκης, may be an error; in any case Σαμοθρᾴκης should be taken as referring to the Samothracian Peraea.[2] That Σιρραῖος is, however, the ethnic of the city which stood on the site of the modern Seres, and was called, apparently indiscriminately, Σίραι, Σέρραι, Σέρρα, and Σίρρα, is clear from inscriptions found on the spot.[3]

The form Σειραῖος occurs in *IG*, XII (8), 206, also of Imperial date. Whether this belongs to the same city of Macedonia or to one of its quasi-homonyms must be left open.

1. For a list of these places see Pape-Benseler, s.v. Σέρραι, Σέρρειον, Σίρρα.
2. S.v. Σέρραιον: ἀκρωτήριον τῆς Θρᾴκης. ἔστι καὶ πόλις Σαμοθρᾴκης. Cf. *IG*, XII (8), p. 40, left col.; Ober-

hummer, *RE*, s.v. *Serreion*. See also Vol. 1, 4, 19, 95.
3. See, e.g., *CIG* 2007: ἀγωνοθέτην τῆς Σιρραίων πόλεως. For the site see W. M. Leake, *Travels in Northern Greece* (4 vols., London, 1835), III, 200–201.

47. 39.332. (Pl. XVIII.)

Stele of Thasian marble, with tang for insertion. Height 0.73 (including tang), width 0.368, thickness 0.07–10; height of letters 0.020–025.

Found 5 July 1939, in the "Sacristy."

Lehmann-Hartleben, *AJA*, 44 (1940), 345–46, no. 1 (cf. p. 493); J. and L. Robert, *REG*, 57 (1944), 222, no. 151a.

ἐπὶ βασιλέως

Θεοδώρου τοῦ Ϛ·

μύσται εὐσεβεῖς

Βεροιαῖοι·

5   Τι.Κλαύδιος Εὔλαιος

Οὐλπία ᾿Αλεξάνδρα

ἡ γύνη αὐτοῦ,

Γα· ᾿Ιτύριος Πούδης·

δοῦλοι

10   Κλαυδίου Εὐλαίου·

Στάχυς
Παράμονος
Θηβαῒς
ἔτους   αξσ

Line 2. Θεοδωρούτους, Lehmann, corrected by Robert, and by J. H. Oliver (letter to Lehmann, 2 October 1940). The last letter is certain: ς, i.e., 6. The Βασιλεύς does not occur elsewhere.

Line 5. Εὐάλιος, Lehmann. Both here and in line 10, where the name recurs, ΑΛ and ΛΑ are equally possible epigraphically, and Εὔλαιος is a more likely name in itself.

Line 8. Βιούδης, Lehmann. Πούδης is certain, a form of *Pudens:* cf. *IGRR,* I, 688, 1333. The more usual form is Πούδενς (ibid., 719–20, 1471–72).

Line 12. Παρώονος, Lehmann. Παράμονος is certain.

The era-date 261 in line 14 apparently refers to the provincial and not to the Augustan era.[1] This gives A.D. 113, which suits well the presence of the name Οὐλπία in line 6, since this name fell out of use after the early years of Hadrian.[2] Another citizen of Beroea occurs in a list of initiates of 38 B.C.[3]

The names call for little comment, save for line 8, where the rare *nomen* Iturius may be connected with the Iturius of Tacitus, *Ann.* 13.19–22, etc.[4] Pudens, who alone of those present has the *tria nomina,* is sandwiched between the Beroeans and their slaves.

1. The date is already given by Lehmann, loc. cit., without comment. The weakness of the generally accepted view that the undescribed era-date in Macedonian inscriptions is that of the provincial era (see, most recently, M. N. Tod, *Studies Presented to David Moore Robinson* [Mylonas and Raymond, eds., 2 vols., St. Louis, 1953], II, p. 388, no. 141*) has recently been demonstrated by F. Papazoglu, *Zbornik filozofskog Fakulteta Beograd,* 3 (1955), 15–28, which I know only from the summary of J. and L. Robert, *REG,* 69 (1956),

136, no. 146 (cf. also ibid., no. 159, for further instance of a date in the Augustan era which is not specified, and for further references).
2. See L. Robert, *Hellenica,* 3 (1946), 5–10; J. and L. Robert, *La Carie,* II, 211, 222–23, 225.
3. *IG,* XII (8), 195 = L. Robert, *Collection Froehner I* (Paris, 1936), 44 (cf. Tod, op. cit., p. 397, ad num. 141).
4. Cf. Stein, *RE,* s.v.; another Iturius occurs in *CIL,* VI, 35503.

48. 53.74. (Pl. XIX.)

Fragment of Thasian marble broken on all sides. Preserved height 0.12, preserved width 0.08, thickness 0.028; height of letters: lines 1–2, 0.015; line 3, smaller.

From Halonia, 30 June 1953.

Unpublished.

[ἐπὶ β]ασιλ[έως τοῦ δεῖνος]
[μ]ύστα[ι εὐσεβεῖς]
————ụπ————
– – – – – – – – – –

The lettering is Imperial, and the sigma of line 2, Σ, suggests a fairly advanced date.

49. 39.338. (Pl. XIX.)

Top right part of stele of white marble. Preserved height 0.20, preserved width 0.16, thickness 0.040; height of letters: line 1, 0.010; lines 2–4, ca. 0.015; lines 2–4 inscribed between guide lines. Above inscription rough incised decoration, circle (theta?) in center, acroterion (?) at right end.

Found 7 July 1939, outside the "Sacristy."

Lehmann-Hartleben, *AJA*, 44 (1940), 346, no. 2.

[ἀγα]θῆ τύχη·
[ἐπὶ βασιλέω]ς Φλ. ῾Ρηγείνου
[τοῦ Δ]ηλίωνος·
[μύσται εὐσ]εβεῖς

– – – – – – – – – – – –

Line 3. Δηλίων, common at Thasos, seems the most obvious supplement here.

The hand is not paralleled in Samothracian Imperial documents, but it is probably of the later second century A.D.[1] Lehmann-Hartleben[2] suggested that the piece may go with the lost Latin fragment of *CIL*, III, 722, on account of the lineation.

1. Of dated hands compare the very similar *Inschr. Olymp.* 100 ff., and, nearer Samothrace, Kalinka, *An-* *tike Denkmäler*, 216 (*IGRR*, I, 730).
2. Op. cit., p. 346, n. 31.

50. 39.348. (Pl. XIX.)

Three joining fragments of Thasian marble, broken above and below. Preserved height 0.385, width 0.308–315, thickness 0.055; height of letters: lines 1–6, 0.030; line 7, 0.018.

Found 6 July 1939, near the "Sacristy."

Lehmann-Hartleben, *AJA*, 44 (1940), 346, no. 3 (cf. p. 493).

– – – – – – – – – – – –

ṭịnianus Q(uaestor) ·prov·Ṃ[ac](edoniae)
Sex·Palp[e]llius Candi-
dus Tullittianus·

                                    A.Vereius·Felix·

                      5   Bato·Batonis·

                                    Purpurio

                                    — — — — — — —

The hand resembles that of **39** and **40**, and the list is probably not later than Hadrianic.

Line 1, init. *ṭinianus,* Lehmann-Hartleben. *ṗinianus* is also possible, but *ċinianus,* which would give the common name [*Li*]*cinianus,* can be excluded. The name is evidently not complete as it stands, even though in the only broken word in the inscription, *Candi|dus,* the part on the lower line is inset. Consequently such names as [*Faus*]*ṭinianus,* [*Fron*]*ṭinianus,* [*Ius*]*ṭinianus,* [*Pa*]*ṗinianus,* etc., are all possible. [*A*]*ṭinianus* can probably be excluded since this would not have been split between the two lines.

Line 1, fin. The bottom of an oblique stroke of a letter is visible after the *v.* Bloch, ap. Lehmann-Hartleben, took this as *A* and restored *A*[*ch*](*aeae*), and Lehmann-Hartleben writes, "The spacing and preserved trace of the first letter of the province allow no alternative." A glance at the photograph shows that the angle of *M* is the same as that of the *A,* and that *M* is thus equally possible. Consequently, since there is no reason why an official of the province of Achaea should be initiated in Samothrace, and since all the other dedications made by known officials are by officials of the province of Macedonia, it is more probable that we should read *M*[*ac*](*edoniae*). The abbreviation Mac(edonica) is used both of the legions of that name,[1] and of the province Macedonia.[2] The reading *A*[*siae*], suggested to me by Professor Syme, is unobjectionable paleographically, and an official of the province of Asia might be in Samothrace en route for Asia Minor, but the parallels provided by the other Samothracian records of officials of Macedonia lead me to prefer the reading *M*[*ac*](*edoniae*).

1. See *ILS* 1060, 1153, 2311, etc. It is, however, less   2. *ILS* 1158.
common than *Maced.* or the full *Macedonica.*

51. 39.79. (Pl. XIX.)

Two joining pieces of stele of Thasian marble, broken below. Preserved height 0.38, width 0.31, thickness 0.135; height of letters: lines 1, 3, 6, 0.04; lines 2, 5, 8, 0.02; line 4, 0.027; line 7, 0.025.

From Chora, 25 June 1939.

Lehmann-Hartleben, *AJA,* 44 (1940), 357 f., no. 3 = *AEp,* 1947, 4.

                              L.Fundanio Lamia

                                    Aeliano

                              Sex·Carminio Veṭ(ere)

```
                         cos.              [A.D. 116
          5    x.K.Mai.mystae pii,        22 Apr.]
               L. Pomponius
               Maximus Flavius
               [Sil]vanus Q·propr
               [prov.Maced.]
          _ _ _ _ _ _ _ _ _
```

Line 3. Veter[e], L-H, followed by *AEp*. The *Vet* appears, however, to reach to the edge of the stone, and there is no room for *-ere*.

Lines 6 ff. L. Pomponius Maximus Flavius [Sil]vanus was presumably quaestor propraetore of the province of Macedonia. He is probably the son of the suffect consul of 121.[1]

Line 8. ...ianus, L-H, followed by *AEp*.

1. See *PIR*[1], III, 566.

52. 38.380. (Pl. XIX.)

Fragment of stele of Thasian (?) marble, left edge preserved. Preserved height 0.28, preserved width 0.20, thickness 0.085; height of letters 0.035.

Said to have been found by A. Salač during his excavations.

Unpublished.

```
          _ _ _ _ _ _ _
          .aspares M..————
                       Se[rvi]
          Eutychus
          Epaphrodit[us]
      5   Tyranni[o]
          _ _ _ _ _ _ _
```

Line 1 is difficult to read. Toward the end of the line, *m* is perhaps followed by I*v*; if so, not *my[stes pius]*.

Lines 2–5 seem to be in a different hand from line 1, but the disposition of line 2 shows that the whole forms part of a single inscription. The lettering suggests a date in the second century A.D.

53. 38.355. (Pl. XX.)

Fragment of slightly concave plaque of Thasian marble, broken on right and at bottom.

Preserved height 0.23, preserved width 0.13, thickness 0.07; height of letters: line 1, 0.045; line 2, 0.030; line 3, 0.028; line 4, 0.024; lines 5–7, 0.015; line 8, 0.010.

From Chora, 1938.

Lehmann-Hartleben, *AJA*, 43 (1939), 145; J. H. Oliver, ibid., pp. 464–66. J. and L. Robert, *REG*, 52 (1939), 492, no. 297: idem, *Hellenica*, 2 (1946), 57, no. 17, and n. 2; Lehmann, *Hesperia*, 19 (1950), 9, n. 30; Hemberg, p. 94, n. 1. As was originally observed by Mrs. E. L. Holsten (see *AJA*, op. cit., p. 145), this inscription forms the top right half of *CIL*, III, Suppl., 7371 (*S,I*, p. 37, and tab. LXXII) = *ILS* 4056 = *IG*, XII (8), p. 39. Pl. XX shows the three pieces associated.[1]

The whole inscription now reads:

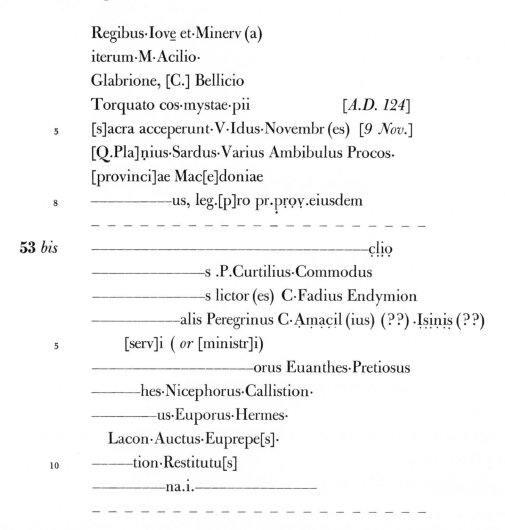

<table>
<tr><td></td><td>Regibus·Iove̲ et·Minerv (a)</td><td></td></tr>
<tr><td></td><td>iterum·M·Acilio·</td><td></td></tr>
<tr><td></td><td>Glabrione, [C.] Bellicio</td><td></td></tr>
<tr><td></td><td>Torquato cos·mystae·pii</td><td>[*A.D. 124*]</td></tr>
<tr><td>5</td><td>[s]acra acceperunt·V·Idus·Novembr (es)</td><td>[*9 Nov.*]</td></tr>
<tr><td></td><td>[Q.Pla]n̲ius·Sardus·Varius Ambibulus Procos·</td><td></td></tr>
<tr><td></td><td>[provinci]ae Mac[e]doniae</td><td></td></tr>
<tr><td>8</td><td>——————————us, leg.[p]ro pr.pr̲o̲v̲.eiusdem</td><td></td></tr>
</table>

— — — — — — — — — — — — — — — — — — —

53 *bis*

— —cl̲i̲o̲

——————————s .P.Curtilius·Commodus

——————————s lictor (es) C·Fadius Endymion

——————————alis Peregrinus C·A̲m̲a̲c̲il (ius) (??) ·I̲s̲i̲n̲i̲s̲ (??)

5   [serv]i (*or* [ministr]i)

——————————————orus Euanthes·Pretiosus

————hes·Nicephorus·Callistion·

————us·Euporus·Hermes·

Lacon·Auctus·Euprepe[s]·

10   ————tion·Restitutu[s]

————na.i̲.————————

— —

The two previously known fragments were found in the "Arsinoeion," and Conze was probably right in suggesting (*S,I*) that the slight concavity of the stone was connected with the construction of the building. Lines 7–8 of the new fragment were not correctly read in the original publication.

1. I am grateful to the authorities of the Wiener Kunst-historiches Museum for providing a new photograph of the two pieces previously known, and for permission to publish it.

Lines 1–2. On deities as eponyms see Robert, loc. cit. There was no room for the *a* at the end of line 1.

Line 6. Ambibulus, here proconsul of Macedonia, is presumably the consul ordinarius of 126.[2]

Line 8. I owe the reading of the difficult *leg* on the Vienna fragment to Professor Syme.

Lines 11 ff. are on the lower, Vienna fragment, the hand of which is very different. The difference indeed is so striking that in spite of the agreement of Conze and Mommsen I cannot believe that it is actually part of the same stone as the upper half, and Professor Syme tells me that he agrees with me. It is no doubt part of another list carved on a similarly concave piece of marble. I reprint it here, for convenience, but as a separate inscription.

53 *bis. Line 2.* The status of P. Curtilius Commodus is not clear.

Line 3. Previous editors read *lictor*, but *lictor* (*es*) is presumably necessary, to include the persons mentioned in line 4.

Line 4. The name at the end was read by Mommsen as *Amacil·Isianus* and by Hirschfeld doubtfully as *C. Amacil·Vialis*. The letters after the *C.* do not resemble much *Amacil.*, but I cannot determine what they are. The last letters seem to be *isiniș*. A very obscure line.

Line 5. The exact title of the slaves who follow cannot be determined. The Greek word for slave attendants in Samothracian documents is ἀκόλουθοι, and Hirschfeld therefore supplied [*pedesequ*]*i*. This is elegant, but *servi* is the word which is so far attested in the Latin lists.[3]

2. See *PIR*, III[2], 68, n. 5. The reading *Pla*]*ṇius* supports the conjecture of Groag (*PIR*, III[2], loc. cit.) that the Ambibulus of this inscription is the Q. Planius Sardus . . . Ambibulus of *ILS* 9486; (cf. *JRS*, 43 [1953], 152). Of the *n* only the top of the right vertical hasta is visible (as already noted in the majuscule copies in *S,I* and *CIL*).

3. *IG*, XII (8), 174, line 9; **36**, line 18.

54. 38.393. (Pl. XXI.)

Left upper corner of plaque of Thasian marble. Preserved height 0.29, preserved width 0.325, thickness 0.48. Inscribed field surrounded by beveled edge. Above, incised pediment with acroteria, and rosette in center. Height of letters: line 1, 0.015; lines 2–4, 0.030.

From Chora, 1938.

Lehmann-Hartleben, *AJA*, 43 (1939), 145; *AEp* (1939), 3.

ἀγαθῆι ❦ [τύχηι]
·M· S· Le[na?]
Ponti[ano]
M·An[tonio]   [*A.D. 131*]
[Rufino]
[cos.]

— — — — — —

The restorations are those of Lehmann-Hartleben, and are no doubt correct. The consul appears elsewhere as Sergius Octavius Laenas Pontianus, and we learn his praenomen for the first time from this document.[1]

There can be no doubt that this is a list of initiates, though only the date is preserved.

1. For the spelling Lenas / Laenas cf. *ILS* 6209, of   Laenate Pontiano.
the consul's name. It occurs as Laenas, ibid., 5287:

55. 53.616. (Pl. XXI.)

Top right corner of stele with molding of Thasian marble. Preserved height 0.12, preserved width 0.035, preserved thickness 0.045; height of letters: lines 1–2, 0.015; line 3, 0.010.

Found 28 July 1953, near the south door of the "Anaktoron."

Unpublished.

[ἐπὶ βασιλέως τοῦ δεῖνος]

μύσται

spat.0.020

[εὐσεβεῖς, καὶ ἐπ]όπτ-

[ης/αι————]τιο[ι?]

—————Τ—————

– – – – – – – – – –

The hand suggests a date in the second or third century A.D.

This insignificant fragment is not without its difficulties. The gap between lines 1–2 suggests a break in sense, as though line 1 marked the end of a rubric, or as if there were a short heading between the two lines. However, μύσται should be followed by εὐσεβεῖς at the head of the list of initiates, and since it is very unlikely that εὐσεβεῖς stood by itself in the space between lines 1 and 2, to the left of the break, I assume that this gap is of no significance and put εὐσεβεῖς on line 2 (as in **59**, below). The next partially preserved word is clearly some form of ἐπόπτης, and my restoration seems the only possible one in the circumstances.[1]

Line 1. στα are in a ligature of the form ᚲA.

Line 3. The final omicron is clear on the squeeze. The letters are probably the end of an ethnic, perhaps [——Βυζάν]τιο[ι].

1. μύσται and ἐπόπται appear together, in a slightly   same formula, but in the singular, in ibid., 188 (re-
different formula, in *IG*, XII (8), 186(a), lines 2–5:   published below, App. IV, p. 112).
ʽΡοδίων ἱεροποιοί, μύσται καὶ ἐπόπται εὐσεβεῖς. The

56. *53.73.* (Pl. XXI.)

Fragment of stele of Thasian marble, left and bottom edges preserved. Preserved height 0.28, preserved width 0.18, thickness 0.065; height of letters: line 1, 0.016; lines 2–3, 0.020–025; line 4, 0.016.

From the church of Hagios Demetrios, Halonia, 30 June 1953.

Unpublished.

Apparently not inscribed in top surviving 0.090.

ἐπὶ βασιλέω[ς τοῦ δεῖνος]·
Κάστω[ρ]
Ἐπικράτ[ους μύστης *or* ἐπόπτης εὐ]-
σεβής

molding.

This crudely carved inscription appears to have been very unsymmetrical. Line 2 must have held the nominative Κάστωρ, and since it is clear from line 4 that only one mystes or epoptes was recorded Ἐπικράτ– (line 3) must be the patronymic. Line 1 must therefore have held the name (but probably no patronymic) of the βασιλεύς.

Line 1. The last letter looks more like omicron than omega, and omicron is possible;[1] but it may be an extravagantly shaped omega.

The hand shows that the inscription is of Imperial date, but a closer approximation hardly seems possible in view of the poor quality of the writing.

1. For βασιλέος cf. *IG*, XII (8), 220, line 2: [ἐπὶ β]ασιλέος Τι. Φλαουίο[υ Τιβερί]ου, κ.τ.λ.

57. *49.995.* (Pl. XXII.)

Fragment of Thasian marble broken on all sides. Preserved height 0.22, preserved width 0.12, preserved thickness 0.15; height of letters 0.020.

Found 30 July 1949, to the southwest of the "Arsinoeion" (next to **45**).

Unpublished.

[ἐπὶ βασι]λέως [τοῦ δεῖνος————————]
[ἀγορ]αν[ομοῦντος τοῦ δεῖνος—————]
– – – – – – – – – – – – – – – – – –

The opening with dating by eponym and agoranomos is confined to list of initiates.[1] There are traces of the bottoms of letters 0.070 above the first preserved line; possibly the remains of an earlier list.

1. Cf. *IG,* XII (8), 187–88.

The lettering suggests a date in the second or third century A.D.

According to an observation of Lehmann (*per ep.*) this fragment may belong to the same building block as **45**.[2] There is no reason, however, to connect the traces of letters mentioned above with the other inscription.

2. "We observed at the time that, to judge from appearances, this was a broken piece of the same building block on which **45** is inscribed. Even though **57** is much later this seems possible."

58. 49.348. (Pl. XXII.)

Fragment of plaque of Thasian marble, broken above and below. Preserved height 0.225, width 0.29, thickness 0.055; height of letters 0.020–025.

Found by F. Chapouthier, 1925; brought from Chora, 5 July 1949.

Mentioned, Chapouthier, p. 234, n. 4; L. Robert, *Coll. Froehner*, p. 53. I am very grateful to Professor G. Daux, Director of the French School at Athens, for permission to publish this inscription.

— — — — — — — — — —

]ος Θεσσαλονεικεύς,

Μ.’Ορφίδιος ’Αγησίλαος

‘Ηρακλεώτης ἀπὸ Στρύμονος,

Κλαύδιος Σύμφορος

5   Θεσσαλονικεύς,

Μάρκιος Μυρισμός

Θεσσαλονεικεύς.

[δ]οῦλοι Εὐσεβ[ίου(?)]·

— — — — — — — — — —

The hand is quite different from that of any other Samothracian inscription, but closely resembles that frequently found in inscriptions of Thessalonike.[1] In view of the number of Θεσσαλονικεῖς who appear in this inscription, I should be inclined to think it was carved by a lapicide trained in the style of that city. Its date is, to judge by the analogues quoted in n. 1, of the third century A.D.

Line 2. The *nomen* Orfidius is rare, represented by C. Orfidius Benignus, *legatus leg. I Adiutr.* in A.D. 69, and his family,[2] and the cons. suff. of A.D. 148, P. Orfidius Senecio.

Line 3. The rho of Στρύμονος is just visible, joined to the tau in the ligature Ϸ. For the ethnic ‘Ηρακλεώτης ἀπὸ Στρύμονος see L. Robert, *RevPhil*, 1936, pp. 113 ff. The site of the city is unknown.[3]

1. See Kallipolites and Lazarides, ’Αρχαῖαι ἐπιγραφαὶ Θεσσαλονίκης (Salonika, 1946, γεν. διοικ. Μακεδ., διεύθ. ἱστ. μνημ. καὶ ἀρχ.), p. 13, no. 7, and p. 43, fig. 8; Pelekides, ’Απὸ τὴν πολιτεία καὶ τὴν κοινωνία τῆς ἀρχαίας Θεσσαλονίκης (Salonika, 1934, Πανεπ. Θεσσαλ. ἀριθ. δημοσ. 77), p. 36, no. 3, and fig. 7. Other inscriptions in these two publications show varying degrees of similarity with the present inscription.
2. See *RE*, s.v. *Orfidius*.
3. For the literary evidence see *RE*, s.v. *Herakleia* (6).

Line 8. As to δοῦλοι there can be no doubt. Their presence establishes beyond dispute that the list is part of a record of initiation. After it one would expect to find the name of the master (cf. **41**, line 9; **47**, lines 9–10; **59**, line 7). The letters Εὐσεβ seem certain, in spite of the fact that only a portion of them is preserved. The second letter is certainly upsilon, though it has the appearance of kappa in the photograph. Thus it seems natural to read Εὐσεβ[ίου], the end of whose name may survive at the beginning of line 1. A possible alternative would be δοῦλοι εὐσεβ[εῖς], but the expression is unparalleled. In either case, it should be noted that there is an oblique horizontal mark after the beta which could hardly be epsilon or iota, but may not be a letter at all.

59. 39.547. (Pl. XXI.)

Plaque of Thasian marble with incised decoration of cornice and acroteria, broken below. Preserved height 0.55, preserved width 0.39, thickness 0.07; height of letters: line 1, 0.035; line 2, 0.025–030; lines 3–5, 0.025; lines 6 ff., 0.020. Rear face prepared for insertion into wall.

Found 10 July 1939, serving as pavement slab in the late Roman floor of the "Sacristy."

Lehmann-Hartleben, *AJA*, 44 (1940), 346 f., no. 4, and fig. 25; J. and L. Robert, *REG*, 57 (1944), 222, no. 151*a*.

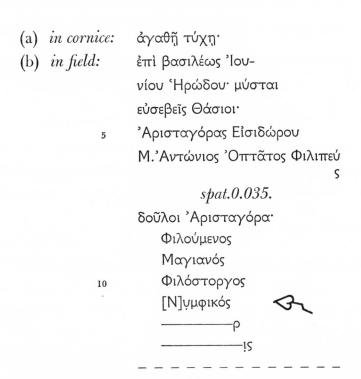

(a)	*in cornice:*	ἀγαθῇ τύχῃ·
(b)	*in field:*	ἐπὶ βασιλέως 'Ιου-
		νίου 'Ηρώδου· μύσται
		εὐσεβεῖς Θάσιοι·
5		'Αρισταγόρας Εἰσιδώρου
		Μ.'Αντώνιος 'Οππᾶτος Φιλιπεύ
		ς
		spat.0.035.
		δοῦλοι 'Αρισταγόρα·
		Φιλούμενος
		Μαγιανός
10		Φιλόστοργος
		[Ν]υμφικός
		————————ρ
		————————ις

The lettering, which is highly ornate in a style particularly familiar in northern Greece (note especially the complex epsilon), is of the same type as that found in third-century documents at Thasos.[1] The absence of Aurelii shows, however, that this inscription must be of the very beginning of that century, or of the late second.

The basileus is unknown. Another of the *gens* Iunia occurs in a first-century list of mystae (?).[2] The name Herodes is very common at Thasos.[3]

The use of the plural ethnic Θάσιοι is illogical, since there were no other Thasians than Aristagoras, Optatus being from Philippi and the slaves without citizenship. Θάσιοι is presumably, therefore, to be understood as "the boat-load from Thasos." [4]

This is the only list of Thasian mystae, though Thasians occur in the theoroi-lists.[5]

1. E.g., *IG,* XII (8), 382; ibid., 387 (for a photograph of which I am indebted to Dr. L. H. Jeffery). For the epsilon (retrograde sigma with transverse bar) cf. also Chapouthier, p. 34, no. 12, pl. VIII (valley of Strymon).
2. *IG,* XII (8), 206, line 2.
3. See the indexes to *IG,* XII (8).
4. Lehmann, loc. cit., p. 348, and *per ep.* explains the Φιλιπεύς differently. He writes (p. 348): "Aside from its well-preserved state and its baroque style of lettering, the inscription offers an amusing detail. As the text reads, the document was originally intended only for people from Thasos, i.e. for Aristagoras and his slaves. In line 6 Marcus Antonius Optatus, a Roman citizen from Philippi, was later added to a stone (probably by a lucrative trick of the administration) for

which Aristagoras certainly had already paid. This line was squeezed in and the scribe got into trouble at the end: he left out one π of Philippeus, used a ligature, and added the ς below. Nevertheless he imitated faithfully the style of the original document. The leaf in line 11 probably marks the original end. Thus lines 12 ff. may have contained names of slaves of Optatus." I cannot myself notice any difference in the hand of line 6, which Lehmann describes (*per ep.*) as "sloppier" than that of the rest of the inscription, except that it is more crowded because it contains more letters. For a final sigma added in this position see *IG,* XII (3), 466, II, line 3.
5. *IG,* XII (8), 161, lines 11–12; 172, lines 16–20.

60. 49.445. (Pl. XXII.)

Limestone block, broken below. Preserved height 0.245, preserved width 0.465, thickness 0.21; height of letters: lines 1–2, 0.030–035; lines 3–4, 0.025–028.

Found by Chapouthier; brought from Chora, 5 July 1949.

F. Chapouthier, *BCH,* 49 (1925), 254 ff.

> ἐπὶ βασιλέως
> Καλίππου· μύστ[αι](?)
> εὐσεβεῖς· Ἥρων
> Ὑγιαίν[ο]ν[τος], Η.ΡΕ
> – – – – – – – – – –(?)

This inscription was dated by Chapouthier to the third or fourth century A.D., and regarded by him as the latest initiate-list then known. The letter-forms might be of any time from the second to the fourth centuries A.D. (⊏ ◊ but Ω), and it is not possible to be more precise.

Line 1. The αι of μύστ[αι] may possibly have been on line 3.

Line 4, fin. There may be a letter joined by ligature between H and E: at the end Ρ is fairly clear. The letters may form part of another proper name, or could conceivably be part of an ethnic. It is uncertain whether the inscription is complete or not. The space between line 4 and the bottom edge is approximately the same as the interlinear space of ca. 0.020.

61. 56.5. (Pl. XXII.)

Fragment of upper right part of stele of Thasian marble, with pediment containing circular object in center. Preserved height 0.23, preserved width 0.18, preserved thickness 0.09; height of letters: lines 1–2, 0.013, omicron 0.010; line 3, 0.008.

Found August 1955, in the neighborhood of the Genoese Towers.
Unpublished.

[ἐπὶ βασιλέω]ς Περ[ικ]λέο—
[υς τοῦ Ἀγ]αφάντου
[ἀγορανομοῦντος —]ανου τοῦ
— — — — — — — — — — — —

This appears to be the opening of a list of mystae.

Line 1. The last three surviving letters of the name are considerably larger than the first three.

Line 3. This line is written in smaller letters than lines 1–2, and there is a lacuna to the left of approximately fifteen letters. There is probably just room for the name of the ἀγορανόμος, e.g. [Σωφ]άνου. The name of the ἀγορανόμος more commonly stands at the end of the inscription, but is found, as here, alongside that of the βασιλεύς in *IG*, XII (8), 188 (below, p. 112) and 221. There are traces of large indecipherable letters in line 4.

APPENDIX IV

IG, XII (8), 188. (Pl. XXIII, stele and squeeze.)
I collated this inscription by kind permission of the second Viscount Mersey on 23 June 1956, at Bignor Park, Pulborough, Sussex.

> ἐπὶ βασιλέως Δείνωνος τοῦ
> Ἀπολλωνίδου
> [ἀ]γορανομοῦντος Ἑρμοκρά[του]
> τοῦ Πυθονείκου,
> 5   [ὡ]ς δὲ Κυζικηνοὶ ἐπὶ Ἑταιρίω-
> [ν]ος τοῦ Εὐμνήστου ἱππάρχ[εω]·
> μύστης εὐσεβὴς καὶ ἐπόπτη[ς]
> Μῖκις Μνησισ[τρ]άτου, φύσει δ[ε]
> Ἀσκληπιάδης Ἀττάλου, Κυζικη-
> 10   νός, ἀρχιτέκτων, ἀποσταλεὶς
> παρὰ Κυζικηνῶν [κα]τὰ τὴν
> πρεσβείαν τοῦ δήμου τοῦ
> [Σ]αμοθράκων ἕνεκα τῆς ἱ[ερο]-
> ποΐας καὶ τῶν ἱερῶν εἰκόνων
> 15   – – – – – – – – – – – – – –
>   – – – – – – – – – – – – –
>   – – – – – – – – – – – – –
>   – – – – – – – – – – – – –
>   ————————————ονος
> 20   ————————ας Ἀσκληπιάδου
>   ————Σαμ.λου————
>   [Μα————————————(?)]
>   ⟨Θ⟩ράσων————————ου
>   ⟨Β⟩άκχιος————————
>   – – – – – – – – – – – – –

The inscription was first seen by the fourth Earl of Aberdeen ("Athenian Aberdeen," Prime Minister 1852–55) in the house of Fauvel in Athens in 1803, as recorded by him in a passage of his *Journal*,[1] reproduced in Walpole's *Travels in Various Countries of the East* (London, 1820), p. 602. Lord Aberdeen, however, though he gave a fairly accurate, if brief, description of the representation on the stone (which he described as a "cippus," though it is a stele),[2] recorded only line 1 of the inscription. Subsequently, Boeckh published the inscription as *CIG*, II, 2158, from two copies, one of Åkerblad and one of Fauvel, out of which he produced an eclectic text.[3] At a later date the stone was regarded as lost by Conze,[4] Rubensohn,[5] and Fredrich,[6] who copied the text of Boeckh and emended it at a few points.

The stone was rediscovered in 1926 by the late S. E. Winbolt at Bignor Park in Sussex. In republishing it and other inscriptions [7] he recorded that they were "almost certainly" brought to England by John Hawkins (1758(?)–1841), the traveler, some of whose papers are reproduced in the same volume of Walpole,[8] and who bought Bignor Park in 1806.[9] Since Hawkins does not appear to have visited the East again after he bought Bignor Park, it may be concluded that he acquired the stone and brought it to England very soon after Lord Aberdeen saw it.

In his republication of the inscription[10] Winbolt was assisted by Dr. M. N. Tod, who, however, did not see the stone. Winbolt recorded that, apart from a few words, which he did not specify, the stone was illegible, and his text is in effect the same as that of Boeckh, with four suggestions of Dr. Tod.[11] Subsequent epigraphical comment appears to be limited to a remark of L. Robert,[12] who, referring to the travels of the stone, added: "à la ligne 14, cette dernière édition [i.e., that of Winbolt] reproduit le texte qui est inacceptable: il faut souhaiter qu'un épigraphiste exercé étudie la pierre." In fulfilling this task I am not likely to satisfy

1. The unpublished MS Journal of Lord Aberdeen's tour of the Near East is preserved in the departmental Library of the Department of Greek and Roman Antiquities in the British Museum, but the Keeper, Mr. D. E. L. Haynes, tells me that the passage quoted by Walpole does not appear there. I do not know whether it is only by chance that this same passage is omitted from Lady Frances Balfour's list of Lord Aberdeen's writings (*Life of George, Fourth Earl of Aberdeen* [2 vols., London, 1923], II, 334–35), though the letters to Walpole printed elsewhere in the *Travels* (pp. 425–46, 489–503) are included.

2. The description of the stone given by Åkerblad, whose note is quoted by Conze, *S,I*, p. 18, n. 6, "inscription sur un marbre taillé en forme d'aedicula," is correctly criticized by Rubensohn, p. 217, n. 48, as confusing the stone with the building represented upon it. Rubensohn, however, was in turn misled by Aberdeen into regarding the stone as round. It is, in fact, a normal pedimental stele (cf. ibid., p. 159).

3. Boeckh, in his lemma, adds the information that the stone was brought from Samothrace to the Hellespont ("ex Samothrace ad arces Hellespontias") by Willis, a British merchant otherwise unknown.

4. See *S,I*, p. 18, n. 6: "Auf einem jetzt wieder verschollenen Inschriftsteine von Samothrake (C. J. gr. II, 2158) . . ."; cf. *S,II*, p. 113.

5. Rubensohn, p. 158.

6. *IG*, XII (8), 188.

7. *JHS*, 48 (1928), 178 ff.

8. *Travels*, p. XII, and pp. 1 ff., 281 ff., 392 ff., 473 ff.

9. See *Dictionary of National Biography*, s.v. *Hawkins, John*, p. 221.

10. Loc. cit., p. 180, no. 3, and p. 181, fig. 3.

11. It does not appear that Winbolt made any attempt to read the stone, or a squeeze. Thus the text must presumably be regarded as copied from *IG*, XII (8), 188. Unfortunately Tod's conjectures are not specifically noted, and can be ascertained only by a comparison of the text with earlier editions.

12. *Coll. Froehner* (1936), p. 60, n. 4.

L. Robert, but it nevertheless seemed to me worth while to record my efforts to read the text.

My study of the stone itself was very unfruitful. Winbolt, we have seen, recorded that he could read little or nothing of the stone, and I am able to say that it is now considerably more illegible. Viscount Mersey informed me that the final deterioration of the surface began in 1930 (that is, after its examination by Winbolt) and was rapid. As a protective measure he secured the inscription under glass; this, however, was removed for my benefit, and I was able to take a squeeze from which, with Boeckh's text to guide me, I have with great difficulty made out a few isolated letters and have been able to control some readings.

I print above the text as given by Boeckh, with the corrections I have been able to make, underlining those letters of which I have not been able to see any signs whatever, and adding a few comments on previous readings. I dot no letters, since if I dotted one I could equally well dot almost all. They must all be regarded, unless otherwise stated, as vestigial. I make no attempt to discuss the interpretation of the building represented on the stele. This representation belongs to a well-known group which has been noticed most recently by Lehmann, and I may refer the reader to his article.[13]

Stele of Thasian marble, complete on all sides, broken in two joining pieces. Height 0.79, width 0.33–37, thickness ?; height of letters 0.017–020. Representation of round building, etc., with two bases, one on either side. In tympanon round object. Height of representation 0.31.

Line 1. Δείνωνος, the epsilon, omitted by both Åkerblad and Fauvel, is visible.

Lines 3–4. Omitted by Fauvel. Rubensohn[14] did not observe this, and claimed that since the copy of Fauvel's copy made by Wescher for Conze omitted these lines, Fauvel had evidently made more than one copy (cf. below, on lines 11–14).

Line 3. Toward the end of the line there are very faint traces of alpha, to justify Tod's Ἑρμο[κράτους?] (though I prefer to print it without the final sigma), as against Boeckh's Ἑρμο[κρίτου?], followed by Conze (Fredrich gives no supplement, but records Boeckh's conjecture in his apparatus).

Line 4. ΛΤΥΘΟΚΕΥΙΟΥ, Åkerblad; Ἀ[γα]θοκ[λ]ε[ίδ]ου? Boeckh; Ἀ[γα]θοκ[λ]ε[ί]ου[ς]? Fredrich; [Π]υθοκ[ρίτ]ου? Hiller; Πυθονίκου, Tod. Πυθονείκου is mostly visible on the squeeze, Πυθο and the epsilon being clear. The alleged alpha at the beginning of the word is a deep oblique crack passing through two or three lines.

Lines 7–10. The double change of name at adoption, although not common, is sufficiently well attested to justify the transmitted text.[15]

13. Lehmann-Hartleben, *Hesperia,* 12 (1943), 115 ff. Lehmann mentions this monument (p. 118, where "Akerbladen" should be "Åkerblad" and ibid., nn. 19, 21, "Wiebolt" should be "Winbolt"), but he is not primarily concerned with it. The brief accounts of the representation were already used by Conze, *S,II,* pp. 113–14, and Rubensohn, pp. 158 ff., in attempts to identify the building. Cf. also Chapouthier, pp. 176–77.

14. Pp. 216–17, n. 47.

15. See, e.g., Paton and Hicks, *The Inscriptions of Cos* (Oxford, 1891), 61: *TAM,* III, 767: *CIG* 2772 (cf.

Line 10. ἀρχιτέκτων, which was read with little variation by both Åkerblad and Fauvel, is not without its difficulties. The first half of the word is quite illegible, and the second half at first sight appears to end very clearly with ΕΩΝ, which would not permit ἀρχιτέκτων, but would permit, e.g., [ἱππαρχ]έων. However, continual study of the marks here leads me to think that the apparently quite obvious epsilon is, in fact, due to post-antique (post-1803?) tampering: the strokes are quite different from those of the other letters, being much thinner and sharper, and there are at the same time signs of a barely visible heavier vertical stroke through the middle of them, which would be the original stroke of the tau. Since I seem to see traces of the two preceding letters, epsilon and kappa (though the latter might be chi), and since both copies agree, I have left ἀρχιτέκτων.[16] At the end of line 9 Κυζίκη was apparently squeezed up, but it is visible.

Lines 11–14. Also largely illegible on the squeeze. Of 11–12 I can make nothing. In 13 Σαμοθρᾴκων can be traced for the most part, and perhaps also τῆς. At the end ν[εω] is not legible, and I find Boeckh's emendation of the copies unlikely (and indeed he himself added, "correctio νεωποίας tamen incerta est"). In line 14 the copies are particularly irreconcilable, as Boeckh shows: "Fauv. .ΠΟΚ..ΑΤΟΙΣ et nihil praeterea, Ak. ΤΑΙΣΑΝΤΟΝΙΕΡΟΝΕΡΜΩΝ, quod recepi uno Ο pro Α ex Fauv. petito," and he gave the text as [τ]ῆς ν[εω]|-ποί[α]ς [καὶ] τ[ῶ]ν ἱερ[ῶ]ν Ἑρμῶν. This was printed by Fredrich—who, however, said of it, "lectio incertissima est"—and again by Winbolt. Rubensohn protested against it, because the copy of Fauvel made by Wescher differed from Boeckh's copy in giving .ΓΟ instead of .ΤΟΙ at the beginning of the line,[17] and he warned against the use of the line as a foundation for further arguments.[18] In fact, however, the squeeze suggests that Wescher's copy was less reliable than that to which Boeckh had access, and Rubensohn's caution was perhaps unnecessary here. The squeeze shows undoubted traces of ποίας (pi, iota, and alpha

---

Lambertz, *Glotta*, 5 [1914], 152 (н); Klaffenbach, *Griechische Epigraphik* [Göttingen, 1957], p. 56); *Inschr. Priene* 266 (iii в.с.), Ἀχιλλείδης Εὐπολ[έ]μου | Σωσίστρατον Πρω[τ]αγόρου | τὸμ φύσει ἑαυτοῦ υἱόν, | κατὰ τὴν διαθήκην (cf. ibid., 267).

16. The occurrence of ἀρχιτέκτων here led to the supposition that the person in question had been responsible for the construction of some sacred buildings in Samothrace, including that represented on the stele: see Boeckh ad loc., and the references given above, n. 13. However, as Rubensohn himself pointed out, p. 223, n. 62, the ἀρχιτέκτονες were a board of magistrates at Cyzicus (Strabo 575: τρεῖς δ' ἀρχιτέκτονας τοὺς ἐπιμελησομένους οἰκοδομημάτων τε δημοσίων καὶ ὀργάνων; cf. Hasluck, *Cyzicus* [Cambridge, 1910], p. 257), so he may have been so called because he was holding that office at the time in Cyzicus, though this does not seem very likely. Honorific decrees for ἀρχιτέκτονες are frequent: see, e.g., *FdDelphes*, III, 3, 184 (*Syll*³ 494); ibid., 4, 96; *Studii și cercetări*,

5 (1954), 92 ff. (Callatis; cf. ibid., pp. 549 ff., J. and L. Robert, *REG*, 68 [1955], 244, no. 163*a*; ibid., 69 [1956], 144, no. 188, where the reference to the previous discussion should read "163*a*").

17. Rubensohn, p. 216, n. 46 (cf. *IG*, XII [8], ad loc.). He prints Wescher's copy of the two lines thus:

ΕΝΕΚΑΣΗΣΝΤ

.ΓΟ . . . . . ΑΤΟΙΣ

The difference between Fauvel's copy as recorded, but not adopted, by Boeckh, and that given by Rubensohn is very slight (Π for Γ, and a kappa after the omicron). Boeckh himself adopted the reading of Åkerblad and not that of Fauvel who, in any case, saw nothing in the second half of the line.

18. Ibid.: "Die Überlieferung ist also sehr unsicher und die Schreibung in der Inschrift auch eine sehr ungenaue. Die Ergänzung Boeckhs muss deshalb mit äusserster Vorsicht aufgenommen werden, und es ist nicht angebracht, Folgerungen irgend welcher Art an dieselbe zu knüpfen."

clear) which should therefore be retained. At the end of line 13, however, I would propose ἱ[ερο]ποΐας instead of ν[εω]ποΐας. We know from other inscriptions that the Cyzicene delegates to Samothrace were called ἱεροποιοί,[19] and an embassy sent to regulate the visits of these envoys would be described as ἕνεκα τῆς ἱεροποΐας.[20] The center of line 14 is virtually illegible, but there are signs of the rho of ἱερῶν. In place of Ἑρμῶν, which is obviously unconvincing, I suggest εἰκόνων which gives good sense, and can be justified by the squeeze: epsilon is visible and possibly kappa (easily confused with rho) and omicron. It may be supposed that the Cyzicenes had made a gift of some εἰκόνες, either statue-groups or pictures, representing some episode connected with the cult of the Samothracian deities.

Lines 15 ff. The rest of the inscription is mostly illegible. The names are presumably those of the other members of the embassy. Boeckh apparently felt that in 20 ff. Åkerblad (Fauvel had nothing after 20) did not observe the line division, and that there was only one pair of names on each line. At the end of 20 he omitted a MN which Fauvel had but Åkerblad had not (cf. his treatment of the sigma given by Fauvel at the end of 12), created a new line (22) out of the MA given at the end of 21 by Åkerblad, and replaced Åkerblad's OY at the beginning of 23 as the end of 22. In all this he may have been right, and I have followed him, control being impossible, though I have thought it safer to put the MA as a separate line in brackets.

The date can now be estimated on letter-forms, of which I record those few which are both significant and sufficiently legible to be utilizable. There are no apices. Circular letters are of full size; theta has a dot and not a stroke. I suspect alpha has a broken cross-bar in line 1, but this is the only instance where the center of the letter is even moderately clear. Mu has slanting vertical hastae, pi a short, right-hand stroke, sigma horizontal strokes. These factors combined suggest a Hellenistic date (ii / i B.C.) rather than an Imperial one. It has been shown above that **29**, in which Asclepiades also occurs as a Cyzicene envoy, should be dated to the late second century B.C. If the explanation offered of the group of names in lines 8–9 is correct, the present inscription should be contemporary or later, since if Asclepiades had already been adopted he would hardly have omitted his adoptive name in **29**.

19. See **29**; *IG*, XII (8), 194, ἱεροποιο[ὶ] | οἱ ἀποστα-λέντες | ὑπὸ τοῦ δήμου | [τ]οῦ Κυζικηνῶν. Rhodian ἱεροποιοί occur in 186 (cf. above, p. 106, n. 1, infra).
20. The title is not otherwise recorded from Cyzicus (Hasluck, *Cyzicus*, so far as I can discover, makes no mention of it), and it may be that the title was be-stowed on theoroi to external cult-centers. As Rubensohn, p. 219, pointed out, the wording of *IG*, XII (8), 194, quoted above in n. 19, shows, in any case, that the ἱεροποιοί were representatives of the state and not, as earlier writers had supposed, members of a private thiasos of Cyzicenes.

v. Miscellaneous

UNDER this heading I include not only all pieces too small to be identifiable, but also complete inscriptions which do not fall into any of the main sections above.

62. 51.501. (Pl. XXIV.)
Fragment of Thasian marble, left and top edges preserved. Preserved height 0.172, preserved width 0.383, thickness 0.086; height of letters 0.038–040.

Found 10 July 1951, ca. 4.0 west of the pronaos of the "Hieron."

Lehmann, *Hesperia*, 22 (1953), 14 f., and pl. 6c; *Guide*, pp. 33, 64, 78; *Guide²*, pp. 33, 65, 81; A. D'Ors, *Studia et Documenta Historiae et Iuris*, 20 (1954), 418; *SEG*, XII, 395.

> ἀμύητον
> μὴ εἰσιέναι
> εἰς τὸ ἱερόν

The large round lettering suggests a date in the first century B.C. The stone itself was probably a rectangular plaque such as was commonly used for public notices of this sort rather than a stele, though the latter form (envisaged by Lehmann) cannot be excluded. Part of the base of the plaque or stele may also have been found.[1] Lehmann's doubts as to whether the text is complete seem unnecessary.[2] The vacant spaces at the end of lines 1–2 (0.050 in both) show that no more was inscribed on these lines, and in any case the formula is complete in itself.

There seems no reason to doubt that τὸ ἱερόν refers to the building close to which the stone was found. In itself the term might refer either to a building within a τέμενος [3] or to a τέμενος

1. See *Hesperia* (above). Since both a stele and a plaque might have a base, the question of the original form of this inscription is not affected by this. In any case, if the base belongs, the plaque will have been free-standing.

2. Ibid., p. 15: "If the text of the *lex sacra* as preserved is complete—the badly destroyed surface at the right does not allow this conclusion to be drawn with absolute certainty . . ." The stone does not appear to me more worn on the right than elsewhere, and quite certainly never inscribed on that part.

3. Cf. ibid., p. 15, n. 77a. See now Habicht, *Gottmenschentum und griechische Städte* (*Zetemata*, 14, 1956), pp. 141 f.

itself.[4] However, granted that it refers to a specific building, it is one thing to say that a building was called a ἱερόν, and another to maintain that that was the specific name of the building.[5] ἱερόν was not a technical term in the way that, for example, ἀνάκτορον could be,[6] and it could therefore be used of a building, without prejudice to its having another name. Thus in the story of the visit of Cleomenes I to the Athenian Akropolis we read ἤιε ἐς τὸ ἄδυτον τῆς θεοῦ ὡς προσερέων· ἡ δὲ ἱερέη ἐξαναστᾶσα . . . εἶπε· ὦ ξεῖνε Λακεδαιμόνιε, πάλιν χώρει μηδὲ ἔσιθι ἐς τὸ ἱρόν.[7] Thus it cannot be maintained that ἱερόν, used substantively of a single building, means more than "the holy building."

Lehmann sees in this prohibition a confirmation of the excavators' opinion that the building to which it applied, and from which the ἀμύητοι were excluded, was that in which the final stage of initiation, ἐποπτεία, occurred.[8]

Sacral prohibitions usually detail the classes of persons to whom access is denied,[9] but direct prohibitions of this type, restricted to the ἀμύητοι, are rare; however, this is not surprising since we have very little epigraphical evidence from the mystery cults.[10]

4. See, e.g., *OGIS* 92 where instead of the usual τὸν ναὸν καὶ τὸ τέμενος (as, e.g., ibid., 54, 59) we have τὸν ναὸν καὶ τὸ ἱερόν, where (given the regularity of the type of formula) it is, I think, clear that τὸ ἱερόν is used of the precinct. So also in the Ephesian inscription, *AnzWien*, 91 (17), 1954, p. 222, no. 3, —νου ἱδρύσατο | κατὰ πρόσταγμα τοῦ θεοῦ | τὸ ἱερὸ[ν] *vv* καὶ τὸν ναὸν | καὶ τὸ τέμενος ἀνέδειξεν ἱερόν, τοῦ θεοῦ προσ|τάξαντος, κ.τ.λ. clearly τὸ ἱερόν refers to the whole precinct. ἱερόν can also be used in a very wide sense, as for instance at Delos, where it is used of the whole sanctuary (τὸ ἱερὸν τὸ ἐν Δήλωι), and at Eleusis—see Rubensohn, *JDAI*, 70 (1955), 2 ff.—and so, I think it is also used at Samothrace: see next note.
5. On this point, therefore, I disagree with Lehmann, who says (*Hesperia*, loc. cit., p. 15): "If the text of the *lex sacra* as preserved is complete . . . [cf. above, n. 2] the 'New Temple' used for the most sacred rites of the mysteries was specifically called τὸ ἱερόν." I doubt very much, further, whether in *IG*, XII (8), 150, lines 8–10, [ἐμ]πρῆσαι τὸ τέμενος τῶν θεῶν καὶ [εἰσ]πηδήσαντας νύκτωρ ἐπ' ἀδικίαι [καὶ] ἀσεβείαι τοῦ

ἱεροῦ, either Chapouthier, who thought (p. 165) that the ἱερόν was a part of the τέμενος, or Lehmann (p. 15, n. 77a), who thought the Temenos was the complex identified by him as the "central terrace precinct" and the ἱερόν was the Hieron, are right. It is more likely that here τέμενος and ἱερόν are synonymous for the whole Sanctuary: see preceding note.
6. See commentary on **63**, below.
7. Herodotus 5.72.3. What actual building Herodotus had in mind cannot be determined: see J. M. Paton, *The Erechtheum* (Cambridge, Mass., 1927), p. 438 (quoted by Dinsmoor, *AJA*, 51 [1947], 110, no. 4).
8. See the references quoted below, p. 119, n. 2.
9. For the normal *leges sacrae* of this type see the references given by me *BS[R]AA*, 40 (1953), 45, n. 2. The relevant material, in so far as it concerns Asia Minor, may now be found in F. Sokolowski, *Lois Sacrées d'Asie Mineure* (Paris, 1955).
10. One example occurs in *Syll*[3] 736 (Andania), line 36: μηδὲ παρερπέτω μηθεὶς ἀμύητος εἰς τὸν τόπον ὅν κα περιστεμματώσωντι.

63. 38.401. (Pl. XXIV.)

Stele of Thasian marble, lower part (0.040 from top) rough picked. Height 0.96, width 0.515, thickness 0.26; height of letters 0.040. Below and to right of inscription representation.
Found June 1938, near southwest of entrance to inner chamber of the "Anaktoron." [1]

1. Lehmann originally maintained (*AJA*, loc. cit.; cf. Hemberg) that of the two chambers the outer main hall was called the ἀνάκτορον and the inner the *adyton*

(or some similar name). This is uncertain, and Kerényi (*Studi . . . Funaioli*, below) has maintained that the ἀνάκτορον mentioned by Hippolytus (*Ref. haer. omn.*

Lehmann-Hartleben, *AJA*, 43 (1939), 138, and fig. 6; *Guide,* p. 35, fig. 20, pp. 46 f., 79 ff. (*Guide*[2], pp. 82 f.); Hemberg, pp. 112–13; Kerényi, *Unwillkürliche Kunstreisen,* p. 110; idem, *Symbolae Osloenses,* 31 (1955), 150–51; idem, in *Studi in onore di Gino Funaioli* (Rome, 1955), pp. 161–62.

Deorum·sacra
qui non accepe-
runt.non intrant.
ἀμύητον μὴ εἰ-
5   σιέναι

The inscription is not easy to date, since neither the Latin nor the Greek hand has very close parallels at Samothrace. The rather soft and flowing Latin hand in some ways resembles that of **36** (of A.D. 19) and **40** (undated). The Greek resembles, in a general way, **46** and **47** of the early second century A.D. Thus a date in the first or early second century A.D. is not unlikely. As explained by L-H in his preliminary publication, the inscription was found face downward in a fallen position at the entrance to the inner chamber of the "Anaktoron." Its text shows that entrance to the inner chamber was permitted only to the μεμυημένοι or μύσται and that consequently a further stage of initiation, probably the τελέτη, occurred there.[2]

Below the inscription is a symbol, presumably apotropaic in purpose, which L-H identified as the κηρύκειον of Hermes-Kadmilos, with two flanking snakes symbolizing the διφυεῖς Κάβειροι.[3]

In this inscription it is clear that *deorum sacra qui acceperunt* are the μύσται. In **53** above, in the phrase *mystae pii sacra acceperunt,* the verbal clause is also epexegetic. If rightly restored in *IG,* XII (8), 207, it again plays no significant role. No Greek verbal equivalent (e.g., τῆς τελετῆς μετεῖχον) is found in the Samothracian lists, though such phrases are frequent in references to initiation in literature.

5.8.9–10, Turchi, *Fontes Historiae Mysteriorum Aevi Hellenistici* [Rome, 1923], no. 174) was the inner room, and the outer main hall the τελεστήριον (see above Vol. 1, **147**). This problem, which is not relevant here since the word ἀνάκτορον does not occur in the inscription, will be discussed by Lehmann in a later volume of this publication.

2. See Lehmann, *Hesperia,* 22 (1953), 14–15; *Guide,* pp. 32 ff. against his earlier views in *AJA,* loc. cit., formulated before the excavation of the building

previously called the "New Temple," and the discovery of **62**, from the wording of which Lehmann infers that the epopteia took place in the "Hieron" (cf. also already *AJA,* 45 [1941], 577, n. 4).

3. "The two snakes symbolize the διφυεῖς Κάβειροι who are mentioned in an orphic hymn as assuming the form of snakes." The reference is to *Hymn. Orph.* 39 (Quandt), lines 5–8, where the Corybant is described as θεὸν διφυῆ. The inverted snakes appear with the stars of the Dioscuri on a silver ring discovered in Samothrace: see *AJA,* 44 (1940), 355, fig. 39.

I know of no other *lex sacra* which is bilingual in Greek and Roman. This text emphasizes very graphically the popularity of the Samothracian cult among Romans.[4]

4. See above, Introduction, p. 17. Nock, *AJA,* 45 (1941), 577, emphasizes the same point.

64. 53.683. (Pl. XXV.)

Fragment of stele of local limestone, right edge with sunk margin preserved. Preserved height 0.32, preserved width 0.21, thickness 0.09; height of letters 0.012, omicron ca. 0.007.

Found 1937. (For the history of the stone see *Hesperia*, 24 [1955], 100, n. 18.)

Lehmann, *Archaeology,* 6 (1953), 33–34, and pl.; idem, *Hesperia,* 24 (1955) 100, no. 40 (and pl. 40); cf. G. Bonfante, ibid., pp. 101 ff.; Lehmann, *Guide,* p. 96, fig. 48, and p. 97 (*Guide²*, pp. 100, 102); Georgiev, *Trakiiskiat Esik* (subtitle, *La langue thrace*) (Sofia, 1957), pp. 37 ff. and fig. 26 (see below, n. 2).

```
          – – – – – – – – – – –
   ————————————ΛΕΓ⊙
   ————————————Ɔ ΔΑ⊙ΗΤΟ
   ————————————ΥΕΛΑ
   ————————————ΒΛ⊙ ⟨ΕΝ⊙
 5 ————————————ṚΑΙΑΝΕ
   ————————————⊙ ⋀ΒΕΚΑ
   ————————————⊙ΛΕΙΤΡΑ
   ————————————ΝΤ⊙ΛΑ
            spat.0.025
   ————————————ΨΕΝΙ
10 ————————————⊙Ν⊙⟨
          – – – – – – – – – – –
```

The upper part of the stone is very worn. I originally thought that there were very faint traces three lines above line 1, visible with the aid of charcoal, and Lehmann also records an E at the end of a line, above the present line 1, but repeated re-examination of the stone has ultimately convinced me that these marks are accidental, if not illusory.

Line 4. Lehmann read E before B, but I see only a vertical stroke, too close to the beta to be epsilon.

Line 6. Lehmann prints a stop in the center before B, and Bonfante, pp. 105–106, develops the linguistic possibilities of BEKA. I am not sure that the mark is deliberate, but there is an undoubted *vac.* before the B.

Line 9. Lehmann read E, before Ψ, but I could not see it. He also read the last letter as T, but it is clearly Ι. Lehmann says, "Lines 10 and 11 could belong to a Greek postscript" (for

Bonfante, ibid., this has become the last *three* lines) —but, other considerations apart, the identity of the hand of the last two lines with that of the preceding lines makes this unlikely.

The lettering is not easy to date. Judging by the normal epigraphical practice of a Greek city-state, one would think of the earlier part, or the middle, of the fourth century. It is certainly earlier than that of **1**.

This is the main text of the non-Greek language in Greek characters, of which other examples exist on the graffiti.[1] The language itself has been studied by G. Bonfante,[2] and I am not competent to pursue the matter.

The stone was found on the island,[3] is local limestone,[4] and was therefore no doubt inscribed on the island. However, the inhabitants of the city in historic times naturally spoke Greek; so the inscription cannot be regarded as a normal document from there. It is possible that the stone is witness to some remote community on the island, but this does not seem likely for habitable areas on Samothrace are few. Alternately, it may emanate from a non-Greek community elsewhere, for instance on the Thracian mainland in which case it might either commemorate a visit to the Sanctuary, or its presence might be purely fortuitous. The most likely explanation, however, is that the inscription is in fact Samothracian, and is an example of that pre-Greek language which, Diodorus records, survived as a ritual language into the Hellenistic or Roman period.[5] If so, then the stone will have come from the Sanctuary, not from the town.

The similarity of terminations in many of the lines suggests that the words may be proper names, and the inscription a list of theoroi or initiates.[6]

1. They are all published by Lehmann, *Hesperia*, 24 (1955), 93–100, below, pt. II, pp. 45 ff.
2. Bonfante, *Hesperia*, 24 (1955), 101–9. Still more recently the text has been republished and studied by Georgiev, loc. cit., who regards the language of the document as Greek, and suggests that it records thanks for the cure of a cough.
3. For the circumstances of its discovery see Lehmann, ibid., p. 100, n. 16.
4. Lehmann says, "The stone material is unusual and was no longer in use after the fourth century." The only other inscribed example of this limestone is **1**, which also belongs to the fourth century: see below,

pt. II, p. 10.
5. See Lehmann, loc. cit. Diodorus 5.47.3: ἐσχήκασι δὲ παλαιὰν ἰδίαν διάλεκτον οἱ αὐτόχθονες, ἧς πολλὰ ἐν ταῖς θυσίαις μέχρι τοῦ νῦν τηρεῖται (see Vol. 1, **32**). μέχρι τοῦ νῦν may] of course derive from Diodorus' source (cf. Schwartz, *RE*, s.v. *Diodorus* (38), col. 678).
6. Lehmann, p. 100 (followed by Bonfante, ibid., p. 106) suggests that "the curious, indented ending of the lines gives the impression that we may have to do with a poem, possibly a hymn or prayer." But the indentation does not appear to be more than is usually found in lists of names (or pairs of names) of differing lengths.

65. (a) 51.716, (b) 51.717. (Pl. XXV.)

Two non-joining fragments of a marble plaque (?), broken on all sides. (a) Preserved height 0.056, preserved width 0.185, preserved thickness 0.055. (b) Preserved height 0.10, preserved width 0.13, preserved thickness 0.06; height of letters: (a) 0.020.

Found 19 July 1951, within the "Altar Court," close to the north wall.

Lehmann, *Hesperia*, 22 (1953), 19–20.

(a) ——————δαιος Κ̣

(b) ——————υρων

Fragment (a) of this inscription bears the same letters as fragment (a) of **9** (the apex of the initial letter apart). As noted in the commentary to **9**, these two fragments were regarded by Lehmann as bearing what survives of an inscription containing exactly the same words as **9**, and inscribed on the main altar within the "Altar Court." [1] At the suggestion of G. Daux, Lehmann supplied in fragment (b) of the present inscription [– ἀπὸ λαφ]ύρων, and correspondingly restored the same phrase in **9**. Now that good grounds exist for supposing that the dedicatory inscription of **9** is shorter than had previously been supposed (see above, p. 42), and that it contained only the simplest dedicatory formula, in which there is no room for the expression ἀπὸ λαφύρων, there is no need to consider further the possibility of a repetition of the inscription here. The question what the present inscription is, and where it was engraved, remains. In themselves the two fragments tell us nothing save that the inscription was on a flat, and not a convex, surface such as the body of a round altar. However, it is certain that it was not the main dedicatory inscription on the main altar of the court, as Lehmann had supposed when he believed it to be a duplicate dedication. Consideration of the relative dimensions of the altar and the inscription enable us to exclude this possibility. The length of the altar can be calculated, as Mr. Spittle tells me, at about 12.00 m. Yet the letters of the inscription, where they are preserved to their full height – in (a) – are only 0.020. That such a small inscription could not form the main dedication of so large a structure is self-evident. Confirmation, if needed, is provided by the dimensions of another altar of about the same size. The altar of the sanctuary of Demeter at Pergamon, dedicated by Philetairos and Eumenes, was 8.60 m. long and 4.50 m. wide, and the letters of the dedicatory inscription were 0.075 high, as might be expected.[2] Thus, quite apart from the fact that it did not contain a duplicate text of the architraval inscription, we may be sure on this ground that this inscription was not the dedicatory inscription engraved on the main altar. Nevertheless, the lettering which seems to be unapicated (though the surface is very worn), the identity of the name in (a) with the name in **9**, and the discovery of the fragments within the "Altar Court" show that a very close connection exists between **9** and **65**. Evidently the present inscription was inscribed on some small object, or a small area of a larger object, within the shrine. In this connection the supplement [– ἀπὸ λαφ]ύρων becomes very persuasive in the light of the analogy provided by the series of χαριστήρια inscribed on the great bathron of the precinct of Athena at Pergamon.[3] There the various victories of Attalus I

1. *Hesperia* (above), p. 19: "They preserve parts of what evidently is a replica of the façade dedication in letters of much smaller size (height 0.02 m.) but of the same style." I would in any case question whether they are "of the same style," but the size of the lettering is

so different that I should not expect them to be.
2. See *AM*, 35 (1910), 437 ff., nos. 22 and 23, and ibid., pp. 376–77.
3. Fränkel, *Die Inschriften von Pergamon* (2 vols., Berlin, 1890–95), 22–28 (= *OGIS* 273–79). The

were recorded, in similar language, in succession along the face of the bathron. In the same manner, Adaios may have commemorated one or several specific victories within his altar court, either on the altar itself or on a bathron or on individual plaques of the type most familiar from Ptolemaic Egypt.⁴ The size of the letters would suit any such arrangement, and the supplement [– ἀπὸ λαφ]ύρων, which is found so used in two dedications,⁵ one Attalid and one Rhodian, would be very suitable in this context.

However, Adaios' connection with military matters is conjectural, and there are other possibilities. In particular, since the dedication of the "Altar Court" was to the θεοὶ μεγάλοι, there is no difficulty in supposing that Adaios erected inside it a subsidiary monument, or monuments, to associated deities.⁶ In this connection the supplement ['Α]δαῖος Κ[ορράγου τὸν βωμὸν τῶν Διοσκο]ύρων——— immediately suggests itself, in view of the close connection, if not identity, of the Dioscuri with the θεοὶ μεγάλοι.⁷ It would be unwise to choose between these two hypotheses and the different types of restoration to which they lead.

monument is reconstructed in *Inschr. Perg.*, loc. cit. 21 (= 273) is the dedicatory inscription embracing the entire monument. Cf. also ibid., *33–37* for a similar series.

4. For examples of Ptolemaic plaques see Breccia, *Iscrizioni*, pls. I–XI, and the brief discussion of the different types in *JEA*, 38 (1952), 66–67, with references to other instances. For royal dedications on such a plaque see *OGIS* 77; Breccia, op. cit., 13 (seemingly). 5. *Inschr. Perg.* 60 (Michel 1218); *IG*, XI (4), 1135 (Durrbach, *Choix*, 40), both already adduced in this

context by Lehmann, *Hesperia*, loc. cit., p. 20, n. 99. In the Pergamene dedications and elsewhere such phrases as ἀπὸ τῶν κατὰ πόλεμον ἀγώνων, ἀπὸ τῶν πολεμίων are more frequent than ἀπὸ λαφύρων. 6. See the examples of altars, etc., dedicated to deities within the sanctuaries of other deities, collected by Nock, *HTR*, 41 (1930), 44 ff. 7. See Hemberg, pp. 98–99. For the prevalence of the form Διόσκουροι see G. Restelli, *RFIC*, 79 (1951), 246–57. For the form Διόσκοροι, which is very common in the Hellenistic age, see ibid., p. 251, n. 2, and Chapouthier, p. 105, n. 6.

66. 54.393. (Pl. XXV.)

Upper portion of plaque of Thasian marble, with molding. Preserved height 0.15, preserved width 0.13, preserved thickness 0.060; height of letters 0.016–018.

Found 25 July 1954, in "accumulation of shapeless marbles on the slope of the hill to the east of the Central Terrace precinct" (Expedition diary).

Unpublished.

βασιλ————————
/ Λ——————————

– – – – – – – –

The lettering is probably of the third or early second century B.C. It is impossible to determine the nature of the document. The absence of ἐπί at the beginning of line 1 suggests that the reference is not to an eponym but to a sovereign.

There are traces of letters in line 2: at the beginning, an oblique stroke above the line ', the angle of which is too steep to be a sigma, and after this the clear top of an apex ^ ; beyond this the tops of two vertical strokes close together, the first probably iota.

67. 39.24. (Pl. XXVI.)

Top part of stele of Thasian marble, with pediment, with antefix crowning stele, right and upper parts missing. Preserved height 0.26, width 0.24, thickness 0.07; height of letters 0.012–013, omicron 0.009.

     Given to the museum by Mr. Makras, 20 June 1939.
     Unpublished.

Διονυσόδωρος
Μητρώνακτος

A funerary stele, probably of the third or early second century B.C.

     Metronax is a frequent name at Samothrace: cf. *IG*, XII (8), Index, s.v.

68. 57.854. (Pl. XXVI.)

Stele of Thasian marble with molding, broken diagonally below. Preserved height 0.44, width 0.44–46, thickness 0.070–080; height of letters 0.017–020.

     Found 29 May 1957, in southern necropolis, leaning against porphyry slab-tomb, S.M. 60B.[1]

     Unpublished.

Ε̣ὐθ[υ]κλείδης
᾿Αγαθώνακτος

The hand, which is elegant, suggests a date in the second century B.C. The first part of the name in -κλείδης is not certain: Π̣υθ[ο]κλείδης is possible.

1. **68** and **69** were found in excavations by Mrs. E. Dusenbery and Mr. A. Vavritsas, to both of whom I am grateful for permission to include the pieces in this publication.

69. 57.855. (Pl. XXVI.)

Pedimental stele of Thasian marble, complete except for acroteria, small portion at bottom right corner and tang, round object in center of tympanon. Preserved height 0.60, width 0.455–485, thickness 0.10; height of letters: (a) 0.025–030; (b) 0.012–015.

     Found 6 June 1957, in sepulchral building in southern necropolis, placed against wall of building.

     Unpublished.

(a) *original inscription:*

...⁶...ων

Διννίου, φύσει δὲ

Σείρωνος,

χαῖρε

(b) *later inscription, inscribed over first line of* (a):

Μητροκλῆα τὴν μητέρα

Στρατονείκην

(a) *Line 1.* The name of the person originally commemorated is no longer legible under-neath the first line of (b) which has been so inscribed as to obliterate almost all traces of the name except the final -ων, which is clear: —κρῶν or —φρῶν seems possible.

Line 2. After Διννίου there is a space of five letters before δέ. φύσει (not, in spite of appearances, φύσιν) is certain.

Line 3. The initial sigma is certain. Σείρων, a rare name, apparently occurs also on a Samothracian coin.[1]

(a) is apparently of Hellenistic date (ii / i B.C.), while (b) is rather crude, and there-fore more difficult to date, but a date in the latter part of the first century B.C. or the first century A.D. seems likely. Probably, then, about three generations elapsed between use and re-use of the stele.

1. *IG,* XII (8), p. 41.

70. 38.39. (Pl. XXVI.)

Fragment of base or altar of Island marble with molding below and two holes in upper sur-face: a dowel hole (0.043 long × 0.046 wide, ca. 0.020 deep) and a clamp hole for a pi-shaped clamp near the preserved edge (0.074 × 0.025, ca. 0.056 deep) broken to left. Height 0.65, preserved width 0.64, thickness 0.16; height of letters 0.025–035, omicron 0.015.

Said to have been found by Salač near the road cut from the "Ruinenviereck."

Unpublished.

[————(?)]σίννων 'Ανδρονίκ[ου]

The dowel hole on the upper surface indicates that there was another slab above, doubtless with an upper molding corresponding to the lower, and the clamp hole at the right end indicates that another block joined on at the end. The stone is not complete to the left, and there may have been a further block or blocks on this side. Evidently the monument was far larger than the surviving piece; the nature of the monument, and the inscription, must remain uncertain. The first name is probably complete, since names in Σιυυ- are common.[1]

1. See the instances in Pape-Benseler. They do not seem to have any particular regional distribution. I   do not recall having come across the form Σίυυων.

71. 49.90. (Pl. XXVII.)

Fragment of building block of Thasian marble, broken above, below, and at left. Preserved height 0.22, preserved width 0.155, preserved thickness 0.09; height of letters 0.010.

    Found 18 June 1949, on surface, southwest of the "Arsinoeion."

    Unpublished.

- - - -

——ρεσ.

spat.0.042

[—?]ευστε

spat.0.040

- - - -

The inscription is evidently Imperial: the sigma has the square form, Ϲ.

    Line 2. [— βασιλ]ευϛ τε — : or, e.g., εὐστέ|[φανος]?

    The space between lines 1 and 2 is unexpectedly large.

72. 56.64. (Pl. XXVII.)

Fragment of epistyle block of Thasian marble, broken at left, above, and below. Anathyrosis at right end; end of clamp hole preserved on upper surface near end. Preserved height 0.27 (inscribed fascia 0.165), preserved width 0.81 (inscribed fascia 0.39), preserved thickness 0.77; height of letter 0.10.

    Found 29 July 1956, in the river bed opposite the northern end of the "Anaktoron."

    Unpublished.

————ϛ *vac.*

This is evidently the last letter of a dedicatory inscription on an epistyle. Lehmann conjectures (*per ep.*) that it may be the last letter of the architraval inscription *IG*, XII (8), 229, which Salviat has seen to be the dedicatory inscription of the Ionic building on the western hill of the Sanctuary, known in earlier days as "Le Temple Ionique," and called by Chapouthier "Le Temple des Cabires."[1] The majuscule copy of this inscription is very

1. See *BCH*, 81 (1957), 609.

formal,[2] but it points to a good Hellenistic date, with which this sigma agrees. In addition, the width given for the fascia of 229, 0.170, is virtually identical with that of our fragment, the width of which, in its present damaged state, is ca. 0.158. Further, the place of discovery is also suitable, since 229 was found on the hill above the river bed, in the vicinity of the building. The only possible argument against the identification might be found in the size of the letter. The letters of 229 were said by Blau and Schlottmann[3] to be "fünfzöllige," while this sigma measures 0.10, i.e., just under four inches. This objection clearly cannot be regarded as decisive, and the positive reasons for the identification are extremely strong. It is remarkable that a woman of private status should have dedicated a structure in the Sanctuary in the third century when all other buildings were apparently dedicated by kings and other prominent persons. Her identity is wholly unknown.[4]

2. Conze, *Reise auf den Inseln des Thrakischen Meeres* (Hannover, 1860), p. 60; *S,II*, p. 102.
3. *Berl. Ber.* (1855), p. 618.
4. Conze, *S,II*, p. 112, n. 1, suggested that the —νδρου Μιλησία of *IG*, XII (8), 229, should be identified with the Εἰρήνη Μενάνδρου Μιλησία of the Eleusinian tombstone, *IG*, II², 9533, and added: "Die Stifterin des immerhin kostspieligen marmoren Säulenbaues von Samothrake wird schwerlich eine gewöhnliche Privatperson gewesen sein. Da sie den Namen ihres Mannes nicht angibt, wird man eine vielleicht einem Diadochen nahestehende Hetaire in ihr vermuthen dürfen." Rubensohn, pp. 225–26, rejects the identification, and it has nothing to recommend it (cf. also Fredrich, *IG*, XII [8], 229: "Quae de hac femina suspicati sunt; *Untersuchungen* II, 112, 1, nihili sunt").

73. 51.665. (Pl. XXVII.)

Fragment of Thasian marble, broken on all sides. Preserved height 0.040, preserved width 0.145, preserved thickness 0.15; height of letters 0.015.

Found 14 July 1951, east of, and near, the pronaos of the "Hieron."

Unpublished.

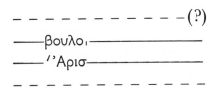

The lettering, probably of the second century B.C., resembles that of **4**. There is the base of a vertical letter at the end of line 1, and the tip of a right oblique stroke to the left of the alpha in line 2. Both are probably the remains of upsilon. The letters are large and perhaps form part of an eponymous date:

[ἐπὶ βασιλέως————]βούλου
[το]ῦ Ἀρισ[τ—].

74. 52.3. (Pl. XXVI.)

Fragment of Thasian marble broken on all sides (except right?). Preserved height 0.12, preserved width 0.105, preserved thickness 0.05; height of letters 0.015–020.

Found 1952, in the neighborhood of the Genoese Towers.

Unpublished.

$$\begin{array}{r} - \; - \; - \; - \; - \; - \; - \; - \\ \text{———————πη} \\ \text{———————της} \\ \text{—————Διον-} \\ \text{——————τ——} \\ - \; - \; - \; - \; - \; - \; - \end{array}$$

Probably Hellenistic.

Line 2 could be restored as [μύσ]της or [ἐπόπ]της, but obviously there are other possibilities.

75. 51.678. (Pl. XXVII.)

Fragment of Thasian marble, broken on all sides except right. Preserved height 0.09, preserved width 0.144, preserved thickness 0.102; height of letters 0.012–015.

Found 18 July 1951, in the west part of the "Altar Court."

Unpublished.

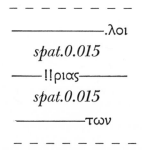

$$\begin{array}{c} - \; - \; - \; - \; - \; - \; - \\ \text{——————.λοι} \\ spat.0.015 \\ \text{——!!ριας———} \\ spat.0.015 \\ \text{—————των} \\ - \; - \; - \; - \; - \; - \; - \end{array}$$

Line 1. The labda is certain, and delta (cf. ἀοιδοί in *IG*, XII [8], 185, and perhaps 203) not possible. Before it there are traces of a letter.

Line 2. The second letter is apparently iota. The letter before that might conceivably be beta, but the circular mark may be accidental. I cannot make anything of the group as a whole.

This is a puzzling fragment, the hand of which appears to have been influenced by Latin forms. It is probably of the second or third century A.D. It may be a fragment of a list of initiates though the three lines are very widely spaced for such a list.

76. 39.1138. (Pl. XXVIII.)

Fragment of Thasian marble, broken on left and right. Preserved height 0.105, preserved width 0.41, preserved thickness 0.138; height of letters 0.065.

From Chora.

Unpublished.

————υτῳ καὶ ἰδ————

— — — — — — — — — — — ?

The letters are evidently of the late Imperial period. The size of the surviving letters, as well as their natural interpretation, might seem to indicate a dedicatory inscription of some sort, but, as Lehmann points out to me, the stone is probably too small to have formed part of the architrave of a building. He suggests a string course in the wall of a building. The stone appears to be complete above and below, and it is difficult to see how a full sentence in letters of these proportions can have been inscribed on one line unless it was considerably longer than an architrave. No restoration is worth attempting.[1]

1. For instance, ἀδ]ύτῳ and α]ὐτῷ are equally possible.

77. 48.504. (Pl. XXVII.)

Fragment of cylindrical altar (?) of Thasian marble, molding below. Preserved height 0.07, preserved width 0.13, thickness 0.035; height of letters (kappa) 0.023.

Found 25 July 1948, in the collapsed debris of the central section of the terrace wall east of the "Arsinoeion."

Unpublished.

\ κ.υ\ι\

I can make nothing of these letters.

78. (a) 50.109, (b) 50.278. (Pl. XXVIII.)

(a) Fragment of Thasian marble evidently recut for use as paving slab, left and bottom edge preserved. Preserved height 0.07, preserved width 0.22, preserved thickness 0.14; preserved height of letters 0.010.

Found 28 June 1950, slightly north of the "Hieron."

(b) Fragment of Thasian marble, top edge preserved. Preserved height 0.060, preserved width 0.165, preserved thickness 0.13; preserved height of letters (το in (b)) 0.035.

Found 4 July 1950, in the same spot as the preceding.

Unpublished.

(a) ⌡1 ˥ʀ—˧ 1 1 11 1

(b) ˥ ʌ ⊤(

Imperial.

The two fragments probably form part of the same inscription: the stones are of almost precisely the same dimensions, and though the height of the letters cannot be determined, their apicated terminals are extremely similar. The two pieces, moreover, were found in the same spot. However, they do not join.

(a) begins, as it now stands, with ΟΛ or ΘΑ, followed by sigma and a series of vertical strokes which look most like the lower parts of ΙΠΠ on a slightly smaller scale than the preceding letters. The part of an oblique stroke which meets the right vertical stroke of the second pi is evidently not part of the main stroke of the letter and may be disregarded.

(b) consists of ΑΤΟ preceded by a letter containing a circular element. This is evidently not omicron, to judge from the existing omicron, and is not likely to be theta either. It is thus probably part of either a beta or a rho. The following letter will therefore be alpha, and not delta or labda.

(a) may be part of a proper name. Θᾳϲιππ– is perhaps the most likely, though it is a new compound.[1] (b) is perhaps part of another name, [Στ]ρατο[κλ–]. Θᾳϲιππ[ος | Στ]ρατο-[κλέους] would thus be possible, or alternatively ——Θαϲ Ἱππ[ο|κ]ράτο[υς]. [ἄ]βατο[ν] is tempting for (b), but rash, and irreconcilable with (a) in any apparent way. The letters are very large, and do not suggest a funerary monument.

1. Names in -ιππος are, as is well known, predominantly Eretrian (see Bechtel, *Hermes*, 35 [1900], 326–31), but this name does not occur among the many instances in *IG*, XII (9) and *IG*, XII, Suppl.

79. 49.439 and 49.628. (Pl. XXVII.)

Two joining fragments, forming top left part of block of Thasian marble. Preserved height 0.335, preserved width 0.385, thickness 0.105; height of letters 0.035–040.

From Chora, 5 July 1949.

Unpublished.

$$\kappa\alpha\acute{\iota} \begin{Bmatrix} \delta \\ \tau \end{Bmatrix} \tau\acute{o}\delta' \ \grave{\alpha}\nu[\acute{\epsilon}\kappa\epsilon]\text{-}$$

νισε τὸ μέρος ——

Ἀσκάμης ὅρον ——

εἰς φυλᾳ ————

. . . ————

– – – – – – – –

This inscription, of the late Byzantine age,[1] is not without its difficulties. The two fragments evidently join, even though there is a surprisingly wide space between the delta at the beginning of the right half of the first line and the break. In line 1 there is a small delta carved above the first tau. Of the two taus one is presumably carved by error. At the end of the line and the beginning of line 2 ἀν[εκέ]|νισε (= ἀν[εκαί]νισε) I owe to Sir William Calder. Evidently some letters are missing at the end of line 1 and perhaps also at the end of lines 2 and 3, though there is a blank space in which a letter could have been inscribed between the last letter of line 3 and the edge. Between lines 1 and 2 are traces of other small letters. Their significance is not clear, nor indeed is it certain whether they form part of the main original inscription: a beta and a very clear theta are visible.

Line 3. Toward the end of the name, mu and eta are apparently in ligature.

Line 5. There are traces of the upper apex of a triangular letter (alpha or delta) at the beginning, followed perhaps by a sigma: Ἀσ—— is possible.

The stone seems to commemorate the restoration of the limits of some property. φυλα may perhaps be a place name, fragmentary or complete.

Accents are added on καί and μέρος and on the first word of line 3, a smooth breathing on εἰς in line 4, and an apostrophus above the delta of τόδ'.

1. For the hand cf. Conze, *Reise Thrak. Inseln*, pl. iii, no. 10, and p. 56 (Samothrace, not in *IG*, XII [8]); *BCH*, 37 (1913), p. 144, no. 50 (Maroneia): Kalinka, *Antike Denkmäler*, 366 (Sofia); Keil and von Premerstein, *Bericht über eine Reise in Lydien und der südlichen Aiolis* (*DenkschrWien*, 53 [2], 1910), 105; *Dritte Reise*, 34 (a.d. 1217); *JÖAI*, 23 (1926), Beibl., cols. 167–68, no. 110 (Eregli, Thrace).

80. 51.727. (Pl. XXVIII.)

Fragment of Thasian marble, broken on all sides. Preserved height 0.06, preserved width 0.05, preserved thickness 0.013; height of letter as preserved 0.030 (total height ca. 0.040).

Found 19 July 1951, "in earth carried off of wagons from [Nike-] precinct excavation area" (Expedition diary).

Unpublished.

Ͱ

There is some roughness in the execution of the letter.

81. 50.461. (Pl. XXVIII.)

Fragment of Thasian marble. Preserved height 0.065, preserved width 0.95, preserved thickness 0.085; height of letter (as preserved) 0.045.

Found 13 July 1950, on the Central Terrace.

Unpublished.

Fragment of a letter ⟍ , ⟨ , or ⟩ . There is an unmistakable curve to the stroke, which is roughly cut.

82. *39.733.* (Pl. XXVIII.)

Right part of rectangular plaque, Pentelic (?) marble, bearing tabula ansata in relief. Preserved height 0.17, preserved width 0.18, thickness 0.066; height of letters: line 1, ca. 0.010; line 2, ca. 0.007–010.

Found 31 July 1939, near the south wall of the "Anaktoron."

Lehmann, *Hesperia,* 20 (1951), 30, and pl. 18*e* (incorrect reading of B. Kallipolites); mentioned, Fraser and Rönne, *Boeotian and West Greek Tombstones* (Lund, 1957), p. 181, n. 39.

A·Balto

spat.0.030

traces of two or three letters, Latin or Greek: possibly ạị pịị *or* MḤ?

The reading of B. Kallipolites, ABATON, given by Lehmann, is impossible, and the conclusion there drawn from that reading must be abandoned.[1]

The letters in line 1, though very thinly scratched, are clear. Since there is a stop after *A,* we presumably have to regard Baltus as a cognomen.[2] I doubt very much whether the inscription and the tabula ansata are contemporary. The well-carved tabula ansata is not likely to have been adorned with such a roughly scratched, unsymmetrically placed, Latin inscription. On the other hand, uninscribed tabulae ansatae, used as a decoration, are not unknown in the Hellenistic period.[3] Probably the inscription was scratched at a considerably later date by some visitor who thought it a good surface for this purpose. The tabula ansata is of the shape characteristic of the Hellenistic age.[4]

1. As also the conclusion of Kerényi, *Studi in onore di G. Funaioli,* p. 162, who, however, wisely adds "falls richtig gelesen."
2. I have not encountered it elsewhere. *Balbo* is not possible.
3. See the instances from Priene and Delos quoted in Fraser and Rönne, *Boeotian and West Greek Tombstones,* pp. 181–82.
4. See ibid. So already Lehmann, loc. cit.

83. (a) *51.627,* (b) *51.628.* (Pl. XXIX.)

Two gilt bronze letters. (a) Height 0.082; (b) height 0.076.

Found 1951, in the "Hall of Votive Gifts."[1]

Lehmann, *Hesperia,* 22 (1953), 8–9, pl. IV, figs. *a–b; Guide,* pp. 67, 90; *Guide²,* pp. 70, 94.

1. A large section of one bar of another gilded bronze letter (accession number 53.64) exists, found west of the "Anaktoron" in 1953. It is of slightly different size and thickness from the two letters noted above, and presumably is from another building.

132

(a) Υ   (b) |

These bronze letters have pegs for insertion on the rear surface. They were evidently inserted in the façade of the "Hall of Votive Gifts." Lehmann quotes other instances of this practice, at Adalia and Corinth, and suggests that relief-letters on stone may represent such bronze letters. I have discussed relief-letters and tabulae ansatae elsewhere,[2] and need say here only that though there is probably a connection between relief-letters in stone and bronze models, it does not seem to me likely that such loose bronze letters should have been the model for relief-letters. On chronological grounds this is improbable, since relief-letters appear to be the earlier phenomenon.[3]

2. Fraser and Rönne, op. cit., pp. 155 ff. and 176 ff., where further examples of loose bronze letters are given.
3. The known instances of loose bronze letters are all Imperial, while relief-letters in stone go back at least to the third century: see Fraser and Rönne, pp. 155–56, 171 ff. Lehmann (*per ep.*) says that there is no reason why such applied letters should not be earlier, and suggests that the upsilon, (a), is pre-Imperial. I am not willing to offer a date for it myself.

84. 56.3 (Pl. XXIX.)
Block of brown limestone, broken on all sides. Preserved height 0.22, preserved width 0.235, thickness 0.33; height of letter 0.15.

Found 1951, in the region of the river bed, near the Theater.

Unpublished.

On front face:

A

Probably complete in itself. The block is perhaps connected with the Theater in some way.

85. (a) 48.137, (b) 48.360. (Pl. XXIX.)
Two fragments of lamps of Thasian marble, inscribed on the rim. Diameter 0.178, height 0.072, rim 0.02 wide.

Found 1948 – (a) 10 July and (b) 26 July – in the inner fill of the "Arsinoeion." Lehmann, *Hesperia*, 19 (1950), 15, and pls. 10, 26 ((a) only).

(a)   θε[οῖς/ῶν]
(b)   [θ]ε[οῖς/ῶν]

The lettering of these two fragments suggests a fourth- or early third-century date.[1] Since they were in the inner fill of the "Arsinoeion," they are inevitably earlier than the foundation of that building (before 281 B.C.).[2] The reading θε[οῖς] would indicate that the lamps were dedicated, probably after use in a ceremony, but Lehmann has suggested (*per ep.*) that they are too heavy for this purpose, that they were "part of the equipment of cult buildings," and that we should consequently read θε[ῶν]. One cannot be certain, but I am inclined to prefer the dative.[3]

1. Lehmann, *Hesperia*, 19 (1950), 15, regarded the lamps as belonging to the sixth century, but ibid., 24 (1955), 95, n. 11, he adopts a later date on account of the lettering, on the advice of G. Daux. Cf. *Guide*, pp. 92–93; *Guide*[2], p. 97.

2. See above, pp. 5–6.

3. See below, pt. II, Index 6, s.v. *lamps* for clay lamps with inscriptions found in Samothrace.

86. (Pl. XXIX.)

Cut on block in the western corner of the outer terrace of the "Temenos." Height of letters 0.038–040.

Lehmann, *Hesperia*, 20 (1951), 13 and pls. 4 f.

```
        Γ
      Γ | |
```

The wall on which the letters are carved was later screened by a limestone wall when the building was complete. They are therefore earlier than the completion of the "Temenos," in the middle of the fourth century.[1]

1. See *Hesperia*, 21 (1952), 24, and below, pt. II, p. 103.

87. No number.

"Hieron" block, 714. Marble threshold, presumably from one of the lateral doors of the "Hieron." Height of letters 0.020.

Now in the Marble field above the terrace wall to the south of the building.

Unpublished.

$$ἐδα——$$

This lettering is undistinguished, and apparently Hellenistic. The inscription is evidently complete and contains an instruction referring to the level of the ground around the blocks: ἐδα(φ —), followed by a horizontal line indicating the level.

88. 54.138.

Fragment of Lartian marble, broken on all sides. Preserved height 0.13, preserved width 0.060, preserved thickness 0.08; height of letter unknown.[1]

Found 9 July 1954, near the northwest corner of the Nike-precinct retaining wall; probably from the old excavation dump. Now in the Louvre, Paris.

Unpublished.

Probably the left angle of a delta.

The marble indicates that the fragment probably belonged to the Nike monument. The irregular formation of the letter suggests that it is a mason's mark rather than part of a monumental inscription.

1. Unfortunately the piece was not available when I was in the Louvre in September 1957, so I have been unable to record the height of the letter which I omitted to note in 1954.

89. 52.281.

Fragment of Thasian marble broken on all sides. Preserved height 0.06, preserved width 0.040, preserved thickness 0.047; preserved height of letter 0.040.

Found 14 July 1952, in Austrian dump, near the Nike precinct.

Unpublished.

A mason's mark?

90. No number.

Fragment of wall block of the "Arsinoeion" inscribed on outer face. Preserved height 0.64, preserved width 1.03, thickness 0.42; inscription 0.16 from top; height of letters 0.03.

Unpublished.

| εας

There is a possible trace of a vertical letter rather more than one letter space to the left of the epsilon, so the inscription may not be complete. In any case the group is strange, and may be part of a proper name carved at a later date, e.g., [Δη]μέας, though it is unusually deeply carved for a casual graffito.

91. 56.81. (Pl. XXIX.)

Slab of Thasian (?) marble broken on all sides save the upper. On upper, preserved side, clamp hole at right end. On back, diagonally placed dowel hole, 0.117 square, 0.016 deep. Preserved height 0.175, preserved width 0.186, preserved thickness 0.046; oblique stroke 0.10, horizontal 0.070.

Found 24 July 1956, in the fill of the late, antique terrace wall, to the east of the "Arsinoeion."

Unpublished.

The presence of the clamp hole, as Lehmann points out (*per ep.*), shows that the preserved surface is the original upper surface, and the letter, if it belong to the original use of the stone, must be read as printed. Alternatively, as Lehmann also pointed out, the "inscription" might be regarded as belonging to a secondary usage of the stone and read ∣ ╱. I do not feel convinced that it is part of a letter at all.

ADDENDUM

To p. 44, n. 7. In *Guide*[2], p. 70, Lehmann has altered this sentence to read thus: "The architrave bore the dedicatory inscription, probably of Arrhidaios, half-brother and eventual successor of Alexander the Great (or, according to others, by an otherwise unknown Macedonian general Adaios)." In view of this statement it is perhaps well to emphasize that although I believe that the dedication was made by Adaios, I explicitly abandoned the attempt to identify him (see above, p. 47; cf. also p. 13), and also left his connection with military matters open (p. 123).

PLATES

1

4

2

5

6

7

8A

8B

App. I A

App. I B

9a

9b

9c

IV

9d

10a

10B

10b

10c

10d

11,2 (East)

11,3 (East)

11,4 (East)

11,1 (West)

11,2 (West)

11,5 (West)

12

13

14

15

16

17a

17b

18a

18b

19

20

IX

21

22a

22

22b

X

23

App. III A

24

25

35

27

37

26

28b

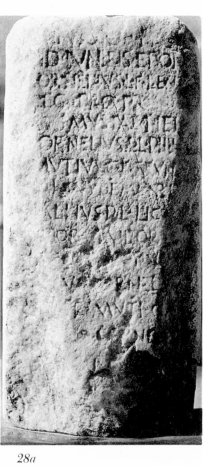

28a

28c

XIII

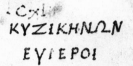

KYZIKHNΩN
EYIEPOI

A d marmorea & ornatissima latin gratis
& latinis litteris epigramma

·M· OPPIVS NEEOS

MYΣIΛAΣ TPHPAPXOΣ
ΔHMHTPIOΣ ΔHMHTPIOY
MOΣXOΣ MENEKPATOY
ZHNΩN ZHNΩNOΣ
AΠOΛΛΩNIOΣ
ΔIONYΣIOY

APMH
POMAXOΣ
ΔHMHTPI
OY

·Q· VISEL
LIVS·L·F·

E ΦOTΣ
O E O Σ A Σ
MOIPAΠOIOΣ
ZHΓINTOΣ
POΛOKΛHOY
P O ΔΛ
N·

PREGE-
PIVS

KYZIKHNΩN IEPOΠOIOI KAI MYΣTHPIΩN
EYΣEBEIΣ EΠIANTIΓENOYΣ TOY EPMAΓOPOY
IΠΠAPXEΩ
ΣΛMOΘPAKEΣ EΠIBAΣIΛEΩΣ APIΔHΛOY
IXOY ΓAPMENIΣKOΣ APIΣTEΩ
ΣENOΣ ΦIΛOΞENOY
AITAI EYΣEBEIΣ AΣKΛHΠIAΔHΣ
AΓAΔOY ΘEPΣIΩN HPOΓEITHΣ
KYBEPNHTHΣ MHNOΦIΛOY

29

XIV

29a

29b

30

32

33

36

31

34

XVI

38

39

40

41

42

44

46

47

XVIII

45

48

52

49

50

51

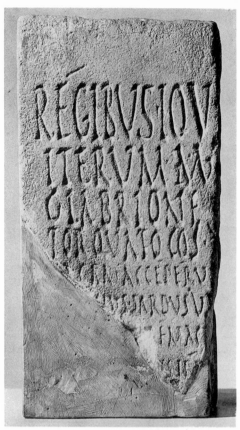

53 left

53 right

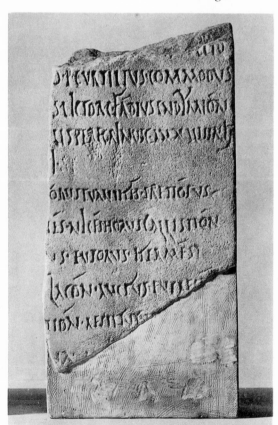

53 bis

XX

54

55

56

59

57

61

60

58

XXII

App. IV

App. IV

XXIII

62

63

64

66

65a

65b

67

68

70

69

74

XXVI

71

72

73

77

75

79

76

80

78a

82

78b

81

83a

83b

86

85a

84

85b

91

INDEXES

Numbers in bold type refer to catalogue items; those in ordinary type

refer to pages, unless otherwise noted.

1. INSCRIPTIONS PUBLISHED IN THIS VOLUME

A. INSCRIPTIONS IN ORDER OF CATALOGUE

Figures in italics indicate the page(s) on which the inscription is published.

75, *128*

76, *129*

77, *129*

78, *129–30*

79, *130–31*

80, *131*

81, *131–32*

82, *132*

83, *132–33*

84, *133*

85, *133–34*

86, *134*

87, *134*

88, *135*

89, *135*

90, *135*

91, *136*

B. NAMES OF MEN AND WOMEN

(I) . GREEK

This index includes all persons mentioned in the inscriptions (other than Latin names, for which see Index 1 B (II)). The ethnic or civil denomination is added when known; in instances in which, although the ethnic is not known, the individual in question is not a Samothracian (for example, because he occurs in a list of theoroi), the name is followed by a dash. Where line references are given, they appear in Roman type following the catalogue number.

Ἀγαθόνικος, Κνίδιος, **22**, 6

Ἀγαθοφῶν, Κνίδιος, **22**, 6

Ἀγαθῶναξ, **68**

Ἀγαθ——, ——, **33** (a), I, 22

Ἀγησίας, ——ιος, **22**, 30

Ἀγησίδαμος, Κνίδιος, **22**, 8

Ἀγησίλαος, Λακεδαιμόνιος, App. I, A, 2

Ἀ̣δαῖος, Μακεδών, **9**, **65**

Ἀθανόδωρος, *bas. epon.*, **22**, 1

Ἀθηναγόρας, ——, **22**, 35

Αἰγ——, **22**, 1

Ἀλέξανδρος, **37**, 4

[Ἀ]μφί⟨λ⟩οχο[ς], ——, **28** (b), 13

Ἁμέτερος, Κνίδιος, **22**, 7

Ἁμ——, Καλχηδόνιος, **22**, 67

Ἀνδρόμαχος, ——, **29** (a), 1

Ἀνδρόνικος, **70**

Ἀντιγένης, Κυζικηνός, **29** (a), 7

Ἀντίγονος, *bas. epon.*, **43**, 1–2

Ἀντίγονος, Λαρισαῖος, **23**, 6

Ἀντίπατρος, ——, **37**, *3*

Ἀπολλόδωρος, Ἀβδηρίτης, **22**, 47

[Ἀ]πολλόδωρος β, ——, **26**, 5

Ἀπολλόθεμις, Μυριναῖος, App. III A (b), 5

[Ἀπ]ολλοφάνης, **17** (a)

Ἀπολλο——, *bas. epon.*, **41**, 11–12

Ἀπολλωνίδης, App. IV, 2

Ἀπολλώνιος, Παριανός, **22**, 52

Ἀπολλώνιος, Τήϊος, **22**, 4

[Ἀπ]ολλώ[ς], ——, **28** (c), 9

Ἀπολλ——, *agoran.*, **36**, 30

[Ἀ]ρίδαμος (I), ——, **28** (c), 12

[Ἀ]ρίδαμος (II), ——, **28** (c), 13

Ἀρίδηλος, *bas. epon.*, **29** (a), 9

Ἀριστα[γόρας], Ἐρυθραῖος, App. III A (c), 5

Ἀρισταγόρας, Θάσιος, **59**, 5, 7

Ἀρισταγόρας, ——, **24**, 4

Ἀριστεύς, Κυζικηνός, **29** (a), 10

Ἀριστόβουλος, Μ̣ήλιος, **22**, 12

Ἀριστόθε[ι]ος, ——, **33** (a), I, 14

Ἀριστοκλῆς, ——, **33** (a), I, 3, 5

Ἀριστόλας, ——, **22**, 33

Ἀριστομένης, Λαρισαῖος, **23**, 4

Ἀρίστων, ——ιος, **22**, 29

Ἀρίστων, ——, **33** (a), I, 13

Ἀρισ——, **73**

Ἀρκέσ[τρατος], Μαρωνίτης, **2**, 13

Ἀρσινόη, *see Index 1 E (I), s.v.*

(II) . ROMAN

a. Praenomina

b. Nomina

c. Cognomina

Ἀγησίλαος, see Index 1 B (II) b, s.v. M. Ὀρφίδιος
   Ἀγησίλαος
Aelianus, see below, s.v. Lamia (Aelianus)
Ἄκαι[ος], see Index 1 B (II) b, s.v. Λεύκιος
Ἀλεξάνδρα, see Index 1 B (II) b, s.v. Οὐλπία Ἀλεξάνδρα
(Sardus Varius) Ambibulus, see Index 1 B (II) b, s.v.
   [Q. Pla]n̦ius Sardus, etc.
Antiochus, see Index 1 B (II) b, s.v. Antiochus Pacci
An——, 36, 19
Apollonides, see Index 1 B (II) b, s.v. P. Paccius C. l.
   Apollonides
Ἀθηνίων, see Index 1 B (II) b, s.v. Λούκιος Ἀθηνίων
Arch——, 44, 4
Auctus, 53 bis, 9

Balbus, see Index 1 B (II) b, s.v. L. Norbanus Balbus
Baltus, 82
Bato (I), 50, 5
Bato (II), 50, 5

Caesar, see Index 1 B (II) b, s.v. C. Iulius Caesar
Callistion, 53 bis, 7
Candidus Tullittianus, see Index 1 B (II) b, s.v. Sex.
   Palpellius Candidus Tullittianus
Cedrus, 36, 19
Chre——, 44, 5
Clenas, 36, 22
Commodus, see Index 1 B (II) b, s.v. P. Curtilius Com-
   modus

Demetrius, see Index 1 B (II) b, s.v. Manius
Διονύσιος, see Index 1 B (II) b, s.v. Κλ. Διονύσιος

Endymion, see Index 1 B (II) b, s.v. C. Fadius Endymion
Εος——, 36, 23
Epaphroditus, 52, 4
Epaphus, 36, 26
Erun——, see Index 1 B (II) b, s.v. [C.] Mutius C. l.
   Erun——
Euanthes, 53 bis, 6
Εὔλαιος, see Index 1 B (II) b, s.v. Τι. Κλαύδιος Εὔλαιος
Euporus, 53 bis, 8
Euprepes, 53 bis, 9
Eutychus, 52, 3

Felix, 36, 29
Felix, see Index 1 B.(II) b, s.v. A. Vereius Felix
Fructus, see Index 1 B (II) b, s.v. . Marius Fructus

Glabrio, see Index 1 B (II) b, s.v. M. Acilius Glabrio

Hermes, 53 bis, 8
[Her]mes, 36, 21
Ἑρμ...ιας, see below, s.v. Ῥοῦφος
Ἡρώδης, see Index 1 B (II) b, s.v. Ἰούνιος Ἡρώδης
Hilarus Primus, bas. epon.(?), 34, 1

Ia——, 44, 2
Ἰουστινιανός, Imperator, see Index 1 E (I) a, s.v.
   Ἰουστινιανός
Is̩in̩is̩(?), see Index 1 B (II) b, s.v. C. A̩m̩a̩çi̩l̩(ius) I̩s̩in̩is̩

Κρίσπος, 43, 4

Lacon, 53 bis, 9
Laetus, 36, 20
Lamia (Aelianus), see Index 1 B (II) b, s.v. L. Fundanius
   Lamia Aelianus
Lenas (Pontianus), see Index 1 B (II) b, s.v. M. Sergius
   Lenas Pontianus
Lentulus, see Index 1 B (II) b, s.v. Cornelius
Lepidus, see Index 1 B (II) b, s.v. M. Aemilius Lepidus
Lict[avius(?)], see Index 1 B (II) b, s.v. [P. M]allius
   P. l. Lict[avius?]

Μαγιανός, 59, 9
[M]atrodorus, see Index 1 B (II) b, s.v. . Cornelius
   [M]a̩t̩rod[orus]
Maur̩[us?], 39, 4
Maximus (Flavius [Sil]v̩anus), see Index 1 B (II) b, s.v.
   L. Pomponius Maximus, etc.
[Me]nander, Chius, 36, 12
Μυρισμός, see Index 1 B (II) b, s.v. Μάρκιος Μυρισμός

Niger, see Index 1 B (II) b, s.v. L. Iulius Sp. f. Pap.
   Niger
Nicephorus, 53 bis, 7

Ὀππᾶτος, see Index 1 B (II) b, s.v. M. Ἀντώνιος
   Ὀππᾶτος
Opt[atus], 36, 21

Paideros, 36, 27
Pamp[hilus], see Index 1 B (II) b, s.v. [M. S]e[rvilius?]
   M. l. Pamp[hilus]
Paneros, 36, 25
Pa——, 36, 28

C. GEOGRAPHICAL NAMES

D. NAMES OF DEITIES

E. OFFICIAL TERMS AND TITLES

(I). GREEK

a. Rulers

b. Constitution and city-organization

c. Magistracies, etc.

ἀγορανόμος, **34**, 2; **36**, 30; **41**, 13; **57**, 2; **61**, 3; App. IV, 3
ἀγωνοθέτης, App. I, B, 8–9
ἀργυρολόγος, **5**, 14
ἀρχιτέκτων (Κυζικηνῶν), App. IV, 11
αὐτοκράτωρ (L. Calpurnius Piso), **18**
βασιλεύς (epon. Samothr.), **22**, 1; **23**, 1; [**27**, 1]; **29**, 9;
   32, 1; [**36**, 1]; **40**, 1; **41**, 11; **42**, 1; **43**, 1; **46**, 3; **47**, 1;
   48, 1; [**49**, 2]; [**55**, 1]; **56**, 1; **57**, 1; **59**, 2; **60**, 1; **61**, 1;
   App. IV, 1; [**73**]
ἐπιμηνιεύων ('Οδησσιτῶν), **6**, 4
ἱερεύς, **6**, 3 (ἐπὶ [ἱερέω θεοῦ μεγάλου Δερζελα(?)], mag.
   epon. Odessi)

ἱερομνάμων, **27**, 2
ἱεροποΐα, App. IV, 14 (ἱ[ερο]ποΐα)
ἱεροποιός (Κυζικηνῶν), **29** (a) 6
ἱππάρχης (Κυζικηνῶν), **29**, 8; App. IV, 6
πρεσβευτής, App. I, B, 17
πρεσβεία, App. IV, 12
πρόεδρος, **2**, 2; **5**, 7 (οἱ προεδρεύοντες); App. I, B, 8
   (οἱ πρόεδροι)
σιτοθέτης, **5**, 4, 12–13, 15
στρατηγός, App. I, A, 3 (στρατηγὸς ἐφ' Ἑλλησπόντου
   καὶ τῶν ἐπὶ Θράικης τόπων)

d. Honors, etc.

ἀναγόρευσις, App. I, B, 9
ἀτέλεια, App. I, B, 15 (ἀτ. τῆι πόλει)
δίδωμι, App. I, A, 19 (ἥ τε πολιτεία καὶ τὰ λοιπὰ τὰ
   δεδόμενα παρὰ τῶν πολιτῶν φιλάνθρωπα)
εὐεργ—, **1**, 2

ἐπαινέω, **2**, 11–12; App. I, A, 18 (περὶ ἐπαίνου); [B, 1]
[πά]τρων, **18**
πολιτεία, App. I, A, 19 (cf. above, s.v. δίδωμι)
πρόξενος, **1**, 6; **2**, 15, 17–18; **23**, 1
φιλάνθρωπα, App. I, A, 20

e. Cult

ἀμύητος, **62**, **63**
ἀνάθημα, App. I, A, 6 (τιμᾶι τὸ τέμ[ενος] θυσίαις καὶ
   ἀναθήμασι)
ἀπαρχή, App. I, B, 21
ἐπόπτης, **26** (ἐπόπται); **28** (c), 11 (ἐφόπται); **29** (b), 1
   (ἐφό[π]της); **41** ([ἐπ]όπ[τ— εὐσεβ—]); **55**, 3
   ([ἐπ]όπτ—); **56**, 3 ([ἐπόπτης(?) εὐ]σεβής); App.
   IV, 7 (μύστης εὐσεβὴς καὶ ἐπόπτης); **18** (ero⟨p⟩tes);
   28 (a), 2 (epop(ta)); **30** (epoptes pius); **31** (epoptes
   p[ius]); **36**, 14 (epoptae)
θεωρία, **6**, 5 (διὰ πρό[τερον θεωριῶν (?)—])
θεωρός, **13** (Παρίων θεωροί); **23**, 2
θυσία, App. I, A, 6; B, 21
ἱερόν, **7**, 7 (εἰς τὸ ἱερὸν τῆς 'Αθηνᾶς); App. I, A, 21
   (ἐν τῶι ἱερῶι τῆς 'Αθηνᾶς); **62**
μυστήριον, **6**, 6 ([τῶν ἐν] Σαμοθράκη μυστηρίω[ν]);
   App. I, A, 7 (μετασχεῖν τῶν μυστ[ηρίων]

μύστης
   μύσται εὐσεβεῖς, **27**; **28** (b), 2; **29** (a), 6–7, 12; **35**
     ([μύσται εὐσε]βεῖς); **41**, 4; **42**, 3 ([μύσται εὐσ]εβεῖς);
     43, 3 ([μύσται] εὐσεβεῖ[ς]); **45** ([μύστ]α[ι εὐσεβεῖς]);
     46, 6–7 (μύστης εὐσεβής); **47**, 3; **48** ([μ]ύστα[ι
     εὐσεβεῖς]); **49**, 4 ([μύσται εὐσ]εβεῖς); **55**, 2–3
     (μύσται [εὐσεβεῖς]); **56**, 3 ([μύστης(?) εὐ]σεβής);
     59, 4–5; **60**, 2–3 (μύστ[αι] εὐσεβεῖς); App. IV,
     7 (μύστης εὐσεβὴς καὶ ἐπόπτης)
   mystae pii, **18** ([mystes] pius); **25** (mystes pius); **28**
     (a), 5 (mustae piei); **31** (mystae piei); **32**, 5
     (mustae [piei]); **33** (a), II, 13–14 (musta pius);
     34, 5 (mustae p[i]ei); **36**, 4 (mystae pii); **39**
     (mist[— pi—]); **40**, 4 (m[ystae pii]); **53**, 4 (mystae
     pii)
συμμύστης, **36**, 7 (symmust[ae] pii)
τέμ[ενος], **19**; App. I, A, 5 (cf. above, s.v. ἀνάθημα)
χ[αριστήριον], **14**

(II). LATIN

a. Magistrates

leg. pro pr(aetore), **28** (a), 4; **53**, 8 (leg. [p]ro pr.
   prov. eiusdem)
lictor, **53** bis, 3 (lictor(es))
magister, [**40**, 5]

proconsule, **53**, 6–7 (procos. [provinci]ae Mac[e]doniae)
pro magistris, **40**, 6 (pro mag[istris])
quaestor, **50**, 1 (Q(uaestor) prov. M[ac](edoniae));
   51, 8–9 (Q(uaestor) propr. [prov. Maced.])

b. *Cult. See Index 1 E (I) e, s.vv.* ἐπόπτης, μύστης, συμμύστης

F. DATES

This index includes only those dates which have a Julian equivalent.

(I). ERAS, REGNAL YEARS, CONSULAR DATES

ἔτους αξσ (A.D. 113), **47**, 14

ἔτους — ('Ιουστινιανοῦ), **20**, 4

M. Antonio, [A. Postumio(?)] (99(?) B.C.), **31**

Cn. Octavio M. f., C. Scribonio C. f. (76 B.C.), **32**

C. Iulio Caesare, M. Lepido (46 B.C.), **33**

M. Antonio, [P. Dolabella(?)] (44(?) B.C.), **31**

L. Cornuficio, Sex. Pompeio (35 B.C.), **34**

M. Iunio Silvano, L. Norbano Balbo (A.D. 19), **36**

L. Nonio, M. Arruntio (A.D. 66 *sive* 77), **40**

L. Fundanio Lamia Aeliano, Sex. Carminio Vetere (A.D. 116), **51**

M. Acilio Glabrione, C. Bellicio Torquato (A.D. 124), **53**

M. S. Lena Pontiano, M. Antonio Rufino (A.D. 131), **54**

(II). MONTHS

X.K.Mai. (22 April, A.D. 116), **51**

VIII.Idus Iunias (6 June, A.D. 119), **36**

id.Iunieis (i B.C.), **28** (a)

A.D.XII.K.Iulias (20 June, 35 B.C.), **34**

(A.D.?) K.Sept. (A.D. 66 *sive* 77), **40**

V.Idus Novembres (9 Nov., A.D. 124), **53**

A.D.XV.K.Nov. (18 Oct., 46 B.C.), **33**

A.D.IV —— (99 *sive* 44 B.C.), **31**

A.D.X —— (76 B.C.), **32**

G. WORDS, PHRASES, ETC.

(I). GREEK

This index does not include the article or common conjunctions, prepositions, pronouns, etc.

ἀγαθῆ(ι) τύχη(ι) (*initio catalogorum*), **39, 45, 46, 49, 54, 59**

ἀγαθῆ(ι) τύχη(ι) (*initio decretorum*), App. I, A, 21

ἀγοράζω, **5**, 11 ([το]ῦ ἀγοραζομένου τὸν [σῖτον], 19 ([— ἀγορ]άζ—)

ἀγών, [App. I, B, 10 (ὅταν — τὸ[ν ἀγῶνα συντελῆι ὁ δῆμος —])]

ἀδιαπτώτως, **5**, 5 (ὅπως δ' ἀγ καὶ ἀδιαπτώτω[ς | ὑπάρχηι] χρήματα)

αἵρεσις, App. I, A, 17 (ἀκόλουθα πράττων τῆι τοῦ βασιλέως αἱρέσει); B, 14 ([— ἀκολούθως τῆι τοῦ βασιλέως καὶ τῆς [β]ασιλίσσης [α]ἱρ[έ]σει)

ἀκόλουθος (adj.), App. I, A, 16–17 (*see above, s.v.* αἵρεσις); B, 14 (*see ibid.*)

ἀκόλουθος (subst.), **28** (b), 10

ἀναγράφω, [**2**, 18–9 ([ἀναγράψαι δὲ τόδε | τὸ ψήφισμα εἰς στήλην λιθινήν])]; **7**, 4–5 ([ἀναγρά]ψαι δὲ τόδε τὸ ψήφισμ[α | εἰς] στήλην); App. I, A, 20 (τὰ λοιπὰ τὰ δεδόμενα ... φιλάνθρωπα ἀναγραφήσεται εἰς στήλην)

ἀνακαινίζω, **79** (ἀν[εκέ]νισε τὸ μέρος)

ἀνανεέομαι, **20** ([τ]οῦτο λοετρὸν ἀνανεοῦτε)

ἀνατίθημι, App. I, A, 21 ([ἀνατε]θήσεται ἐν τῶι ἱερῶι); B, 22 (ἵνα ἐκ τῶμ προσόδων θυσίαι τε συντελῶνται καὶ ἀπαρχαὶ [ἀνα]τιθῶνται τοῖς θεοῖς); [19, 1, [ἀνέθηκαν?]]

ἀξιόω, App. I, A, 12 (ἀξιωθεὶς προδανεῖσαι χρήματα), 13 (βουλόμενος ὑπακούειν πάντα τὰ ἀξιούμενα)

ἀπαγγέλλω, **5**, 14 (ἀπαγ[γ]έλ[λειν πρὸς τὸ πλ]ῆθος)

ἅπας, **5**, 16

ἀποδίδωμι, **5**, 3 (ἀποδιδόναι τὴν τιμ[ὴν | τοῦ σίτου]); **6**, 7 (ἀποδιδ—)

ἀποστέλλω, App. I, A, 9 (ἀποστέλλων τοὺς διαφυλάξοντας ἱππεῖς); App. IV, 10 (ἀποσταλεὶς παρὰ Κυζικηνῶν)

ἀσφάλεια, App. I, A, 8 (τῆς τε κατὰ τὸ χωρίον ἀσφαλείας)

ἀφικνέομαι, App. I, A, 16 (τῶμ πρὸς αὐτὸν ἀφικνουμένων)

151

βέλος, App. I, A, 10 (ἱππεῖς [τε καὶ] πεζούς στρατιώτας καὶ βέλη καὶ καταπάλτας)

βούλομαι, App. I, A, 13 (βουλόμενος ὑπακούειν)

γεωργέω, App. I, B, 20 (τοὺς κληρουχήσοντας καὶ γεωργήσαντας τὴν χώραν)

γίγνομαι, 5, 13 ([ἐάν τις γ]ένηται ἔκγδεια); 23, 1 (οἵδε πρόξενοι ἐγένοντο)

γράφω, 5, 4 (ἐν τῶι γεγρα[μ|μένωι χρ]όνωι)

γυμνάσιον, 8, 4

γύνη, 10, 2 (βασιλέω[ς Λυσιμάχου] γύ[νη —]); 47, 7 (Οὐλπία Ἀλεξάνδρα ἡ γύνη αὐτοῦ); 69 (a), 2 ([γ]ύνη δὲ Σείρωνος)

δέω, 5, 12 (ὧν ἂν δεήσηι)

διακεῖμαι, App. I, A, 5 (ε[ὐσεβῶ]ς διακείμενος πρὸς τοὺς θεούς), 14 (διακείμενος δὲ καὶ πρὸς τὸν δῆμον)

διαλέγομαι, App. I, B, 17 (διαλέγεσθαι δὲ αὐτῶι)

διανομή, 5, 1 (καὶ αἱ δια[νομαὶ(?) —])

διατελέω, 2, 6 (φίλος ὢν καὶ εὔνους διατελεῖ τῆι πόλει)

διαφυλάσσω, App. I, A, 10 (ἀποστέλλων τοὺς διαφυλάξοντας ἱππεῖς)

δίδωμι, 5, 15 ([τοὺς δὲ ἀργυρολόγου[ς διδόναι τοῖς] σιτοθέταις); App. I, A, 12 (χρήματα ἔδω[κεν]); B, 15 (ἀτέλειαν δοῦν[αι])

δοκέω, 5, 16 (ὅτι ἂν αὐτοῖς δοκῆι)

δοῦλος, 41, 9; 47, 9; 58, 8; 59, 7

δύναμις, 6, 7

ἔγγονος, 2, 14 (εἶναι αὐτὸν καὶ [ἐ]γ[γ]ό|νους πρ[οξ]ένους)

ἔδα(φος), 87 (ἐδα—)

εἰκών, App. IV, 14 (ἕνεκα . . . τῶν ἱερῶν εἰκόνων)

εἰμί, App. I, B, 17 (εὔκαιρον φαίνηται εἶναι)

εἴσειμι, 62, 1 (μὴ εἰσιέναι); 63, 4–5 (μὴ εἰσιέναι)

ἕκαστος, 5, 7

ἐξαγωγή, App. I, B, 15 (σίτου ἐξαγωγήν)

ἐπελθεῖν, 5, 18 ([ἐπελθεῖ]ν ἐπὶ τὴ[ν β]ουλ[ήν]); 7, 2 ([ἐπε]λθεῖν ἐς —)

ἐπιδημία, 8 (B), 4 ([— τὴν ἐ]πιδημίαν χ[ρησίμως ἐποιήσατο —])

ἐπιμέλεια, App. I, A, 15 (πᾶσαν ἐπιμέλειαν ποιεῖται)

ἐπιμελέομαι, [App. I, B, 9 (— τοὺς πρ]οέδρους καὶ τὸν ἀγων[οθέτην ἐπιμεληθῆναι τῆς ἀναγορεύσε]ως)]

ἔτος, 20 (πρὸ ἐτῶν β (i.e.?)); cf. also Index 1 F (I), s.v. ἔτους

εὐδοκ—, 8 (B), 3

εὔκαιρος, App. I, B, 16 (ὅθεν αὐτῶι εὔκαιρον φαίνηται εἶναι)

εὔνους, App. I, A, 14–15 (διακείμενος πρὸς τὸν δῆμον [εὐνό]ως)

εὐσεβής, App. I, A, 4–5 (ε[ὐσεβῶ]ς διακείμενος); cf. also Index 1 E (I) e, s.vv. ἐπόπτης, μύστης

εὐτυχῶς, 20, 3 (εὐτ[υχῶς]?)

θυγάτηρ, 10, 1 ([βασ]ίλισσα Ἀρ[σινόη βασιλέως Πτολε]μαίου θυγάτηρ)

ἴδιος, 2, 8 (καὶ κοινῆι καὶ ἰδίαι τοῖς ἐντυγχάνουσι τῶν πολιτῶν); App. I, A, 16 (καὶ κοινῆι τῆ[ς πό]λεως καὶ ἰδίαι τῶμ πρὸς αὐτὸν ἀφικνουμένων)

ἱερός, 5, 9 (μετὰ τὰ ἱερὰ προδό|[ματα —]); App. IV, 14 (ἕνεκα . . . τῶν ἱερῶν εἰκόνων); cf. also Index 1 E (I) e, s.v. ἱερόν

ἱππεύς, App. I, A, 9 (ἀποστέλλων τοὺς διαφυλάξοντας ἱππεῖς)

καθίστημι, App. I, B, 19 (εἰς τὸ . . . κατασταθῆναι τῶμ πολιτῶμ τοὺς κληρουχήσοντας)

καλ—, 8 (A), 3

καταπάλτης, App. I, A, 10 (ἱππεῖς [τε καὶ] πεζούς στρατιώτας καὶ βέλη καὶ καταπάλτας)

κατατάττειν, 5, 9 (κατατάττειν μετὰ τὰ ἱερὰ προδό[ματα])

κοινός, 2, 8 (see above, s.v. ἴδιος); App. I, A, 15 (see above, ibid.)

κυβερνήτης, 29, 13

λοετρόν, 20

λοιπός, App. I, A, 19 (ἥ τε πολιτεία καὶ τὰ λοιπὰ τὰ δεδόμενα παρὰ τ[ῶν πο]λιτῶν φιλάνθρωπα)

μέγας, 20 ([τ]οῦτο λοετρόν — [τ]ὸ μέγα); cf. also Index D, s.v. θεοὶ μεγάλοι

μέρος, 79 (ἀν[εκέ]νισε τὸ μέρος)

μετέχω, 2, 16 ([μετέχ]οντ[ας] πάντων [ὧν καὶ οἱ ἄλλο]ι πρό[ξ]ενοι); 6, 7 ([τῶν ἐν] Σαμοθράκῃ μυστηρίω[ν μετέχοντος(?)]); App. I, A, 7 (ἔσπευσεν παρα[γενό]μενος εἰς τὴν νῆσον μετασχεῖν τῶμ μυστ[ηρίων])

μήτηρ, 69 (b) (Μητροκλῆα τὴν μητέρα Στρατονείκην)

μισθός, App. I, A, 11 (εἴς τε τοὺς μισθούς . . . ἔδωκεν)

νῆσος, App. I, A, 7 (παρα[γενό]μενος εἰς τὴν νῆσον)

ὅρος, 79

ὀχύρωμα, App. I, B, 18 (διαλέγεσθαι δὲ αὐτῶι τοὺς πρεσβευτὰς καὶ περὶ τοῦ ὀχυρώματος)

παραγίγνομαι, App. I, A, 6–7 (cf. above, s.vv. μετέχω, νῆσος); 23 (θεωροὶ πα[ραγενόμενοι]) παρακαλέω, App. I, B, 18 (διαλέγεσθαι αὐτῶι τοὺς πρεσβευτὰς ... καὶ παρακαλεῖν αὐτόν)

παραχρῆμα, 5, 16 ([διδόναι τοῖς] σιτοθέταις ... [— παραχρῆ]μα ἐξ ἁπάσης τῆς π[ρο|σόδου])

πᾶς, 5, 8; App. I, A, 9, 13, 15

πεζός, App. I, A, 10 (ἱππεῖς [τε καὶ] πεζοὺς στρατιώτας)

πλοῖον, 19, 3 ([οἳ] ἐν πλοίῳ)

ποιέω, 8 (B), 4 ([— τὴν ἐ]πιδημίαν χ[ρησίμως ἐποιή-σατο —]); 17 (a), 5 ([ὁ δεῖνα ἐ]ποίη[σεν])

πράττω, App. I, A, 17 (ἀκόλουθα πράττων τῆι τοῦ βασιλέως αἱρέσει)

προδανείζω, App. I, A, 12 (ἀξιωθεὶς προδανεῖσαι χρήματα)

πρόδομα, 5, 9–10 (μετὰ τὰ ἱερὰ προδό[ματα])

πρόνοια, App. I, A, 9 (πᾶσαν πρόνοιαν [ποιεῖ]ται)

πρότερον, 6, 5 (διὰ πρό[τερον θεωριῶν? —]); 8 (B), 5 (——ας εἰς πρότε[ρον —])

σῖτος, 5, [4], [7], [11]; App. I, B, 15 (σίτου ἐξαγωγήν)

σπεύδω, App. I, A, 6 (ἔσπευσεν ... μετασχεῖν τῶμ μυστ[ηρίων])

στήλη, [2, 19 ([εἰς στήλην λιθίνην])]; 7, 6 (ἀναγράψαι ... εἰς στήλην λιθίνην καὶ ἀναθεῖ[ναι]; App. I, A, 20 (ἀναγραφήσεται εἰς στήλην)

στρατιώτης, App. I, A, 10 (ἱππεῖς [τε καὶ] πεζοὺς στρατιώτας)

συμπράσσω, App. I, B, 18 (παρακαλεῖν αὐτὸν συμπράξαι τῆι π[όλ]ει)

συνάγω, 5, 18 ([διδόναι τοῖς] σιτοθέταις ὅτι ἂν αὐτο[ῖς | δοκῆι ... ὅταν συν]αχθῆι)

συντελέω, [App. I, B, 10 (ὅταν — τὸ[ν ἀγῶνα — συντελῆι ὁ δῆμος —])]; App. I, B, 19 (εἰς τὸ συντελεσθέντος αὐτο[ῦ] κατασταθῆναι τῶμ πολ[ι|τῶ]ν τοὺς κληρουχήσοντας), 21 (ἵνα ἐκ τῶμ προσόδων θυσίαι τε συντελῶνται)

τάσσω, [App. I, A, 2–3 ([Ἱππομέδων] Ἀγησιλάου Λακεδαιμ[όνιος ὁ ταχ|θεὶς ὑπὸ τ]οῦ βασιλέως Πτολεμαίου στρατ[ηγός])]

τιμάω, App. I, A, 5 (τιμᾶι τὸ τέμ[ενος])

τιμή, 5, 3 (ἀποδιδόναι τὴν τιμ[ὴν | τοῦ σίτου])

τόπος, App. I, A, 4 (τῶν ἐπὶ Θράικης τόπων)

ὑπακούειν, App. I, A, 13 (βουλόμενος ὑπακούειν πάντα τὰ ἀξιούμενα)

ὑπάρχω, [5, 6 (ὅπως δ'ἂγ καὶ ἀδιαπτώτω[ς | ὑπάρχηι] χρήματα)

φαίνομαι, App. I, B, 16 (εὔκαιρον φαίνηται εἶναι)

φιλία, 7, 2

φίλος, 2, 6–7 (φίλος ὢν καὶ εὔνους διατελεῖ τῆι πόλει)

φυλή, 79 (φυλα— (Φυλα—?))

φύσις, App. IV, 8 (Μῖκις Μνησισ[τρ]άτου, φύσει δ[ὲ] Ἀσκληπιάδης Ἀττάλου); 69 (a), 1–2

χαῖρε, 69 (a)

χράομαι, App. I, A, 11 (τοὺς χρησομένους τούτοις)

χρεία, 2, 7–8 (χρείας παρεχόμενος καὶ κοινῆι καὶ ἰδίαν)

χρήματα, 5, 6 (ὅπως δ'ἂγ καὶ ἀδιαπτώτω[ς | ὑπάρχηι] χρήματα τῆι πόλει); App. I, A, 12 (χρήματα ἔδωκεν)

χρήσιμος, 8 (B), 4 ([— τὴν ἐ]πιδημίαν χ[ρησίμως ἐποιήσατο])

χρόνος, 5, 5 (ἐν τῶι γεγρα[μ|μένωι χρ]όνωι)

χώρα, App. I, B, 20 (τοὺς κληρουχήσοντας καὶ γεωργήσοντας τὴν χώραν)

χωρίον, App. I, A, 8 (τῆς τε κατὰ τὸ χωρίον ἀσφαλείας)

ὠνή, 5, 6–7 (χρήματα ... εἰς τὴν ὠ[νὴν σίτ]ου)

ὡς, 6, 3 (ὡς δὲ ἐν Ὀδησσῷ ἐπὶ —); 29 (a), 10 ([ὡς δὲ] Σαμοθρᾷκες ἐπὶ —); App. IV, 5 ([ὡ]ς δὲ Κυζικηνοὶ ἐπὶ —)

(II). LATIN

de suo, 16

idem, 53, 8 (leg. [p]ro pr. ρ̣ρ̣ο̣ν. eiusdem)

iterum, 53, 1 (regibus Iove et Minerva iterum)

minister, *see below, s.v.* servus

prece, 29 (b), 8–9 (prece p̣ịṷṣ)

sacra, 53, 5; 63 (sacra acceperunt)

servus, 36, 18; 52, 2; 53 *bis*, 5 ([serv]i *sive* [ministr]i)

153

2. GREEK AND LATIN WORDS

A. CIVIC ORGANIZATION AND MAGISTRACIES

ἀγοραστής, 10 n. 39
ἀγωνοθέτης, 28
ἀργυρολόγοι, 32
ἀρχιτέκτων, 115
βασιλεῖς (οἱ), 13
βασιλεύς, 24
βουλή, 24, 28, 32
ἐπιμηνιεύων, 35
εὐεργέτης, 22
θεωρός, 10 n. 39

ἱερομνάμων, 76
ἱεροποιός, 115–16
κατὰ ψήφισμα, 61
magister, 95
οἱ ἐπὶ τοῦ σίτου, 32–33
πρεσβευτής, 10 n. 39
προεδρεύω, 28
πρόεδρος, 24, 28
πρόσοδος, 29, 31
σιτοθέται, 32

B. CULT

διφυεῖς Κάβειροι, 119
ἔνδενδρος (Dionysos), 84
θεοὶ Σαμοθρᾷκες, *see Index 6, s.v.* Samothracian gods
ἱερόν, 117–18

ἱερὸν Σαμοθρακικόν, 36
Σωτῆρες (Ptol. I *et* Berenice), 6 n. 18
τέμενος, 118 n. 4

C. NAMES

Ἀδαῖος, 45–46
Ἀρριβαῖος (Ἀρραβαῖος), 46
Ἀρριδαῖος, 45–46
Aufidius, 54–55
Βενδι—, 76
Κόρραγος, 46

Orfidius, 108
Paccius, 87
Πούδης, 100
Σείρων, 125
Τάρυλα, 90
Ulpia, 100

D. VARIA

ἀδιαπτώτως, 27–28
ἀκόλουθος (subst.), 105
ἀνανεοῦτε, 60
ἀπὸ λαφύρων, 122–23
διανομή, 26
ἔκγδεια, 30
εὐδοξία, 38
εὐτεχνῶς, 60
εὐτυχῶς, 60
εὐχήν, 49
ἱερέω(ς), 34 n. 5

κατατάττειν, 29
κηρύκειον, 119
λοετρόν, 60 n. 4
μέγεθος, 30–31
οἶκος, 49–50
patronus, 57
πλῆθος, 30–31
πρόδομα, 29
τελέτη, 119
-εύς (names in), 86

3. ANCIENT AUTHORS

4. INSCRIPTIONS PUBLISHED ELSEWHERE

A dagger before the publication indicates that an improved text is given.

A. GREEK

AJA, 1 (1885), 21, no. 2: 10 n. 39
†   43 (1939), 138: *see* **63**
†   44 (1940), 345, no. 1: *see* **47**
†   346, no. 2: *see* **49**
†   485 f.: *see* **18**
AJP, 60 (1939), 452 ff.: 8 n. 30, 11
AEp, 1926, 34: *see* **31**
AnzWien, 91 [17] (1954), 222, no. 3: 118 n. 4
AEMÖ, 11, p. 41, no. 55: 35 n. 7
Archaeology, 6 (1953), 33–34: see *Hesperia,* 24 (1955),
    100, no. 40
AM, 35 (1910), 22–23: 122 n. 2
Breccia, *Iscrizioni,* 13: 123 n. 4
              105: 49 n. 3
              p. xvi, no. 2: see *AJA,* 1 (1885),
                21, no. 2
BMI 444: see *IG,* XII (8), p. 38, I and II
     451: 46 n. 16
BCH, 37 (1913), 144, no. 50: 131 n. 1
     46 (1922), 50: 46 n. 20
†   49 (1925), 245 ff.: *see* **9**
†   254 ff.: *see* **60**
†   256 ff.: *see* **31**
†   52 (1928), 395 ff.: *see* **6**
         426 ff.: 26 n. 3
†   70 (1946), 537 ff.: *see* **9**
Chapouthier, p. 34, no. 12: 110 n. 1
Conze, *Reise auf den Inseln des Thrakischen Meeres,* 10:
    131 n. 1
CIG 2007: 99 n. 3
    2772: 114 n. 15
    5117: 55 n. 3
Dörpfeld, *Troja und Ilion,* II, p. 448, no. III: 12 n. 49
Dunant and Pouilloux, *Recherches sur l'histoire et les
    cultes de Thasos, II,* no. 169: 24 nn. 3, 5; 37 n. 1
Durrbach, *Choix d'inscriptions de Délos,*
             40: see *IG,* XI (4), 1135
             48: see *ibid.,* 666
             50: see *ibid.,* 1025, 1055
             116: see *Inscr. Délos* 1753
             141: see *ibid.,* 1712

FdDelphes, III, 1, 104: 55 n. 1 (*infra*)
     3, 184: 115 n. 16
     4, 21–23: 57 n. 5
       96: 115 n. 16
Herzog and Klaffenbach, *Asylieurkunden aus Kos,*
               4 ff.: 35 n. 8
               8: 8 n. 31
Hesperia, 19 (1950), 15: *see* **85**
†   21 ff.: *see* **20**
    20 (1951), 13: *see* **86**
    22 (1953), 8 f.: *see* **83**
          14 f.: *see* **62**
†   18 ff.: *see* **9**
          19 f.: *see* **65**
    24 (1955), 100, no. 40: *see* **64**
Histria, I, 8: 35 n. 7
       pp. 496–97: 36 n. 13
Inschriften von Magnesia 18: 70 n. 4
Inschriften von Olympia 54: 35 n. 8
          100 ff.: 101 n. 1
Inschriften von Pergamon 21: 122–23 n. 3
          22–28: 122 n. 3
          33–37: 122–23 n. 3
          60: 123 n. 5
Inschriften von Priene 156: 43 n. 4
          266: 114–15 n. 15
          267: 114–15 n. 15
Inscriptiones Creticae, I, p. 35, no. 3: 53 n. 2
IG, II², 9533: 127 n. 4
    V (1), 1379: see *BCH,* 52 (1928), 426–32
        1390: 118 n. 10
    IX (1), 694: 32 n. 25
    IX, I², 176: 35 n. 8
        187: 35 n. 8
        192: 35 n. 8
    (2), 517: 9 n. 35
        1228: 90
    XI (4), 666: 32 n. 28
        1025: 32 n. 28
        1051–52: 35 n. 8
        1055: 32 n. 28
        1135: 123 n. 5

B. LATIN

5. PAPYRI, ETC.

6. GENERAL INDEX

160

BOLLINGEN SERIES LX

SAMOTHRACE

EXCAVATIONS CONDUCTED BY THE

INSTITUTE OF FINE ARTS, NEW YORK UNIVERSITY

KARL LEHMANN
Editor